"Christopher Renstrom does someth... ...ar and makes the vast subject of astrolog... ...ives. A pleasure to read!"

—**ISAAC MIZRAHI**, bestselling author of *I.M.: A Memoir*

—

"Extraordinary knowledge of astrology is woven into every page—accessible, humorous, and profoundly insightful. Everyone needs this book!"

—**CHANI NICHOLAS**, bestselling author of *You Were Born for This*

—

"Renstrom's 'seasonal' approach to astrology is fresh and new and always hits the mark."

—**PATTI STANGER**, *The Millionaire Matchmaker*

—

"A gift for the new student and seasoned practitioner alike! Applies characteristic diligence, clear and novel organization, and masterful command of the language of the heavens to provide a new twist on the fundamentals of Western astrology."

—**MICHAEL LUTIN**, astrologer and columnist

—

"Christopher Renstrom combines a deep knowledge of history with a wise and humorous take on the way we live now. *The Cosmic Calendar* is essential reading for anyone who wants a deeper understanding of how to use astrology to get the most out of life."

—**J. COURTNEY SULLIVAN**, bestselling author of *Friends and Strangers*

THE
COSMIC
CALENDAR

THE
COSMIC
CALENDAR

Using Astrology to Get in Sync
with Your Best Life

CHRISTOPHER RENSTROM

A TarcherPerigee Book

tarcherperigee

an imprint of Penguin Random House LLC
penguinrandomhouse.com

TarcherPerigee with tp colophon is a registered
trademark of Penguin Random House LLC

Most TarcherPerigee books are available at special quantity
discounts for bulk purchase for sales promotions, premiums,
fund-raising, and educational needs. Special books or book
excerpts also can be created to fit specific needs. For details,
write: SpecialMarkets@penguinrandomhouse.com.

ISBN 9780525541080
ebook ISBN 9780525541097

Printed in the United States of America
1   3   5   7   9   10   8   6   4   2

Book design by Ashley Tucker

To Wendy Wilburn and Janet Robins for being there for me—
both in season and out

CONTENTS

INTRODUCTION

In 46 BC Julius Caesar changed the world. He had been invited to a dinner party on Queen Cleopatra's barge and found himself seated next to one of her court astronomers, Sosigenes. The two men became absorbed in conversation and were inseparable all night. The discussion was about calendars. The Roman calendar had been a mess for decades. It was based on the Moon, so intercalary months needed to be added every eight years in order to align it with the seasons. Although lunar calendars were commonplace throughout the Mediterranean, Roman priests had been adding and subtracting months willy-nilly to extend the terms of politicians in office they favored and shorten the terms of those they disliked. Indeed, their manipulation of time was wreaking havoc on shipping, commerce, and tax collecting.

Sosigenes suggested switching over to the Egyptian calendar, which was based on the Sun. Centuries earlier the Egyptians had calculated that it took the Sun 365¼ days to return to the place in the sky where it was at the spring equinox. He demonstrated to Caesar that by dividing the year into twelve months—one month of 30 days alternating with another of 31—he could create a consistent year of 366 days and then reduce February by one more day in order to sync the calendar to the Sun. That way, instead of having to add or subtract an entire month every eight years, all Caesar had to do was add one day to February once every four years. This was the origin of the Julian calendar—named after Julius Caesar, of course—and it standardized timekeeping throughout the republic. Sundials and obelisks (both Egyptian inventions) soon became all the rage as Roman citizens were able to clock for themselves the time of day, month, and year. Moreover, this change of calendars gave birth to Western astrology—which had been based on the Moon since the twilight days of Babylon and would, from Julius Caesar on, be based on the blazing Sun.

Your birth chart is a calendar. One that's unique to you because it's a picture of the heavens at the moment of your birth. You can think of it as a screenshot of the sky—*your* sky—and this individualized star map will guide you throughout your entire life. It tells you when you are in season or out, and when's a good time to start a venture or think better of it; it shows you grace periods where you can breeze right past obstacles and it gives you a heads-up on future rough patches where you can expect resistance. And like the calendar, this can all be done according to the Sun—which is why it's so important to know where the Sun is in your birth chart. Not everyone was born with the Sun shining overhead. Many of us were born when the Sun had already set. People born in the early-morning hours aren't going to be like people born in the late afternoon any more than people born in the middle of autumn are going to have the same outlook on life as those born in the spring. This book will also describe your individual elemental temperament as depicted by the planets in your birth chart. This will be easy for you to understand because everything relates back to the Sun. The Sun represents you in your birth chart, and we will be using it as the "You Are Here" planet throughout this book.

How to Use This Book

You will need a copy of your birth chart and for that you will need to know your birthday and year, birth time, and birthplace. You can download a copy of your birth chart from my website: RulingPlanets.com.

If you don't know your birth time, then use 12 PM. Astrologers often use noon as a default time because it still gives a general idea of where the Moon is. You may not be able to distinguish if you're a day or night birth, but at least you'll get a list of the planets for your birthday and that will still allow you to use this book.

1. **Identify your Sun sign** (you can do this by looking up your birthday on page 39).

2. **Find your season:** Are you spring, summer, autumn, or winter?

3. **What's your mode:** Are you an unstoppable force? An immovable object? Or are you the one trying to make an impossible situation work?

4. **Are you a day or night birth?** This is significant because if you're a night-time birth, then the Moon is going to be just as important as the Sun in your chart—maybe even more so.

5. **What's your elemental makeup?** This is what really unpacks the birth chart. The four elements—water, earth, air, and fire—describe the cornerstones of your personality: your emotional life, material welfare, social skills, and spiritual beliefs. Based on the seasons, the four elements are rarely evenly distributed in a birth chart, and how they work with (and sometimes against) the Sun speaks to your temperament.

6. **Explore the Sun in the signs.** This section describes the Sun as it passes through the twelve zodiac signs in calendrical order. You can use this to read about yourself—along with loved ones and friends—but you can also use it to identify your ruling planet. This is the planet that rules your Sun sign, so you'll want to look it up (along with the sign that it's in) to read more about how your Sun's energy will be directed in life. Finally,

you can use this Sun sign section to get a fuller grasp of the seasonal dis-
position of the other planets in your chart.

7. **Get to know the planets.** This section describes the planets in your chart
   along with the signs that they are in. Each planet will refer back to your
   Sun (i.e., you)—which is why some planets will be helpful, some will be
   challenging, and some will leave you scratching your head. Furthermore,
   this section describes what it's like to have Mercury and Venus as morning
   stars versus evening stars, what it means when a planet is retrograde, and
   where certain planets are in domicile, detriment, exaltation, or fall.

8. **Learn to use your astrology chart as a personal calendar.** This part of the
   book shows you how to turn your chart into a calendar using the seasons
   and elements. Not only is it useful for timing decisions, romances, and
   sit-down talks with your kids, but it can also help you negotiate problem
   areas of your birth chart where the energy gets stuck or you experience a
   disconnect. There's no such thing as a "bad" chart because the Sun is
   always moving through the twelve signs of the zodiac. It may take days,
   weeks, or months, but the Sun will always "come out tomorrow" because
   at some point it will be in season or it will pass through a zodiac sign of a
   similar or the same element. This easy-to-use method will help you to
   plan for that and, more importantly, to do things in your own time.

UNDERSTANDING YOUR COSMIC CALENDAR

ASTROLOGY IS A CALENDAR

Astrology is not a science. Astrology is not a religion. Astrology is a calendar. It's why nearly every major civilization on the planet—Middle Eastern, Indian, Chinese, and Mesoamerican—developed some form of astrology. It was in order to tell time.

In astrology, everything is seen from the Earth's point of view. Yes, we all know that the planets actually orbit the Sun, which sits at the center of our solar system. However, in astrology the horoscope (better known as the astrological chart) is set up to show that *the planets orbit us.*

It's not such a far-fetched concept when you consider how the Sun rises in the east in the morning, travels across the sky during the day, and then sets in the west at night. Can't we all tell time by where the Sun is? Isn't the quality of heat and light at 6:00 in the morning different from 2:00 in the afternoon, 5:30 in the evening, or 9:00 at night? That arc that the Sun travels across the sky is the same arc that the planets follow. Mercury, Venus, Mars, Jupiter, and Saturn—and even the ones we can't see with the naked eye like Uranus, Neptune, and Pluto—all follow the same path across the sky. They rise and set just like the Sun and the Moon do. And yes, the Sun and the Moon are considered planets in astrology. "Planet" comes from the Greek word *planetoi*, which means "wandering lights." The Greeks used this word to describe the difference between the lights that moved in the sky—like the

Sun and the Moon—versus the lights that didn't: like the zodiac constellations.

And that's the first thing you need to know about reading your astrology chart: planets move and zodiac signs don't.

Imagine the face of a clock. And all you can see on that clock are the twelve numbers. Twelve numbers. Nothing else. Now if I were to ask you, "What time is it?," and all you could see was a clock with twelve numbers—would you be able to tell me the time?

Of course not. Because you would be missing the hands, right? You'd need an hour hand, a minute hand, and maybe even a second hand to tell me the time.

The zodiac signs are like the numbers on the face of a clock. There are twelve signs just like there are twelve numbers on a clock and twelve months in a year. They never ever change their order.

The planets, however, are like the hands of a clock. They are in constant motion. The planets are what astrologers use to tell time.

This is why, when you look at your own astrological chart, the signs are on

| Aries the Ram | Taurus the Bull | Gemini the Twins | Cancer the Crab | Leo the Lion | Virgo the Maiden |
| Libra the Scales | Scorpio the Scorpion | Sagittarius the Archer | Capricorn the Goat | Aquarius the Water Bearer | Pisces the Fish |

the outside of the wheel (just like the numbers on a clock) and the planets are inside the wheel (just like the hands of a clock). The planets point to the signs. This is what astrologers mean when they say something like your Sun is in Aries and your Moon is in Capricorn. This would be like an hour hand pointing to 9 and the minute hand pointing to 12.

Imagine what life must have been like before the calendar. You would have had no way of knowing that the flowers that bloomed in the spring wouldn't last forever or that winter, once the temperatures dropped and the snows began, didn't mean the end of the world for all time. Life would have seemed capricious, dangerous, and pretty depressing. Like the other creatures on the planet we would have been bound to our body clocks—eating when we're hungry, sleeping when we're tired, having sex, giving birth, and dying without much thought for the future. So what lifted our sights from the day-to-day grind of gathering some fruit here or running down an antelope there to envision a better life? The stars.

Newgrange is a prehistoric monument located in County Meath on the eastern side of Ireland. It looks like an enormous emerald mound. Built around 3200 BC during the Neolithic period, Newgrange is older than Stonehenge and it is older than the great pyramids of Egypt. The entrance of the monument is aligned with the rising sun on the winter solstice so that every year around Dec. 21 the sun shines directly through a rectangular opening above the entrance, down a long dark passageway, and fills the central chamber with light for about seventeen minutes. This is the only time of year when Newgrange's pitch-black interior is naturally lit. Today the light enters about four minutes after sunrise, but calculations based on the precession of the Earth show that five thousand years ago the first light would have entered exactly at sunrise. So on the shortest day of the year when the world was cold and bleak, here arrived a promise of light. Whether that promise was meant to assure the people who inhabited Newgrange millennia ago that there would be a new year to come or whether it promised hope for a life hereafter, we cannot know. All we do know is that this monument could not have been built if these prehistoric people weren't already using the heavens to tell time.

Astrology was never about superstition and fear. If anything, astrology was created to counteract our greatest fears. Understanding that the phases of the Moon added up to a month; that the four seasons wherein the Sun rose in the spring, peaked in the summer, set in the autumn, and grew distant in the winter could be measured in 365 days; and that the planets themselves always returned without fail to the place in the sky where they were first spotted gave humankind a sense of continuity and stability. The regular orbit of the heavenly bodies was reassurance that there truly was an order to things and that life wasn't random and chaotic. This is why symbols of the zodiac can be found in churches, synagogues, temples, and government buildings throughout America, Europe, and Asia. They're not there for decoration or to ward off evil spirits. They're there to remind us that *we all live in time*. It doesn't matter how we clock it, zone it, lapse it, or extend it—time transcends all sciences, religions, economies, and cultures. Everything rises, peaks, falls, and dies away—but the story of how it does that in time and what happens along the way is as diverse and singular as the lives that are born into this world.

We all live in time, but time also lives within us—and that's what your horoscope is. It is your time stamp for when you came into the world: a screenshot of the sky on the day that you were born. Your horoscope serves two functions. It paints a psychological portrait of you based on the positions of the ten planets, and it acts as your own personal calendar telling you when you are in season or out. You see, astrology was never about a fixed fate, because time isn't fixed. Astrology describes the relationship between a moving heaven above interacting with a growing horoscope below. You know how we talk about syncing our mobile devices to the cloud? Well, your horoscope works in an analogous fashion. The more in sync you are with *your* time, the more you'll be able to make the most of your booms, recover from your busts, and live a fully realized life. Astrology never tells you what to do, but rather when to do it.

THE SEASONS

There are twelve signs of the zodiac—one for each month of the year. The best way to remember the order of the signs is to group them into seasons. Aries, Taurus, and Gemini are the spring signs. Cancer, Leo, and Virgo are the summer signs. Libra, Scorpio, and Sagittarius are the autumn signs, and Capricorn, Aquarius, and Pisces are the winter signs.

Spring Signs:

Aries　　　Taurus　　　Gemini

Summer Signs:

Cancer　　　Leo　　　Virgo

Autumn Signs:

Libra　　　Scorpio　　　Sagittarius

Winter Signs:

Capricorn　　　Aquarius　　　Pisces

The next thing you need to do is to quarter that seasonal cycle into equinoxes and solstices. Equinoxes and solstices set the four cornerstones of the year.

THE EQUINOXES

You'll notice that Aries and Libra are placed exactly opposite each other on the horizon line, like two people facing each other on a seesaw. That's because these are the signs of the equinox. *Equinox* means equal day and equal night, and that's what we all experience every year when the Sun enters Aries on or around March 21 or when the Sun enters Libra on or around Sept. 22. This is when—from the Earth's point of view—the Sun crosses over the equator, moving from one hemisphere to the other.

In the spring the Sun moves into the Northern Hemisphere and that's when the trees bloom and the first green shoots push up through the earth. In the autumn the Sun moves past the equator again and into the Southern Hemisphere. Autumn is when the foliage changes color and the leaves begin to flutter down from the trees.

The Equinoxes

Starting on the first day after the spring equinox, the days get longer and the nights grow shorter until the Sun reaches the summer solstice. Similarly, on the first day that follows the autumnal equinox, the days get shorter and the nights grow longer—like a shadow—and this will continue until the Sun arrives at the winter solstice.

THE SOLSTICES

Solstice literally means "Sun at a standstill." Now the Sun doesn't really come to a standstill. If it did, we'd all be in a lot of trouble. But that's the way it looked to the people who were clocking it for centuries, and solstices mark the two times of year when the Sun is farthest from the celestial equator. It was at these points that the Sun appeared to stop in the sky. It couldn't get any higher (summer) and it couldn't get any lower (winter). The summer solstice (which occurs in Cancer), marks the longest day and the shortest night of the year. It takes place on or around June 21. Summer is when the Sun feels closest and warmest to us. And the winter solstice (which occurs in Capricorn), marks the shortest day and the longest night of the year. It takes place somewhere around Dec. 21. Winter is when the Sun feels the most cold and distant. This is illustrated with Cancer and Capricorn being given the 6 o'clock and 12 o'clock positions on the chart.

Spring people (Aries, Gemini, and Taurus) are regarded as the "young signs." They're the up-and-comers. Eager to make their mark on the world, they see life as chock-full of opportunities, and they want to capitalize on each and every one of them. They are guileless and a tad naïve, and there's no denying that their enthusiasm is infectious. They're the eternal kids who will never grow up. Quick starters and big talkers, they have difficulty with bringing things in for a landing.

You can think of the summer people (Cancer, Leo, Virgo) as the "sunbathers." Born in the season of abundance when roadside stands are spilling over with ripe fruit and vegetables, they have no reason to believe that life will ever let them down. They are the most self-assured and confident of the signs. Their way is the right

The Equinoxes and the Solstices

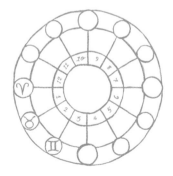

way. Whether their aims are ambitious or modest, they know that they have a guaranteed place at the table. It's why they don't do well with setbacks.

Autumn personalities (Libra, Scorpio, and Sagittarius) are the "comeback kids." Born during the time of year when the Sun is "setting," these signs have all experienced firsthand what it's like to take a fall after being on top. They also know that if you cave in to self-doubt and fear, you'll never pull yourself up by the bootstraps and get back on your feet. This indomitable will to rise again makes them the seasoned players of the zodiac.

Winter people (Capricorn, Aquarius, and Pisces) are slow to warm up. No strangers to hardship, they expect to shoulder heavy responsibilities in life and pride themselves on their resourcefulness, perseverance, and playing the long game. Whereas spring signs see life as starting out, the winter signs see life as winding down, so the challenge is to get them to try new things and to see the world through fresh eyes. They are the "old souls" of the zodiac. Now these descriptions have nothing to do with personal evolution or how many past lives you've clocked down here on planet Earth. They're solely based on the Sun. Were you born at the time of year when the Sun was just starting out? Peaking? Setting? Or set?

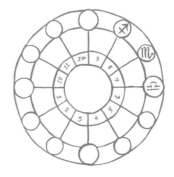

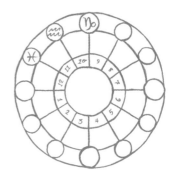

MODES

Each season—spring, summer, autumn, and winter—is made up of three signs, and they follow in strict order of appearance: cardinal, fixed, and mutable. These are called *quadruplicities* or if you want to be hip—modes.

Cardinal signs are zodiac signs that rule an equinox or a solstice. These are the signs that start the season, so they possess the most initiative. When

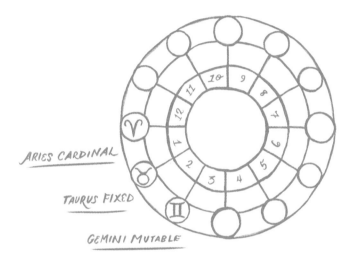

ARIES CARDINAL

TAURUS FIXED

GEMINI MUTABLE

you're in cardinal mode, you give direction but don't take it. Cardinal signs are the unstoppable forces of the zodiac, and they won't take no for an answer; however, they don't approach life in the same way. Aries attacks a situation head on; Cancer makes a wide circle around its objective before closing in; Libra invites people to combine forces, thereby augmenting its strength; and Capricorn, the climber, goes over the head of anyone who tries to get in their way. Cardinal signs go the distance and will always achieve their ends. It's why they are the most goal-oriented of the zodiac signs.

A fixed sign always follows a cardinal sign, and because it sits in the center, it is considered to be the heart of the season. In other words, spring has sprung when the Sun is in Taurus, summer is hottest in Leo, gardens fade and go to seed in Scorpio, and the world is coldest in Aquarius. Fixed signs always say no before they say yes. No before yes means it's up to you to sell them on your idea. It's a show-me mentality. Fixed signs never relinquish their veto power, which makes them the immovable objects to cardinals' unstoppable force. Their strength is in resistance. And like the cardinal signs they resist in different ways. Taurus plants it, Leo gets heated, Scorpio stares you down with a withering gaze, and Aquarius just freezes you out.

Mutable signs end the season. And it's because they're transitional signs—always looking back at what's come before while anticipating what will come next—that they are depicted as double-bodied. Either there are two figures—like Gemini the Twins and Pisces the Fish —or they are a composite figure, a mix of two beings, like Virgo, which is represented in antique star maps as a woman with wings, or Sagittarius, which is half man and half horse. Dualistic by nature, these signs introduce flexibility into a zodiac squeezed between unstoppable forces and immovable objects. It is in their nature to be accommodating. Their aim is to facilitate matters, to find a way to make the situation work. Gemini is the go-between, Virgo is the helper, Sagittarius accents the positive, and Pisces elicits sympathy.

ELEMENTS

After grouping into seasons and dividing into

modes, you want to join the signs by elements. The difference between modes and elements in astrology is like the difference between consonants and vowels in the alphabet. Consonants provide the building blocks, but it's the vowels that make the sounds. Vowels animate words. Similarly, in astrology it's the elements that make the zodiac signs come to life. And like vowels, they have their own distinct behaviors.

The four elements—water, earth, air, and fire—are the cornerstones of astrology. Water is the lowest on the scale; then comes earth, then air; and fire is the highest. This has nothing to do with one element being more evolved than another. What the ancients were trying to do by setting up this ascending order was to describe the nature of the elements themselves. It is the nature of water to go down. Rain falls from the sky, water flows downhill (not up), and a leak will always seek the lowest point before it seeps out. This is why water is at the bottom. Earth "sits" on water, as you see when approaching land from a boat. It's the solid ground we stand on. Air is all

FIRE	Aries	Leo	Sagittarius
AIR	Gemini	Libra	Aquarius
EARTH	Taurus	Virgo	Capricorn
WATER	Cancer	Scorpio	Pisces

around us. It fills our lungs, carries the clouds, and creates the atmosphere we live in, while fire flies up and out. The biggest source of heat and light is the Sun, which rises and sets above our world. Water seeks depth. Earth seeks to amass. Air seeks to circulate. And fire seeks height. That's why fire crowns the elemental scale.

WATER

Water represents our emotional life. It gives us depth and it gives us feeling. When you think about how two thirds of our planet is covered by water and how 60 percent of our bodies are made up of water, you realize just how essential this element is. Life can't exist without water. Our emotional life can't exist without our feelings, memories, imagination, and dreams. Water rules our unconscious—the mysterious part of ourselves that lies submerged beneath our conscious, waking minds. This is where we emerge every morning feeling replenished and renewed, and this is where we return every night, in need of the restorative waters that only sleep can bring. Our consciousness is really just an island if you think about it—a small piece of real estate supported by a deep vast psyche.

The water signs are Cancer, Scorpio, and Pisces. These are the emotional signs of the zodiac. Think of the word *emotional* for a moment. When someone is described as being emotional, doesn't it usually mean that this person is being hysterical, crazy, or out of control? Yet the water signs are famously nonexpressive. For water signs, feelings are meant to be felt. It's why they don't talk about them or even try to explain their reactions. If you ask a water sign what they feel, you usually get a monosyllabic response. Water signs won't wax poetic like a fire sign will or analyze behavioral patterns like an air sign. Water signs have a profound mistrust of the spoken word. Now this doesn't apply to words in general. Some of our greatest writers, poets, and lyricists were born under water signs. These are people who understand that words are incantations that can cast a spell on a reader or a listener—opening up their hearts to the magic of their inner lives. A water sign's mistrust of the spoken word comes from the fear of their words being used against them. They've experienced too many times being misquoted or having their words twisted around to mean something they never felt. Quote what a water sign said back to them in an argument—or worse yet, try to pin them down to semantics—and you will see them grow fuzzy-headed; they'll get angry and confused like a witness grilled on the stand. They will respond with "That's not what I meant." They will flip-flop in all directions like a fish out of water. Theirs isn't the world of cool, systematic logic. They're suspicious of facts, mistrustful of stats, and they can smell a hastily manufactured rationale from miles away. Water signs know full well that words in the wrong hands can become weapons.

Water signs believe that we all draw from the same wellspring of emotion. The way that someone falls in love in New York City is no different from the way someone falls in love in Tokyo or Somalia or Iceland. Everyone knows what it feels like to be swept away, to experience hope or exhilaration, just like everyone knows what it's like to be hurt, to feel rejected, angry, or despondent. So if we all know what it's like to feel joy, then why would you ever want to make anyone else miserable?

This is what gives people born under Cancer, Scorpio, and Pisces their empathy and compassion. They feel other people's pain. They don't try to avoid the subject, tell you to get over it, or accuse you of being self-sabotaging. The water signs have the presence of heart to sit with you in your hurt. A water sign calms, soothes, and comforts.

Water signs can also imagine other people's emotional lives. It's not hard to put themselves in somebody else's shoes and to see the world through their eyes. Sometimes people who aren't water signs find this bewildering. They might say, how can you feel bad for a criminal who was so cruel and who intentionally caused so much harm? Yet water signs know that every person was once a child, and perhaps it was the pain and neglect suffered in childhood that made them turn out this way. Water signs know that all saints were once sinners. Treating people the way that you would want to be treated, turning the other cheek, and forgiving the trespasses of those who trespass against you isn't always something that comes naturally, but it does to the water signs. Forgiveness is a strength, not a weakness.

The hardest thing for a water sign to accept is that not everybody swims as deeply. Most people prefer to walk along the shore, hang out in the shallows, or maybe do some snorkeling. They're not all deep-sea divers. Each of us deals with rejection in our own way, but for water signs this can be a terrible betrayal. That's because so much of the back-and-forth is based on the silent undercurrents that run between two people. There's an unspoken understanding, a psychic rapport that allows water signs to read moods, decipher gestures, and know the exact moment to say the right thing. It's phantasmal and nebulous, to be sure, but this is what makes water signs so prescient. Which is why it's so important for water signs to know when to take someone at their word—even if that person's turning their back on the greatest thing that ever happened to them or making a huge mistake. At the end of the day, people's mistakes are theirs to make. Someone can share the same feelings as you but simply choose not to go there. This kind of acceptance doesn't come easy, but it will give you a fortitude and makes more sense than trying to set up "personal boundaries." What are boundaries to someone who's as deep and fluid as you?

You don't have to be born under a water sign to have a lot of water in your chart. If you have four or more planets in water signs, then your chart's pretty watery as far as an astrologer is concerned. If you have a lot of water in your chart, then you're going to attract people who are psychologically damaged, emotionally challenged, or carrying around a lot of personal baggage. They are in search of your water—like nomads in the desert looking for an oasis. We often think of emotional people as being needy, but they're not. If you have a lot water in your chart, then you have a lot of love to give. If anything, you have *too much* love to give, which is why you need people to come drink from your well so that you don't feel too heavy. People with a lot of water tend to be withdrawn, depressed, and isolated. When they give of themselves emotionally, the water circulates, which lightens the mood and buoys their spirits. It's kind of like the water cycle, if you think about it. Excess water is drawn up into the atmosphere to form clouds, and once the clouds become too heavy, that water returns to the Earth as rainfall. Water signs don't seek out the emotionally walking wounded because they're masochists. They draw them into their orbit in order to keep their energy flowing.

People with a lot of Cancer, Scorpio, and Pisces in their charts carry the water for us in this parched world. They fill our lives with intimacy, move us with their sensitivity, and enthrall us with their creativity. They carry qualities we don't always value but couldn't possibly live without. Without imagination we wouldn't be able to envision life any differently than what we see in front of us. Without memory we wouldn't remember who we used to be in those times when we've forgotten who we are. Without solace we wouldn't be able to collapse into somebody else's arms sobbing, and without hope we wouldn't be able to love again. People with watery charts have a hard time seeing themselves as empowered beings, but once they make the switch from bucket to reservoir they start to grasp the idea that theirs is a renewable energy source. The water in the water bottle you purchased last week is as old as the first drops of water that fell on the Earth millennia ago. It keeps going round and round. It keeps getting recycled. Water literally reincarnates. That's why water has always been connected to the immortal life of the soul.

EARTH

Imagine a water planet where coral reefs abound, fish swim free, and kelp forests stretch out in all directions without interruption. Now imagine throwing some land masses down on top of it. That's Earth.

Earth is the element we live on. It provides the ground beneath our feet, the bodies we inhabit, and the sustenance we need like food, shelter, and livelihood. Everything we produce physically—whether it's a burp or a great work of art—is ruled by earth. Earth is the domain of the material world—things that you can touch and feel with your body. And these objects come in a variety of shapes and sizes. Some may be warm and cozy while others may be cold and sharp. There are objects in easy reach and objects that are much harder to come by. And then there are the high-end luxury items versus the cheap knock-offs. Earth signs know that there is a wealth of disparity in this material world we live in and not everything is of equal value. This is why earth signs are always sizing up their situations in terms of how much value they really have.

There is only one question that drives the earth signs: *How do you live in a world where everything ultimately falls apart?* This is why the earth signs—Taurus, Virgo, and Capricorn—are always fretting about the time that's passing, how much money's in the bank, and what the expiration date is on the food squirreled away in the back of the refrigerator. An earth sign's greatest fear is to be kicked to the curb. They never want to be without, and it's the specter of that abandonment that gives them their drive, discipline, and determination.

Water signs are compassionate, sympathetic, and empathetic. They believe that we all draw from the same emotional reservoir, which is what makes them so willing to share, embrace, and make sacrifices. Earth signs aren't exactly sold on that idea. They are big proponents of the idea that good fences make good neighbors. They believe that if you stay on your side of the fence and I stay on mine, then everything's good. Minding your own business is an earth sign credo. You don't have to tell an earth sign to set boundaries. They came into this world with border walls up and deflector shields on.

What this comes from is the body. Earth signs are physical. They are ruled by their appetites and cravings, their need to acquire and secure. Earth is the element of health and wealth. As long as you have your health, you can work; as long as you can work, you can make money; and as long you have money, you can take care of yourself. It's as simple as that. Sex is ruled by earth, but love isn't. Love belongs to the domain of water. The reason that sex is ruled by earth is that it's a physical craving that can be easily satisfied. It's not unlike grabbing a snack when your blood sugar is low or a cup of coffee in the afternoon to perk you up. Whatever the need, you take care of it and get back to work. Now this isn't to say that earth signs are unromantic. It's just that it takes a while to wean them off the take-out menu and to sell them on haute cuisine, but once done they quickly become connoisseurs. You just have to help them make the switch from quantity to quality.

Yet that idea of separateness is key to understanding the earth sign mentality. Earth signs know on a molecular level that everyone is born alone and dies alone, which is why there is always this feeling of apartness that inhabits their every exchange. They are the most existential of the zodiac signs; it's very hard for people born under Taurus, Virgo, and Capricorn to entrust someone else with their welfare. They never know if that person's going to come up short, be part of the problem instead of the solution, or turn out to be a no-show. It's much better for the earth sign to be the reliable one and not the other way around. That way there are no surprises.

You don't have to be born under an earth sign to have a lot of earth in your chart. If you have four or more planets in earth signs, then your chart's pretty earthy as far as an astrologer is concerned. If you have a lot of earth in your chart, then you're going to define yourself by your duties, responsibilities, and obligations. These are the things that get you out of bed in the morning and keep you on track. Mortality is never far from your thoughts. You might laugh at this idea—*mortality* is such a heavy word—but that's why you fret so much about your time, your schedule, your money, and your food. You're always afraid of running out. People with a lot of earth tend to be anxious and worry a lot. This is what makes them the workaholics of the zodiac. Never the grasshopper, always the ant, earth signs are industrious. They need to build, to grow things, and produce. It's a good day if they've checked off everything on their to-do list. It's an even better one if they got paid handsomely for it.

Yet earth signs are deeply committed to taking care of the people they love. It is in their nature to shelter, provide, and protect. But they aren't enablers. They're big believers in the saying "Give a man a fish and he eats for a day, but teach a man to fish and he eats forever." Self-sufficiency is the earth sign credo, which is why they're big on teaching their children how to take care of themselves. Yes, it may be boring to have to sit through the long lecture on why things work the way they do, to sit helplessly by as the earth sign parent takes apart an appliance so that you can see all the inner workings and then shows you how to put it back together again. There's nothing point-and-click about getting the answer you seek with an earth sign—but what you get in the end is the step-by-step process of how to do it yourself, and that comes in handy when you have to change a tire by the side of the road in the dead of night or troubleshoot a problem with your computer when under deadline.

Earth signs have no patience for slackers. And they can be pretty hard-nosed when it comes to the troubles of others. They have to be convinced that you're truly in need before they will help you out, and even then, don't expect a handout. They'll want you to pay back what you owe, either in installments or in sweat equity. Is this about the money? Absolutely. But it's also about learning to live within your means. Learning to live within your means isn't just about frugality. It's about knowing your limits, economizing your efforts, and making the most of your resources. Earth signs know that we don't value things if we don't work hard for them. We just consume them and come back for more.

Earth signs aren't big on vision, but they need one. They need something to lift their sights or else they become slaves to their routine. Earth's great talent is to take what's on the drawing board and to give it physical form. Earth signs can turn a blueprint into a building, a business plan into a thriving company, or a dream into a reality. A lot of people talk about their Mona Lisas, but only an earth sign could paint one. If you have a lot of earth in your chart, then you have an instinct to shape and mold, to model and to fix. Put this in service to a dream, a hope, a cause, or a higher purpose and it's amazing what you can do. For an earth sign, paradise doesn't reside in the hereafter, but in the here and now. This world is your plot of land to seed, till, and harvest.

AIR

Water signs believe that we all draw from the same emotional wellspring. Earth signs believe that we are separate beings with our bodies forming natural borders around each of us. Air signs take a bird's-eye view of the situation. Gliding above earth, which sits above water, air signs recognize that no person is an island. Each of us relies on—and in turn is relied on by—others. It is the nature of life, even on a molecular level, to organize itself into larger bodies. To group, to cluster, to assemble. The air signs know that we are better together than we are apart. This is why the air signs are the bridge builders of the zodiac. They are constantly reaching out across the divide that separates one person from another. But how do you connect to someone who may not be on the same page as you emotionally, spiritually, economically, or politically? You need words.

Words are important to air signs. Not only do words describe and explain what's going on with you to somebody else who hasn't a clue, but you can use words to get what you want. How you word a request, for instance—opting to be polite and deferential rather than bossy and brusque—will likely result in success. Prevailing upon others to see reason when tempers are heated requires you to be both eloquent and clearheaded, while giving direction to those you are leading needs to be done in the simplest language possible in order to be effective. Words communicate and words bind. That's why when you give your word it's the same as signing a contract as far as an air sign is concerned. You word is your bond.

"We" is the favorite word of air signs. The air signs are Gemini, Libra, and Aquarius. And by the way, you don't have to be born under an air sign to have a lot of air in your chart. If you have four or more planets in air signs, then your chart's pretty airy as far as an astrologer is concerned. If you have a lot of air in your chart, you're going to see yourself as being part of a pair, a relationship, or a group. You will rarely refer to yourself in the first person singular. It's almost always first person plural. And this isn't because you're assuming the royal *we* or are trying to hide behind someone else's skirts. For an air sign it's important that everyone be heard. They know full well that this invites contrary views, heated exchanges, and dissonance rather than harmony, but that's all right because air signs don't want everyone to be of the same mind. To be on the same page? Yes, because air signs know that they'll never get anything done if they don't coordinate efforts. But of the same mind? No. If anything, air signs relish a good debate. Air signs are famously inquisitive, experimental, and theoretical. You don't broaden your horizons and inform your world by insisting on conformity. Air signs may not always have an open mind, but they certainly possess a curious one. They always want to know what everyone else is up to.

This can sometimes give the impression of being superficial, of caring too much about what others think. And sometimes that's the case, but the important thing to remember about air signs is that their most precious resources are their human resources. It doesn't matter if you're their dog walker or their spouse—every person has a part to play in the ecosystem of an air sign's life. This is why they're constantly texting, messaging, posting, and "liking." Air signs fuss over their relationships like a florist arranging a made-to-order bouquet. Each person is unique and precious, a bloom that needs to be tended to.

Air signs have been likened to social butterflies flitting from person to person, but they're actually more like busy bees in a hive. A hive is different from a herd. Herd mentality is when people just follow along in a group. In a hive, however, each member is assigned a specific task that serves a particular function. Specialized and hierarchical, a hive couldn't function independently of its members; the whole is always greater than the sum of its parts. It's why air signs gravitate to large organizations, institutions, and agencies. There's something about being part of a collective effort, knowing where their place is in the roster, and hearing the uninterrupted buzz of background chatter that puts their nervous minds at ease. Indeed, air signs do their best thinking in a group—the noisier and more distracting, the better. Nothing makes an air sign more miserable than to be separated from others. They may say that's what they need to focus, but within moments they'll turn on the news or pop in a pair of earbuds to listen to a podcast. They need company to think.

Rule of law is important to an air sign. You might not think that at first because they're constantly pushing the envelope, but it's the answer—not the question—that matters most. There really is a right way of doing things as far as air signs are concerned. And it's usually logical, impartial, and provable. That's why they're the first ones to whip out the contract when there's a dispute, to reference time-stamped emails if someone's recollection of events is iffy, or cite facts and stats when arguments get too heated and personal. They don't do this because they have to be right—although they do often assume that they're smarter than most; they do this because they believe in an ordered Universe. Everything can be explained—even if we don't possess the ability to explain it yet.

However, for an element that can be so people-oriented, it's remarkable how insensitive air signs can be to others' feelings. Don't expect an air sign to read a mood. They'll happily scroll through their text messages while you sit there across the table in angry silence. And it's not because they're trying to avoid you. They simply assume that if you're quiet it's because you've got nothing to say. It's important to remember that words are everything to an air sign, so you have to spell things out if you're upset. And then you have to make time to analyze what's going on and to discuss all the particulars in great detail. Air signs believe in the talking cure—partly because their own emotional lives are a complete mystery to them, so talking about their feelings is an opportunity to decipher those feelings, and partly because they believe in the healing properties of conversation. Conversation—no matter how heated or cool—affirms a connection, and as long as two warring parties remain in the same room, there's always hope of making peace. Air signs famously insist on not going to bed angry—even if that means staying up all night to work out your differences.

So are air signs emotionally challenged? Yes. It's like water signs who clam up, earth signs who refuse to share, and fire signs who can't imagine how you could possibly live without them. Each element has its blind spot, and for air it's their emotions. There's just a mental disconnect that takes place when things get too upsetting, deep, or personal. The emotions are there but the circuitry isn't. This is why air signs are drawn to other people—in order to connect and to learn about themselves. It can be frustrating when they accuse you of doing things that they do all the time, but then air signs can be like children looking to dump their vegetables onto your plate so they can present a clean one for dessert. It's natural for air signs to project—which is why being in a relationship with them can sometimes feel like you're undergoing Freudian analysis— but what you get in return is someone who is committed to you. A relationship is like a covenant to an air sign. It's why they take so long to say yes, but once they do, that bond is solid and everlasting.

FIRE

Ancient people believed that the stars in the heavens were the bonfires of the gods. And as they crackled and popped, they spat out sparks that floated aimlessly for a while in space before being drawn down through the seven planetary spheres. As each spark descended, it was blessed by every planet in turn until it arrived in the body of a baby at the exact moment of birth. When that baby took its first breath, that spark threw open its eyes, lit up its mind, and made it cry out. The spirit entered the body of the infant and resided within it—like a homeowner entering their house at night and turning on all the lights. Fire is literally the spark of life, the spirit that animates our bodies, gets us up and going and eager to experience all that the world has to offer. Fire signs want to live, live, LIVE!

Spirit is not the same as soul. When we describe someone as "spirited," we usually mean that that person is excitable, vibrant, and bursting with energy—like a flame. They're indomitable, volatile, and fiercely independent. "Soulful," on the other hand, implies quiet, contemplative, and even melancholic—qualities that are the opposite of fire. If you were born under the zodiac sign of Aries, Leo, or Sagittarius, you are ruled by your enthusiasms, stoked by your passions, and spurred on by your beliefs. You express everything that is going on inside you, and you express it immediately. There's no holding back. No sitting on feelings, waiting on ceremony, or putting yourself in somebody else's shoes. Fire signs experience everything in the moment. They are the most candid, spontaneous, and impulsive of the elements. They're also the ones most likely to walk back what they just said. If you have a lot of fire in your chart, then apologizing for things you say and do is nothing new. One would think this would be humbling, but it's not. You accepted a long time ago that your words and actions are just going to rub some people the wrong way, and that's OK as long as you are true to yourself.

For air signs it's the other person who's important. Their greatest resources are their human resources, which is why they place such importance on relationships. *We* is the keyword for an air sign. To understand a fire sign's way of thinking, take the *w* in *we*, flip it upside down to make an *m*, and you get *me*. Nobody places a higher value on individuality than a fire sign does. Fire signs know that if it weren't for that special spark that makes each person unique and different, we would all be living in a world of cookie-cutter cutouts. Fire signs make a personal difference.

You don't have to be born under a fire sign to have a lot of fire in your chart. If you have four or more planets in fire signs, then your chart's pretty fiery as far as an astrologer is concerned. People with a lot of Aries, Leo, and Sagittarius in their charts know they are special. They may go through their bouts of doubt and insecurity like everyone else, but they know deep inside that they were born to do great things, that they possess a special gift or have a higher calling. People like this used to be portrayed in ancient times with jewel-encrusted crowns, halos, or tongues of fire flickering overhead—symbols that showed that they were stamped with the sign of the divine. They were privileged, set apart, and favored by the gods. Nowadays we call them stars. Stars radiate that certain something that makes them stand out in a crowd, rise to the top of their field, and have Instagram accounts with bazillions of followers. Other people may fret over their personal brands and authentic selves, but fire signs don't have to do that. They just are. They have an intuitive sense for being in the right place at the right time for when good fortune smiles down on them. If you're lucky and can find a fire sign to stand next to, there's a good chance that some of that good fortune will rub off on you, too.

The biggest challenge for a fire sign is sustainability—learning how to economize their efforts, moderate their pace, and take their time sizing up a situation before jumping into it. Fire signs tend to leap first and ask questions later. Part of this stems from that urgency that propels them forward—fire signs are very future oriented and believe that the best is yet to come—and part of it stems from the fact that they are more sensational than emotional in temperament. Emotions are ruled by water. Emotions are deeply personal experiences that don't need to be expressed or shown because they are simply *felt*. Sensational personalities (like fire signs) are drawn to peak experiences. They live for the highs. When you fall in love it has to be the best romance EVER! When you get angry it can't just be a hissy fit. You have to be really LOUD and DRAMATIC! When you're ashamed you can't just retreat to a corner. You have to WEEP and CONFESS for everyone to see. Everything is on public display. And of course if you're going to experience highs, you're naturally going to experience lows, and those lows can be immobilizing. This is why fire signs avoid anything that's too heavy, gloomy, or depressing. They have a fear of being extinguished.

Fire signs don't think twice about walking out on jobs, relationships, and obligations that have become dead ends. Like a wildfire they have no problem hopping over divides and barriers if there's something combustible and more enlivening on the other side. They're always looking for fresh starts. Yet this element can have a hard time learning from its mistakes. It's not reflective like water, self-incriminating like earth, or analytical like air. Like the Sun dawning on a new day or the legendary phoenix rising from the ashes, a fire sign roars to life with the strike of a match, so dwelling on the past or raking yourself over the coals is not for them. It's almost like they were born with a psychological reboot button. They're much more focused on doing better next time, and because there will always be a next time, they can adopt a "that was then, this is now" attitude regarding everything that has come before. This is why they keep running into the same problems in love and at work without the faintest clue of why it's happening again. For an element that champions the right for each person to be true to themselves, they can have a real problem with accountability. They just don't want to be seen in a bad light.

Fire signs need a lot of reassurance and love. You wouldn't think it from the way they present themselves, but they do. You never want to poke holes in their dreams—even if they're way out there. Be supportive instead and maybe try going along for the ride. Not only will you open up your world, but you may wind up having the adventure of a lifetime.

HOW THE SKY WORKS

This is how the sky works in an astrology chart. The Earth orbits the Sun in a counterclockwise direction. The Earth's orbit around the Sun gives us the seasons. As the Sun moves through the signs in a year—the Sun is in Aries in April, Taurus in May, Gemini in June, and so on—you will see it move in the direction mapped out in the following figure. The Sun in a zodiac sign will always tell you what time of year it is. That's why Aries, sign of the spring equinox and the first sign, is followed by Taurus, Gemini, and so on, all moving in a counterclockwise order.

As the Earth orbits the Sun, it also rotates on its axis. The Earth's rotation on its axis gives us day and night. The side that faces the Sun is day, and the side that faces away is night. The Earth rotates on its axis in the same counterclockwise direction, from west to east. This is what creates the illusion of the Sun moving in a clockwise direction. This is why the Sun rises in the morn-

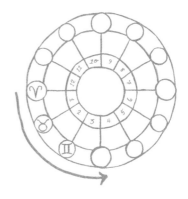

The Earth orbits the Sun in a counterclockwise direction so the order of the signs is counterclockwise

ing on the left, moves across the sky, and then sets on the right at night. Remember that everything in astrology is seen from the Earth's point of view, and that's how the Sun looks to us in the sky during the day.

So why does the Sun do this in an astrological chart when everyone knows that the Sun rises in the east and sets in the west? Because we live in the Northern Hemisphere. The easiest way to spot where the Sun is in the sky is to stand with your back to the north. The Sun's path across the sky—like that of the planets at night—lies farther south than where we are situated in America, Europe, and Asia. That's why the Sun— along with the planets—rises in the east on the left and sets in the west on the right. Astrology was invented in the Northern Hemisphere, so our astrological charts are constructed with this point of view in mind.

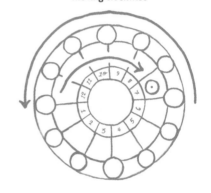

The Earth rotates on its axis from west to east, creating the illusion of the Sun moving clockwise

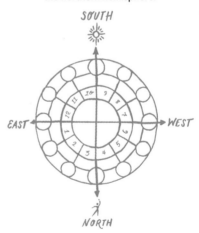

The Sun's path across the sky lies farther south than where we are situated in the northern hemisphere.

DAY CHART

If you were born in the day, the Sun will appear above the horizon in your astrological chart. And this is where the Sun wants to be because this is when the Sun gets to shine. Daytime people need to be seen and recognized. You want to impress others and get your name out there. Everything you do is on display and you are acutely aware of being watched and judged. This is great if you have the sort of ego that presents well, because you will endeavor to climb to the top and be the *best* that you can possibly be. The funny thing about the Sun above the horizon is that even if it's in a shy and retiring sign—like a Cancer or a Virgo—you will still find yourself thrust into the public eye. The

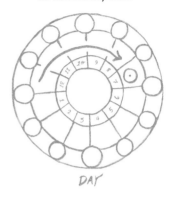

The Sun appears above the horizon in a day chart

DAY

downside is a desperate need for attention. We can't see the other planets when the Sun is out in the daytime, and like the Sun you may seek to outshine others by hogging the spotlight. Learning to share space, listen, and give credit where credit is due is something that daytime people really have to work on. There's also a big fear of disappearing from view—especially if you were born near sunset.

The most comfortable placement for the Moon in a daytime chart is below the horizon. That way it doesn't have to compete with the Sun because it is in its own time of day: night. This gives the Moon equal strength. The Moon can do what it does best, which is to provide a private life—a place to come home to at the end of the day. By drawing a line between your public and personal spheres, the Moon allows you to leave behind the stresses of the day. You can reconnect with family, unwind after work with friends, or pursue a personal

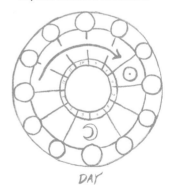

The most comfortable placement for the Moon in a day chart is below the horizon

DAY

hobby or endeavor that's more beloved to you than your day job. Without that line of demarcation you would be on call 24/7, and that can lead to exhaustion and burnout. The Moon's nature is to temper, cool, and restore. Think of the Moon below the horizon in a day chart as the roots of a tree. You never see them, but you know they're what's holding that tree in place. How well you grow and flourish in life will always be based on your root system.

NIGHT CHART

If you were born at night, the Sun will appear below the horizon in your astrological chart. This is the time of day when the Sun is not seen. But just because the Sun has disappeared from view doesn't mean it's not around. You may not be seen, but your presence is always felt. You prefer to be the power behind the throne and not the person sitting on it. Leaders on thrones may get overthrown. Nighttime people like to blend in with their surroundings. Keeping a low profile allows you to come and go as you please. Your "night vision"

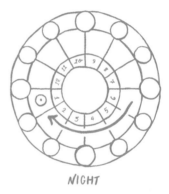

The Sun appears below the horizon in a night chart

NIGHT

also gives you the ability to recognize the hidden potential in people and things. It's what makes you an excellent developer, scout, or investor. You know a diamond in the rough when you spot it. But sometimes you can focus so much on a work in progress that it never sees the light of day. This is especially true of people born just before sunrise. Your big challenge is to get things up and going even if you feel like you're still not ready. Chances are you're better prepared than you know.

The most comfortable placement for the Moon in a nighttime chart is above the horizon. This shows that the Sun has set and now it's the Moon's turn to shine. This makes the Moon as strong as—if not stronger than—the Sun, so if you have a nighttime chart, your Moon sign may play as powerful a role in your horoscope as your Sun sign. A nighttime chart with the Moon visible makes your mother the more dominant parent in your life. The Moon rules the body, so providing food, shelter, and clothing are top priorities. Your well-being—as well as the well-being of others—is of uppermost importance. There is nothing objective, dispassionate, or removed about you. Your body is yourself and the personal is political regardless of where you stand on the issues of the day. For you it's less about your accomplishments and more about what you produce—which makes sense given that the Moon is the planet of growth. Think of the Moon above the horizon in a night chart as the branches of a tree. It provides shade from the Sun and is overladen with the fruits of your labor.

The most comfortable placement for the Moon in a night chart is above the horizon

And what if you were born with a day chart with the Moon above the horizon, or a night chart with the Moon below the horizon? Does that mean you're messed up? Hardly. First of all, it's impossible to be born with a chart where all the planets are in their ideal positions. No such astrology chart exists. Indeed, the art of interpretation is in figuring out how to access a planet's strengths or redirect its challenging energies. Consider the Latin phrase *Astra inclinant, sed non obligant:* "The stars incline us, they do not bind us." The biggest purveyors of astrology in the ancient world were sailors because they used the stars to steer their ships by, and the same goes for your horoscope. That's what it's here for. To help you navigate your way through all the risings and settings, the high noons and the dark nights so that you can live the best life ever.

THE ANGLES

The final piece to understanding how the sky works in an astrological chart is the angles. Let's return to the image of the clock, since we've already determined that the Sun moves in a clockwise direction through the sky. You can think of 9 o'clock as the *ascendant*. This is where the Sun rises over the horizon. Next, 12 o'clock is called the *midheaven*. This is where the Sun reaches its highest point in the sky. Then 3 o'clock is the *descendant*—where the Sun sets at night. And 6 o'clock is called the *imum coeli*, which is Latin for "bottom of the sky," It's better known as the IC. This is the midnight place where the Sun ends one day and begins another.

All of the other planets—from the Moon to Pluto—follow the same path that the Sun travels across the sky. They will all rise at the ascendant, peak at the midheaven, set in the descendant, and drop anchor in the IC. Of course, they will do this at different times of the day

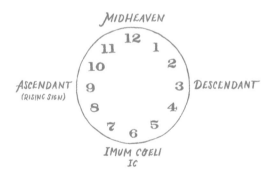

and often in different zodiac signs. Sometimes you will see several planets clustered together around one angle, and sometimes you will see them dispersed to the four corners of a chart.

Any planet close to an angle—that is, any planet that appears at the 9 o'clock, 12 o'clock, 3 o'clock, or 6 o'clock position—increases in strength and will play a prominent role in your horoscope regardless of your Sun sign, Moon sign, or rising sign. You will want to pay very close attention to these.

THE SUN, MOON, AND RISING SIGNS

The three most important features of an astrological chart are the Sun sign, the Moon sign, and the ascendant—better known as the rising sign. They're so important that you could pretty much read a chart with just these alone. That's why it's a good idea to read all three when you read your daily horoscope. The Sun represents what you *know* about yourself to be true. The Moon represents what you *feel* about yourself to be true. And the rising sign is the face that you *show* the world. It's how people see you but it's also how you will, in turn, act because that's the role you feel that you're expected to play. Sometimes this works in accordance with your chart and sometimes it doesn't. The rising sign is such an important feature that it deserves its own book—which I'll be working on next. But for now let's keep the focus on turning your astrology chart into a calendar, and for that we need to turn first to the Sun.

THE SUN

THE SUN

The Sun is the most important planet in your astrological chart. If each planet represents a hand on the face of the celestial clock, the Sun is like the hour hand. It's when you came into the world. That's why it's the easiest planet to find. Look up the zodiac sign that the Sun was in on your birthday (see below) and that's your Sun sign. A person's Sun sign will always tell you the time of year that person was born. (See the box on page 43 for a bit more about these dates, and what happens at the end of one sign and the start of the next, which we call the cusps.)

ARIES March 20–April 18

TAURUS April 19–May 19

GEMINI May 20–June 20

CANCER June 21–July 21

LEO July 22–Aug. 21

VIRGO Aug. 22–Sept. 21

LIBRA Sept. 22–Oct. 22

SCORPIO Oct. 23–Nov. 21

SAGITTARIUS Nov. 22–Dec. 20

CAPRICORN Dec. 21–Jan. 18

AQUARIUS Jan. 19–Feb. 17

PISCES Feb. 18–March 19

The Sun is your life force: the source of your vitality and strength. That's why you always want to do things in your "season." If you're a summer baby, you want to fall in love in the summer. If you're a winter baby, you want to compete in the winter. This is when you are in peak form. Conversely, the time of year when the Sun is farthest away from you—that's six signs away from yours on the zodiac wheel or six months away on the calendar—is the time of year when you will feel the most drained, under the weather, and vulnerable. You don't want to make any important decisions or take on any big commitments when the Sun is opposite your birthday month because you are "out of season." You aren't functioning at top capacity.

Think of your Sun sign as your patch of sky. Since each sign rules a month, that means there are thirty days out of the year (give or take a day) that belong to you. Every birthday, you can look forward to the Sun coming around full circle to revive, reorient, and reboot you. You are made robust and vigorous again when the Sun is in your sign. This is also why so many people pass away just around their birthday. It's their spirit struggling to get back to that place in time when they feel strongest. And if their body can no longer house their spirit, then it's the time when they feel most capable of letting go and sending their spirit back to the stars.

But the Sun sign is more than just your time of year, it's also your identity. The Sun symbolizes "what I know about myself to be true." Think about that statement for a moment. It's not "what I feel, think, want, or would like to believe about myself to be true." It's "what I *know* about myself to be true." There's a certainty to that, a centeredness. Just like the Sun in our solar system. Without the Sun the planets wouldn't stick around. They'd fly off in all directions. The Sun's job in a horoscope is to put you at the center of your own universe. That's why it's always been connected to the ego. And egos are important things. They're not cats in need of stroking or dogs in need of praising. They're a necessary part of the human psyche. Your ego is the gravitational pull that holds all those aspects of yourself together—your desires, dreams, memories, thoughts, spiritual experiences, anxieties, and fears—they are all locked into orbit by your ego.

Father Signs, Mother Signs

There are three signs of the father in astrology: Aries, Leo, and Capricorn. If you were born under one of these signs, then the father plays a prominent role in your life. Leo is the Good Father, Capricorn is the Dark Father, and Aries is Coach Dad. The reason for these descriptions has less to do with your father and more to do with the time of year you were born. For instance, the Sun is at home in Leo because July 22–Aug. 21 is the heart of summer. It's when days are hottest and brightest so you will see your father as a strong presence, good-natured, and lionhearted. Capricorn, on the other hand, is the zodiac sign of the winter solstice. This is the time of year when days are shortest, nights are longest, and the Sun feels weak and cold. This is why Capricorn is the sign of the Dark Father. That doesn't mean your father's bad. It's more like he's unavailable, stern, or hard to get to know. And finally, the Sun is young and exuberant in Aries. Aries is the first sign of the zodiac, and indeed New Year's used to be celebrated on April 1 until the date was changed to Jan. 1 by Pope Gregory XIII in the sixteenth century. It took a while for the new New Year's to catch on (they didn't have Twitter back then), which is why people who continued to celebrate New Year's on April 1 were called fools by those who had made the switch. They were the target of pranks and practical jokes and this is the origin of April Fool's Day. Nevertheless, the spring equinox is still celebrated as New Year's in Persia, Turkey, and Afghanistan. Britain and the American colonies were longstanding holdouts until they finally changed their calendars to Jan. 1 in the 1750s. In any case, the Sun is regarded as being the most up-and-at-'em in Aries, which is why this is the sign of Coach Dad.

Cancer, Virgo, and Scorpio are the zodiac signs of the mother. Cancer is the Good Mother because it rules the summer solstice, where days are longest and nights are shortest and the earth is bursting with life; Scorpio is the Dark Mother because it falls in the heart of autumn, when the crops have been harvested and summer gardens have gone to seed; and Virgo is the zodiac sign of Mother/Daughter relationships. The only zodiac sign to be depicted as a woman, Virgo represents both fruit and seed because daughters are the only children of mothers capable of giving birth.

The easiest way to gauge the Sun's strength in your astrological chart is to determine whether it's in domicile, detriment, exaltation, or fall. The Sun is at home in Leo (domicile) because that's the heart of summer; it's out of season in Aquarius (detriment) because Aquarius is six months away from Leo and lies in the heart of winter; the Sun arrives in Aries because that's the sign of the spring equinox (exalted); and it departs in Libra (fall) because Libra rules the autumnal equinox. Now admittedly these can sound like judgments—and to a certain extent they are—but a judgment is not a definition. If anything, determining planetary strength helps us read an astrological chart in more nuanced ways. A planet—whether it's the Sun, Venus, Jupiter, or Pluto—will do the very best job it can to exert its influence. However, there are certain zodiac signs where it will express itself more vigorously versus ones where it will struggle to do what it needs to do. And this isn't necessarily a bad thing. For instance, you may have noticed that both Libra and Aquarius—zodiac signs where the Sun is either in fall or in detriment—are air signs, which means that the emphasis is going to be on *we* rather than *me*. Air signs are relationship signs, so people born under Libra and Aquarius form alliances in order to succeed. They have no problem combining efforts and don't mind sharing the credit or recognition. And that's because they have a "weak" Sun. Their egos aren't insisting that they get all the glory. As you can imagine, this isn't going to sit well with people whose astrology charts feature a strong Sun and who want to shine on their own. All of this is to say that good placements aren't always good, just as bad placements aren't always bad. It's something to keep in mind as you read about the Sun and how it appears in each of the twelve signs.

A Note about Cusps

The Sun sign dates I've listed (see page 39) are formatted in the way that you would see them in a newspaper astrology column or online horoscope. They are general approximations based on cusps.

Cusp refers to the day in the calendar when the Sun moves from one zodiac sign to the next. For instance, on April 19 the Sun leaves the zodiac sign of Aries and enters the zodiac sign of Taurus. But this isn't set in stone. One year the Sun may change signs on April 19 but in another year it might change signs on April 20.

The reason for this is that we actually live according to two years: the sidereal year and the calendar year. The *sidereal* year is the time that it takes the Earth to complete a single orbit around the Sun, which works out to 365 days, 6 hours, and 9 minutes. The *calendar* year—which is based on the spring equinox (which is also what we use to set our clocks by)—works out to 365 days, 5 hours, and 48 minutes. There is a difference of 20 minutes between our sidereal and calendar years. That difference adds up over time so that every four years we reconcile the two by adding an extra day—Feb. 29—to the calendar. Hence the leap year.

However, astrology columnists make adjustments for the Sun's change of signs every year, which is why when you check your online horoscope on Jan. 1 you will see that some of the zodiac sign cusp dates have changed by a day, but by no more than a day.

This is what gave rise to the notion that people born on the cusp (i.e., on the day that the Sun changes signs) were a mix of the two signs, but that's not true. You're either one sign or the next. That's why it's always a good idea to get your chart done so you can see which sign you were born under.

SPRING SUN SIGNS

THE SUN IN ARIES

Spring is a ferocious season. Seeds sprout, branches flower, and weeds pop out from undercover ready to choke the life out of any fresh growth. It's a race to see who's going to establish territory right away. It's an exciting time and an uncertain time because the threat of frost laces the air and you never know when it's going to descend and wipe out the first ranks. You were born around that time of year when even the clocks have been set forward an hour in order to give you your competitive edge. Leaning forward is built into your sign. And like a runner at the starting line you crouch into position, clear your mind, and wait for the gun to go off.

Aries is really good at exploding out of the gate. Often described as impulsive and heated, you're in fact quite disciplined and focused on whatever you set your sights on. A lot of preparation goes into who you are. Like the kid who wakes up first thing in the morning to train for a swim meet or the child who can't hang out with her friends after school because she has to go to ballet class, you make sacrifices and will do whatever it takes to be the best that you can be. You pursue your passion with the determination of a heat-seeking missile. You were born under the first sign of the zodiac, but first doesn't always mean best—or that your position at the front of the line is secure. Winning hands can be trumped, records get broken, and accomplishments are there for the sole purpose of being surpassed. You more than anyone know that you're only as good as your last performance.

Part of this comes from your father. Aries, Leo, and Capricorn are three zodiac signs where the father plays a prominent role in the horoscope. Aries is the sign of Coach Dad. Coach Dads are the ones who argued with the referee on your behalf, grilled you the night before your big quiz, and tried to show you how to change a tire when you were three. Coach Dads want to make sure that you can take care of yourself in any situation. They're not coddling or indulgent. If anything they point out your shortcomings, chuckle when you mess up, and ask you to hit the ground and give them fifty push-ups at the very moment you need a shoulder to lean on. But there's no doubt that they're in your corner. Your Coach Dad would have told you that you can always do better, and because of him you do. Coach Dads want winners, not whiners.

The hardest thing for an Aries to accept is weakness. You can't stand it in others and you have zero tolerance for it in yourself. This is why you can't help laughing when someone screws up. And it's not because you delight in others' mishaps. If anything, you're a champion for those less fortunate than yourself. Yet laughter masks your deep anxiety about weakness. Your ruling planet is Mars—named after the Roman god of war. You have to be battle ready. You have spartan tastes and if you could sleep on a bed of nails every night you would. You're constantly on guard against getting soft, losing your edge, or being lulled into complacency. This is why Aries people often have such a hostile reaction to weight gain. It also explains why you don't do well with praise or flattery. When someone gives you a compliment you automatically assume they're BSing you—and you'll even respond with a brusque remark. That's because praise and flattery remind you of how much you need appreciation, recognition, and approval, and needs are a no-no in the Aries lexicon. Being needy makes you whiny, wimpy, and spineless. Your reaction to people who want to talk to you about their hurt feelings is to roll your eyes and to tell them: GET OVER IT.

Like Superman or Wonder Woman, you're on call 24/7 to help out in a pinch. And you will. But you don't stick around after you've raced into the burning building to fetch the baby or rescue the cat from a tree. You're on to the next crisis. And in some ways it can be said that you're a crisis junkie. That's why so many Aries people join the police force, the military, or an EMS unit. You are astrology's first responders. You say that you're doing it for truth and justice, but you're actually doing it for the rush. If you could spend the rest of your life spinning like a ninja from crisis to crisis, you would.

Yet superheroes need victims to save, which explains why loved ones and friends are a hot mess, and your co-workers are incapable of stapling two pages together without asking you for help. They're waiting for you to come save the day. And it doesn't matter how many times you say that this is the last time you're going to fly to the rescue, you always do. You may resent how often the people in your life overuse their Bat-Signal privileges, but why shouldn't they if that's the only time they get to see you? Heroic acts don't save people in the end because they invariably foster dependency. That's why coaching them in how to fend for themselves may be the best lesson of all.

You also have a complicated relationship with authority. People say you're a natural-born leader, but in truth you will avoid taking on a leadership position whenever possible. That's because you like taking orders. You can stand at attention confidently knowing that someone else is in charge. But that person in charge has to be above reproach. They must be bold, tough, uncompromising, and in the right. Like any sidekick, you're into hero worshipping. You want to be at their side watching their flank, enforcing their rules, and providing backup when needed, *but* you are no obedient underling. The moment they switch from leader to tyrant, you'll be the first to call Goliath out, put a stone in your slingshot, and take him down. But again, no sooner do you do this than you automatically pass the reins of authority over to someone else. You're a soldier, not a general.

You're really good at striving and not so good at arriving. You have a problem finishing things. Some say it's because you lose interest or are dismayed when the initial excitement wears off, but it comes from being born under the sign of the spring equinox. You're an opener, not a closer.

The Sun is exalted in Aries. *Exalted* means "celebrated." The reason the Sun is exalted in Aries is that it's a young Sun—like at sunrise. It's not the noonday sun that's peaked and sits established on his throne. Yours is the young hero who's just starting out and has something to prove. Yours is the new face people look to, the fresh voice that gets their attention, the independent spirit that gets them to question their limits. And this optimism and idealism never goes away. It doesn't matter how many times you're laid low, kicked to the side of the curb, or cheated by scoundrels—you will always pick yourself up and charge back into the arena. You are heroically uncompromising, unapologetically passionate, refreshingly candid, and surprisingly . . . innocent. Yes, innocent. You still show a child's trust at sixty. And this is a special trait in a world where cynicism passes for wisdom and skepticism guards the castle keep of a closed mind. It takes a lot of courage to believe in the best in people and a lot of persistence to help them to achieve it. These are heavy expectations and you shoulder them gladly.

THE SUN IN TAURUS

There are people who build their houses out of straw and people who build them out of sticks. Yours is a strictly brick-based construction. Your aim is to create a solid foundation with impenetrable walls and an unshakeable roof so that you can withstand anything life has to throw at you. Like the bull that your sign is named after, you were born with a thick skin. You can take insults and slights that would leave others devastated. When stress levels rise, yours is the cooler head in the room that remains focused on finding a solution. And when critics begin nitpicking your job performance you often surprise them by being . . . agreeable. Your perspective is that either they have something valuable to impart or they don't. If they have something valuable to say, then you're the one who stands to benefit by listening to them. And if they don't know what they're talking about, you'll smile and nod and wait for them to move on before quietly going about doing what you were doing all along. You don't like conflict or drama. It takes a lot to make you angry, but when something pisses you off you see red. You'll stomp around and even snort. But you're not one to stay mad for very long. Afterward you'll quickly revert to your calm, peace-loving self.

Yours is a pastoral sign. It's why you come across as relaxed and low key. You may not while away the hours watching sheep graze and stringing together garlands of flowers, but there's nothing stopping you from wanting to live that way. You're built for comfort, not for speed. You would love nothing more than to stroll out to your favorite spot every day, park it, and take in the view. Your space means a lot to you. Whether it's your craft room, your man cave, your she-shed, your favorite table at a restaurant, or your bike in spin class, your spot is your spot and everybody knows it. Yours is the most territorial sign of the zodiac and you will push back against anyone trying to horn in on your turf—which is funny because you have no problem horning in on theirs.

You're very subtle about it. It begins with you leaving some overnight things at your boyfriend's apartment or draping your jacket over the back of an occupied chair so that when that person returns from the restroom you happen to be sitting in their seat. Little under-the-radar annexations like that. "What's mine is mine" is a favorite Taurus catchphrase, but because Venus is your ruling planet it makes sense to add "and what's yours is mine, too."

People like to give you things. That's one of the plus points to being born under Venus, the planet of love and beauty. You are the living embodiment of the law of attraction. You don't have to go after what you want in life because it often comes to you. Let other people hunt down clients or race after the golden apples that roll across their path; you know that the best opportunities are the ones that drop into your lap. But the Venus equation of combining forces with someone because you get twice as much done for half the effort doesn't always sit well with you. You like it in principle, but you don't like having to split the profits. Taurus has a hard time with sharing. You were the kid in kindergarten who refused to put your toy back in the toy box at the end of playtime because you thought you could keep it. And indeed the worst thing that anyone can ever do to a Taurus is to ask to borrow something like a sweater or a book. The Venus part of you will feel obligated to say yes because Venus is all about good manners, but the earthy part of you will agonize over it because earth signs have a desperate fear of being deprived. How long does this person want it? What happens if it's damaged? Will it even be returned? Rather than lose sleep over it, a Taurus will either say no outright or buy a cheaper version to lend out instead, just for the peace of mind.

One would think that Taurus people would be spoiled brats given your love of luxury and indulgence, but you're beasts of burden at heart. You're not averse to putting in the long hours or going the extra distance to make sure that the job is done right. You know that somebody has to pull that plow and carry that load. You're a staunch provider and no one you care about will ever go hungry or want for anything on your watch. It's funny. You won't share, but you will provide. Maybe it's because providing puts you in charge, whereas sharing makes you beholden. In any case, you're happy when the people in your life are happy. But there's more to your work ethic than keeping the wolf from the door. You really love to work. You're one of the few people who look forward to coming in to the office, studio, or workstation every day. And it doesn't matter if you're a barista or a CEO— you will put your all into whatever it is you do. Plus you love money. Taurus people have a real green thumb when it comes to finances. You don't see money as evil any more than you see money as being in short supply or the exclusive domain of the top one percent. Your love of money is like a gardener's love of plants. You understand its behavior and you have a natural talent for cultivating and nurturing it. Money is an organic, living, breathing thing to you. Although some bean counters and number crunchers are born under the sign of Taurus, there are just as many Taurus people who can make businesses grow and investments flourish based on their instinctive feel for the lay of the land. They don't need facts and stats to tell them that wilting leaves mean trouble underfoot or that cascading blooms are the result of having put in the time and done the right prep work. Taurus may not be a fast producer, but you're a prolific one and your yields will only increase over the years.

If you're like most people born under Taurus, you tend to put on the pounds. You are always hungry. And this isn't necessarily the result of stress, carbs, or boredom. You were born under the sign of the Bull, and bulls graze. Constantly. Now obviously some pastures are better to graze in than others—and this is where healthy choices are important. This doesn't have to be joyless. Teach yourself how to cook if you don't know how to already. And educate yourself about what goes into your body. You were born in spring so not only would you enjoy the produce section of your supermarket (you love to squeeze and smell things), but you would also enjoy learning how to mix and match flavors. There's a whole world outside the snack aisle that's better tasting and is better for you.

Few signs are as present as yours. You don't get too caught up in the future, nor do you get fixated on the past. You build a pen around your here and now and put your focus squarely on that. You know that the best way to make the world a better place is to start with your corner of it. No warring. No preaching. No berating. Just love and beauty. And the lovelier you make your corner of the world, the more that people will want to emulate it. Perhaps the greatest gift you have to give is showing people how to live.

THE SUN IN GEMINI

Life for you began with your first playdate, and you were a hit right off the bat. No clinging to your mother's pants leg or going into meltdowns for you. You were too busy working the room—giving your new playmates perfunctory hugs, quickly assessing their toys—identifying the ones that looked fun versus the ones that were "educational"—and within minutes making up a game for everyone to join in. And this is what Geminis do best. You dissolve those invisible barriers that people erect in social situations by being disarming, asking them questions about themselves, and sharing a fun fact or a gossipy bit of information. You don't dominate a group any more than you will wait to be invited. You break the ice. It's why people like you so much. You get them talking. You may never be the most popular kid in school, but you're friends with him. The geeks may never embrace you as one of their own, but you're always welcome to hang out. And should you find yourself drawn into the mean girl orbit, you know how to socialize with them just long enough to enjoy the celebrity without ever becoming truly identified with them. You tap-dance in and out of friendships and associations—keeping people guessing as to how long you'll stay. You're always around, but nobody has exclusive rights to you and in time people come to accept that this is who you are.

The air signs rule over the three types of relationships—siblings, couples, and groups. Gemini, the zodiac sign of the Twins, naturally rules over sibling relationships, which play a big factor in how we all get along with people in life. Everything you learned about winning and losing, competition versus cooperation, and give-and-take you learned from your sibling. And if you didn't have a sibling growing up, then you probably had a friend who was like a sister or brother to you. You don't really "relate" to your mother or father when you're a child. Parents are power figures you turn to for love and approval. They tell you what to do and you pretty much have to obey them as long as you live under their roof. They're not contemporaries. But a sibling is right there next to you. This is the person you're in cahoots with. Your sibling is the one you follow or the one who follows you if you're the older one. Your sibling might be someone you admire, someone you want to be close to and even emulate. Or your sibling may be the one you fight with, complain about, or rat on. Then again, all things being Gemini, there's nothing saying you can't flip-flop. With siblings you never know who's on top or who's on the bottom from one day to the next, but chances are your sibling will still be the one you go to with a secret problem that you can't discuss with anyone else.

Geminis "twin." And it doesn't have to be with your real sibling. You can twin with a friend, spouse, co-worker, or child. Now this doesn't mean you'll start dressing alike and speaking in a made-up secret language. It's more like a sixth sense that you have for identifying someone who gets you in a symbiotic way. You may start out strangers but you'll soon become inseparable. Is your twin the pretty one? Then you get to be the smart one. Or maybe your twin is the moody one? Then that means you're the lighthearted one. Geminis love taking on roles like a shopper trying on clothes in the dressing room. You want to see which ones suit you. This doesn't mean that you're a chameleon. But you learn about yourself through people—like an infant mirroring their parents' facial expressions. You will mimic and imitate, but it's not in order to model yourself after someone else. It's to see if you like living that life or not.

The dark side of this is Evil Twin Syndrome. Feuding siblings are as old as Cain and Abel, and we all know how that turned out. And like Abel, you can have a certain blind spot when it comes to someone who means you harm. For some bizarre reason, Geminis love their frenemies. It's amazing the lengths you'll go to to rationalize their unacceptable behavior, explain away their lies, or keep giving them money after they just ripped you off. And it doesn't matter how much the people in your life try to sound the alarm. It's like you're incapable of severing ties. If anything, you encourage your other half to "raise Cain." And what if you're the Cain in the equation? You might be hopelessly drawn to someone who brings out the worst in you. Your focus is on exposing this person, counteracting their every move, or unseating them altogether. It can become a bit of an obsession as you bend the rules and twist the facts in order to get your way. Loved ones and friends say walk away, but you may be so fixated on the one-upmanship that you can't. You see, Geminis aren't really split personalities at all. What they do is *split* their personality and then give half of it over to the "twin." It's less *The Strange Case of Dr. Jekyll and Mr. Hyde* and more *What Ever Happened to Baby Jane?* When a love relationship, business partnership, or family tie deteriorates into this kind of doppelganger dysfunction, it's always best to quit cold turkey. You may not think you can part company—that you two are forever joined at the hip—but guess what? You can—and need to for your own psychological well-being. There's more to life than being the flip side of a coin.

Your ruling planet is Mercury, named after the messenger of the gods. Swift-footed and quick-witted, Mercury was always racing back and forth between heaven and earth communicating the will of the gods to mortals and then reporting back to the gods on their reactions. You can think of Mercury as the ancient world's version of tweeting. And like Mercury, your mind moves too fast; you speak in 280 characters and find it nearly impossible to sit still. You're always coming from or going to something. Mercury is the reason you're often cast in the role of spokesperson and go-between. It's your job to represent the powers that be. They depend on you to make the deals, broker the agreements, and get warring parties to return to the table when negotiations have broken down. No one is better at herding cats than you. You know how to pique interest, feign indifference, sweeten an offer, taunt, or make yourself scarce until everyone gets nervous and comes looking for you. And this playful quality makes you both engaging and a little suspect. People aren't always sure if you're playing for fun or playing for keeps.

What makes a Gemini a Gemini is how companionable you are. You just show up when people need you. Whether you're on hand to help a customer find an item or walk a client through a bureaucratic maze of benefits and services, Geminis are the people who can get you from here to there. Geminis strike up friendships on the spot. The friendships may not last forever, but then again they may not need to. You're the perfect person to get stranded at the airport with because not only will you figure out the next flight to get on—your fluency with apps and agents and the grace and ease with which you navigate them is unrivaled—but you'll also come up with something fun to do in the meantime.

SUMMER SUN SIGNS

THE SUN IN CANCER

Summer is a lullaby season. Days are long, nights are short, and you can sleep outside beneath the stars if you like. Everything you could possibly want for is in reach. You can pluck fruit from the trees, pull vegetables out of the soil, or hook a fish while lazily dozing on the riverbank. Summertime is when the living is easy because Mother Nature is here to provide. And like an infant suckling at the breast, you can nestle peacefully knowing that you can eat, sleep, and poop with nary a worry in the world.

Now you might laugh and say, "I wish!" but this dream of a time of plenty lies at the back of every Cancer's psyche. Maybe it's a prenatal memory, an archetypal fantasy, or simple wishful thinking, but this image has the power of history and it's so insistent that even if it never happened to you, you will live as if it had. And it doesn't matter if your mother wasn't a particularly nurturing person or if the circumstances of your childhood were harsh and unpleasant, you will still be warmed by this nostalgic idyll, so much so that you will aim to make the childhood of your own children better than the home you were raised in.

Mothering is wired into your cosmic DNA—and that goes for men born under Cancer as well. Cancer, Virgo, and Scorpio are the three zodiac signs where the mother plays a prominent role in the horoscope. Cancer is the sign of the Good Mother. You can't resist the impulse to pick up things and to hold them; to cuddle, coddle, and cradle. It's obvious with babies and children, but it's also apparent with animal rescues, beloved objects, and even places that you return to over and over. You just have this need to hold things close, to drink in their scent, and—should the occasion allow—even to hum to them. It's all part of the maternal bonding. And this bonding is very important because it makes something foreign familiar. It's one thing to feel people's pain but it's quite another to care about it, and for a Cancer this can only be done on a one-on-one basis. There has to be a personal investment. Pledges can be broken and promises left unfulfilled, but bonding is like the mother penguin who can pick out her chick from among the hundreds of little ones slipping and sliding on the ice or a mama bear who goes racing to the rescue of a cub in distress. It links you to a person, place, or thing both intimately and psychically. And once forged, that tie is unbreakable. It's useless telling yourself not to get attached. You always get attached. It's in your nature.

You were born under the zodiac sign of hearth, home, and family, so blood ties will always take precedence. This is why you talk to your mom every day (even if she doesn't approve of your spouse or understand what you do for a living), why your pantry's well stocked (even if you live alone), and why you're always making up the bed for your boomerang kid (no matter how many times they move out and say that this time it's final). You keep the home fires burning. But "home" isn't strictly defined by kin and children. The reason clients and customers ask for you by name is that they know you truly care. You treat them like family, not like a target audience. Friends know you're always there for them regardless of the crisis or the time of day, and even strangers feel like they can take you into their confidence because somehow you understand exactly what it's like to be in their shoes. People born under Cancer—like those born under Scorpio and Pisces—have the ability to stir the waters of the unconscious in everyone they meet.

Scorpio may have the sex appeal and Pisces the fantasy, but your pull is memory. This is why people feel an instant familiarity with you—why they're always asking if they've met you before or saying that you remind them of someone they knew back when. Your presence puts them at ease like a warm glass of milk or a bowl of chicken soup.

So if you're supposed to be so maternal and loving, why do you act so shy and retiring? Maybe it's because when people look at you they see a free meal. This comes from being born under the sign of the Crab, which ranks lowest on the zodiac food chain. Summer is famous for feasting on soft-shell crabs and lobster rolls. It's the time of year when crustaceans migrate toward shore to warmer waters to shed their shells and swim naked until they grow new ones. Cancers are acutely aware of their vulnerability. You love too much, care too deeply, and worry constantly. If you know (metaphorically speaking) that you are the most popular item on the menu for swooping gulls and lip-smacking tourists, you're not going to approach things head-on like an Aries. You're going to hide beneath the rocks and lie in wait until you can sneak up on your prey and seize it.

Cancer is ruled by the Moon, which belongs to Diana, goddess of the hunt in Roman mythology. And like a hunter, you know how to cover your tracks and blend into the background. You're a keen observer and a patient study. Stealth and strategy is how people born under Cancer get what they want. The more attracted you are to a prize, the more you will feign disinterest—even pretending to be bored or brusque to throw people off the scent. Like the crab, Cancers approach their prizes indirectly—starting off in a wide circle that grows narrower as you close in. This is what makes Cancers such great bargain hunters and collectors. It also makes you a natural for covert operations. But there is such a thing as being *too* good at blending into the background—so much so that people don't even know you're there. For instance, that person you're crushing on may have no idea you even care, that buyer you're waiting on to make the first move may be waiting for you, or you might be so low key in your job interview that a prospective employer simply assumes you're not interested. It's times like these when you have to communicate what you're feeling or you really will get passed over.

Geminis may be the split personalities of the zodiac, but it's Cancers who have the multiple ones. Your ruling planet, the Moon, will travel through all twelve zodiac signs in just one month, as opposed to the Sun, which takes twelve months to complete that circle. No planet changes its appearance in the sky more quickly and dramatically than the Moon, and the same goes for your moods. When you're waxing you can be loving and generous to a fault, and when you're waning you're likely to be remote and uninterested. A lot of people get thrown off by this and can start to panic, but those who know better just give you your space, confident that when you reemerge you'll be as sharing and caring as you were before. You're a cyclical creature, after all.

Families have changed since the days of freshly mowed lawns and white picket fences. Single moms, gay dads, and mixed-race households are all part of the neighborhood now. Yet what these different variations on a theme have in common is *belonging*. Belonging is a basic necessity like food, water, and shelter. It testifies to our humanity, especially in a world of closed doors, shuttered hearts, and raised walls. Belonging isn't defined by tradition, nativism, or roots. Traditions get reinterpreted as they're passed down. And roots can be dug up and replanted somewhere else. Yet it's nice to know that constant through all these vacillations and shifting sands is an astrological sign that keeps the light on for all of us trying to find our way home, a sign ready to provide a roof overhead and a bed to sleep in, a sign that knows that its nature is to nurture and that will never be an either/or choice.

THE SUN IN LEO

There's only one you. And you take being you very seriously. Now this doesn't mean you will supervise every facet of your life with the hyperfocus of a Hollywood celebrity. You're not going to monitor your body fat percentage on an hourly basis, keep spreadsheets of your followers on social media, or plunge your face into a bathroom sink full of ice every morning to freeze your pores. Leos are often accused of being vain, but you're not *that* vain. Who wants to work that hard? Besides, you already know that you're the best thing to happen in people's lives. Your smile brightens their day, your good humor puts them at ease, and—when you need to—your command of a situation gets them to step back briskly into line. Few zodiac signs are as comfortable exercising authority as a Leo. It comes from being born at the top of the food chain.

You were also born under the only ruling planet that's actually a star: the Sun. And like the Sun, you are unique and stand alone. You don't orbit people; people orbit you. And it's not like this is something you deliberately set out to do. Right from the start you were singled out as being special. You didn't ask your homeroom teacher to favor you or to be voted the most popular kid in your class. It just sort of happened on its own. You exude a magnetism and charisma that people naturally gravitate to. They're happy when you arrive on the scene because it's like the Sun rising on a new day. They know that everything's going to be all right because you provide the solar power that makes things happen. Your name on the marquee sells tickets. Your athletic performance wins the game. Your star turn in the kitchen transforms an excellent dinner into a sublime experience. Whatever your talent, skill, or personality, you can't help but be outstanding.

Aries, Leo, and Capricorn are the three zodiac signs where the father plays a prominent role in the horoscope. Leo is the sign of the Good Father. But what does *Good Father* mean nowadays in a world of gender fluidity, sperm donors, and single-parent households headed by women more than men? Is *Good Father* even a relevant term anymore? Let's face it: not all dads are good, just like not all kings are just and not all leaders know where they're going, but that doesn't keep us from wanting them to be that way. We all want someone to look up to. Someone to be the bigger person, to take the high road, and to take us aside and explain why bad things happen when they do. A Good Father shows up. He protects, provides, and disciplines. He leads by example and helps his children get back up on their feet when they stumble. And perhaps, more important, he sets his children up for success by making sure they have the education, means, and backup to make it in the real world. It's up to the Good Father to show them the ropes and to be there to catch them when they fall. These are qualities that Leos espouse—and that goes for women born under Leo as well. This sense of guardianship and responsibility isn't just exclusive to children. Anyone who relies on you is a child as far as you're concerned, which is why you will show this same kind of stewardship toward students, employees, or teammates if you're the captain.

Anyone who's ever watched Animal Planet knows it's the lionesses who do all the work, and the same is true of female Leos. You're the ones who raise the cubs, patrol your territory, and bring home the bacon—or in your case the antelope and/or zebra—often while pursuing a career. Female Leos are hardly stay-at-home cats. If anything, that role is going to be played by your mate. People assume that it's the female Leos who expect to be pampered and spoiled all day when actually it's the males. In many cases it's the female Leo who's the higher earner, is more successful, or has the name recognition. Yet interestingly enough you will downplay your accomplishments so as not to outshine your mate. You will stand behind him—just like the lioness stands behind hers. And not only will you stand behind him, you will also stand by him. Female Leos are fiercely loyal. Anyone who messes with a loved one better be ready to mess with you. Lions are the most social of all the big cats. Family is very important to you. You take pride in your pride.

The Sun is in domicile in Leo. *Domicile* means "at home," and it's during the summer that the Sun is most powerful. But the Sun in summer is different from the Sun in spring. It's hotter and more overbearing. And this is something you have to watch out for when dealing with others. It's in your nature to dominate a situation. You know you belong on top, and you have the force of personality that ensures you'll stay there. This is why you can come across as arrogant, high-handed, and dismissive. And when you're born under a sign that's used to people orbiting you, there are going to be times when you're not exactly open to others' input, much less their criticism. But these aren't deal breakers. The people in your life are used to you getting your way. You may be high maintenance, but you're worth it. No, the downside to having an overbearing Sun is that you can stifle growth without meaning to.

When you walk around in a golden globe of light like you do, it's hard to imagine not being "on" twenty-four hours a day. It's up to you to enlighten, inspire, and uplift. The expectation is for you to have it all. But nobody does. You're only human. However, Leos don't do well with shortcomings. And it's not because you're afraid of being outshone or outdone. It comes from a naïve belief that if you're not good at something, how could anyone else be? And this is especially true with loved ones.

Let's say you bombed at math—then it will be impossible for you to see how your child could succeed at it even if she's a math whiz. You just can't see how somebody else can be good at something you weren't. So you'll withhold support. And this doesn't come from wishing her ill. Ironically, it comes from being protective and not wanting to see someone you care about fail. You don't want to create false hope. But because you have a blind spot when it comes to yourself, you may not see how you are actually standing in the way of another person's growth. Just because you didn't succeed doesn't mean that the same will hold true for them. The best thing you can do is step out of the way and not be an obstacle. Eventually, you will recognize what everyone else did all along, and once you do, yours will be the loudest roar of approval.

No sign places such a high value on individuality as you. It takes a lot of courage to be yourself, and that's why Leo rules the heart. You're lionhearted. But not all Leos will be the best quarterback, the most brilliant mind, or the most famous star. And you don't have to be because what you will be is the center that holds the lives of those you love and work with together. You will be a shining example of what each person can be as long as they are true to themselves. Yes, you may be bossy, insist on having the last word, and have an unflinching need to be right all the time, but it's all a genuine expression of who you are. Leos are here to remind us that there's only one you, and since you only get one life to live, then you better give it your best shot.

THE SUN IN VIRGO

You were born under the feminist sign of the zodiac. Now that doesn't mean you're going to don a pink wool cap, grab a sign, and join a protest march, but you are acutely aware that the differences between men and women are more than anatomical and that these differences translate to society in general. There's a difference in status, power, and pay. It's not fair, but the simple truth is there are people who have more and people who have less. This is why you taught yourself how to do more with less. Not *make* do with less—*do* more with less. Virgos are known for their ingenuity and resourcefulness. Of all the twelve signs, only Virgo depicts a woman. That's saying a lot, considering that astrology has been around for more than twenty-five hundred years. Virgo has always been depicted as a woman—alone and unmarried—living in a man's world.

Being a Virgo doesn't mean you'll always be single or that you're a prude. What it means is that nobody owns you. This stems from centuries of women being treated like disposable items. The history of women in the ancient cultures where astrology hails from is not pretty. Unwanted female infants were often left to perish on hillsides. Teenage girls were married off to men twice their age. And if they didn't die in childbirth (something that happened with alarming frequency), they might find themselves abused by husbands who had absolute control over them physically and financially.

And women who lived alone and minded their own business? They never knew if they might be accused of witchcraft one day and hanged in the public square all because a greedy neighbor had an eye on their land and wanted to purchase it for cheap.

Now obviously there were some good marriages over the centuries that begat happy families and flourishing societies, but this dark history of female oppression looms in the background of your sign. That fear of being used and abused is never far from your thoughts—and that goes for men born under Virgo as well. So how do you live in a world where the rules of the game are fixed against you? By using your head!

The best way to outsmart people is to be better at playing the game than they are. It's why rules are so important to you. You know which ones to obey, which ones to bend, and which ones to quote verbatim should anyone ever challenge you. Being well versed in methodologies allows you to move on to another approach if the previous one didn't work, and having an eye for detail means you can spot the treasure in the trash, the defect in the design, and any hidden technicality lying underfoot waiting to entrap you. Yours is an extremely adroit sign thanks to your ruling planet, Mercury. Planet of the mind, Mercury makes you cerebral and analytical, but it also makes you shrewd, cunning, and quick.

Virgo is the zodiac sign of work and service. You have a reputation for being fastidious, doing what you're told, and going the extra mile. And it's true that you will fulfill—if not surpass—your employer's expectations. It's almost physically impossible for you to leave a job half done, and nothing makes you happier than to check items off your to-do list. But you're not some Labrador retriever who fetches sticks and gleefully accepts a pat on the head in return. You learned a long time ago that the secret to ruling the roost isn't to shout orders or bully people into submission. The secret is to make yourself indispensable.

When you wait on people hand and foot you become more familiar with their hands and feet than they do. You can anticipate their every need, predict how they're going to react, and even nudge them in the direction you want them to go. Over time that person you serve will entrust you with more and more responsibility. They might ask for your input, defer to your judgment, or charge you with certain duties. Virgos know that people in power will give up a lot for the sake of convenience. The easier you can make their lives, the more they will hand over. And this is how Virgos gently turn the tables on those who have the upper hand: by managing the routine of their everyday lives.

People will take up your time, test your patience, and hog all the attention, but the one thing they cannot have is your body. It's why you watch what you put into it and go to great lengths to protect it. Your body is your most trusted friend. Your mind can be tricked, your heart can be played with, and your spirit can be fooled into taking things on faith, but your body will always tell it like it is. There are a lot of things you'll put up with in life—pressures in the workplace, demands at home, financial stress, and toxic personalities—but once any of these begins to take a toll on you physically, that's it. You are out of there. And it doesn't matter what's at stake or who you leave in the lurch. Your health is your wealth, and you won't sacrifice it for anything.

Yet for someone who serves but is never subservient, it's ironic how you will allow yourself to become a slave to routine. Imagine being asked to clean a room. Now we all know Virgos will clean every nook and cranny, polish every piece of furniture, arrange every pillow, and adjust every picture, but once the job is done and you are free to leave this room behind, you might be surprised to find yourself hesitating at the threshold. Why? Because you have no idea of what comes next.

It's not unlike a prisoner who awakes one morning to discover that her jail cell door has been left open. Rather than seize this opportunity to escape, she will go back inside and close the door behind her. And in a similar fashion you will return to the room you just cleaned and make a mess of it.

You'll overturn the furniture, empty the garbage on the floor, and undo everything you've just done. Why? Because it is safer to stay in a situation where you know the routine than it is to move on to one where you don't. It's why Virgos constantly pick apart what they do. People think it's because you're perfectionists, but it's actually an elaborate form of procrastination. Focusing on what's wrong keeps you from identifying and then building on what's right.

A to-do list is not a life purpose. It's a list of chores that changes every day but stays the same. Life purpose is when you connect to doing something that's unique to you and truly fulfilling. Chances are you already know what that is, but you've created such a laundry list of what you need to do beforehand that you're working harder, not smarter, toward getting there.

The secret to your success is in finding your niche. This is what will make you truly indispensable. Virgos are the experts, but you're not experts because you're know-it-alls; you're experts because you've taken a talent or skill and honed it into an expertise. You've practiced the craft, learned the discipline, and mastered that specialty that people didn't know they needed until you showed up. Once you find this you can go anywhere in the world. You can set your terms, name your price, and be your own boss. Doing that thing that nobody else can do ensures that you will always be in demand and that no one will ever lord over you.

Cancer, Virgo, and Scorpio are the three zodiac signs where the mother plays a prominent role in the horoscope. Virgo is the sign of Mother/Daughter relationships. Whether you're a man or a woman, it's likely your mother faced challenging circumstances that forced her to place adult responsibilities on your shoulders at an early age. Being a Virgo, you rose to the occasion and over time she may have seen you more as a helper than someone who needed help. She may have turned to you for support and even guidance. Virgo children are famously precocious and can come across as being more mature than they really are. But this can create a Catch-22. The more capable and self-sufficient you proved yourself to be, the more your mother would have treated you like a peer—unintentionally depriving you of the recognition and approval that every child needs. Yours is the sort of relationship that improves with adulthood. You may never recover what was lost between a mother and child, but what you'll gain is a sister and a friend.

AUTUMN SUN SIGNS

THE SUN IN LIBRA

Autumn is a sobering season. There's a chill in the air as the leaves spontaneously explode in a blaze of glory before falling reverently to the ground. Summer is over, the Sun is saying good-bye, and Mother Nature is closing up shop. You were born around the time of year when the clocks have been set back an hour in order to make the most of the remaining daylight. It's extra time to finish what you're doing—to dot the *i*'s, cross the *t*'s, and make sure that everything's complete. It's why you're so careful about your choices and never make a move without considering the repercussions. What if you forgot something valuable? Left out an important detail? Or brought matters to an end too soon? You know that when something's final it's final. There are no do-overs.

Libras are often accused of being indecisive, noncommittal, and too worried about what others think. This gives the impression that you can't make up your mind. Actually, you know your mind pretty well, but what you don't know is somebody else's. Gemini, Libra, and Aquarius rule the three types of relationships—siblings, couples, and groups. You were born under the zodiac sign of partnership. You know that combining forces automatically increases your chances for success. It's why you're on the lookout for that special person with whom you can start a family, build a business, or collaborate on a project. As a Libra you never do anything alone. Not if you can help it. Why go it alone when you can pair up with someone and get twice as much done for half the effort? Getting people on board with what you want to do is a top priority. Nobody's going to want to partner with you if you're mean-spirited, self-absorbed, or rude. They will, however, if you make them feel valued, smart, and like what they say matters. And what they say does matter. You are genuinely interested in different points of view. Asking people what they think, how they would handle a situation if they were in your shoes, or if they can explain something that you don't understand gives you the benefit of their insight, their experience, and their knowledge. You learned a long time ago the value of attracting people into your life who bring things to the table that you don't already have. Most people like to hear themselves talk; you'd rather take in what others have to say.

Zodiac means "circle of animals," and it's telling that yours is the only astrological sign that's an inanimate object. The scales are one of the oldest instruments of measurement in our civilization. Composed of a beam affixed to a pole where two plates hung at opposite ends, scales were used to determine the market value of goods bought and sold on trade routes where cultures rarely—if ever—spoke the same language. Scales were the great equalizers. Nobody disputed their judgment. They were considered impartial. They also made for convincing optics because if someone accused the merchant of cheating, the merchant could always point to the scales and say, "Hey, this is what the scales say. I have nothing to do with it." It's something we all experience when we step on the bathroom scale. We may recoil in horror at the number that appears—explaining it all away as "water weight"—but the scale doesn't lie. You have to accept its verdict. Indeed, the scales were so well respected for their fairness that one of our earliest images of Libra is the Egyptian god of the dead, Anubis, placing the heart of a deceased man on one plate while counterbalancing it with a feather on the other. If the heart was heavier than the feather, then the soul was considered evil and tossed into the gaping jaws of Ammit, a hellish creature that was part crocodile, lion, and hippopotamus. And if the soul weighed the same as the feather? Then it was seen as righteous and given entry into the afterlife.

Weighing souls in the balance may sound a bit heavy, but it explains why you ask so many questions, seek out counterarguments, and insist on hearing the other side of the story. You often find yourself refereeing situations where opinions are split and camps are polarized. Maybe you're the mediator called in to settle a dispute, the arbiter of taste who decides what's fashionable, or the one who bestows the award that will set one person apart from all the rest. And you take your job seriously. It's why you resist being pinned down, baited, or made to make a commitment before you're ready. You strive hard to take your personal thoughts and feelings out of the equation and put your faith in impartial systems like weights and measures, standards of excellence, and the rule of law. To you, nothing's worse than making a bad judgment call that everyone has to live with.

The Sun is in fall in Libra, making you the least self-centered of all the zodiac signs. This doesn't mean you don't have an ego. Everyone does. You wouldn't be you without one. But what it does mean is that you will put yours aside in order to do what's right by your relationship. You don't do things for yourself. You do them for *us*.

A relationship is made up of three parts: you, your partner, and the relationship itself. It's not unlike the scales, if you think about it, with you in one dish and your partner in the other. Your relationship is a living, breathing covenant. And you will look after it the way you would look after anything entrusted to your care. You will curb selfish tendencies, make adjustments, and work to reconcile differences. And you expect your partner to do the same. A successful marriage brings out the best in both of you, while an unsuccessful one means somebody's getting tossed to the croc. And that somebody isn't going to be you.

It isn't easy running a three-legged race in a world where everyone's out for themselves. It takes a lot of energy to pool resources, coordinate efforts, and know when to take the lead and when to follow. People may roll their eyes at the way you check in with your spouse, run plans past him for approval, or ask her if she's OK with a decision you're making, but you don't do this because you're codependent. You do it to keep your partner present. Partnering may promise twice the gains for half the effort, but it also doubles your jeopardy because you never know when the person in the other dish is going to mess up, check out emotionally, or be more trouble than he's worth. It's your job to keep the relationship together.

One would think that you're incredibly self-sacrificing with all the hand-holding that you do, but that's not the only way to keep a marriage alive. Your ruling planet is Venus, after all, named after the Roman goddess of love and beauty, which is why Libras are famous for love triangles. It's your favorite geometric shape! But the reason you might take a lover isn't because you're looking for a way out. It's so you can satisfy those parts of yourself that aren't being satisfied by your partner. Maybe you need more intimacy, intellectual stimulus, spiritual connection, or just plain sex. You may not see it as doing any harm. What's wrong with getting your needs met somewhere else as long as you're discreet? It's all in service to the greater cause, right? But like most things that look good on paper, they often lose something in translation. Claiming that you were having an affair for the good of your marriage is going to be hard to explain to a spouse who thought things were simpatico or a friend with benefits who's fallen in love with you. This is when your design for living could lead to some entangled situations.

Venus is the planet of civility. She's the reason we eat with forks and knives, say "please" and "thank you," and apologize even when it's the other person who did something wrong. Good manners seem laughable in a world where people shriek and holler, but civility is the only thing that's going to get them to return to the table after they've retreated into their separate corners. Anyone can insult, threaten, and bully, but it's a Libra who knows how a kind word can get someone's attention, a goodwill gesture rebuilds trust, and offering an olive branch uncrosses more arms and unlocks more hearts than any poke in the chest will. Libras never lose sight of the fact that we're all in it together—whatever our shortcomings, offenses, and failures— and since we are all in it together, wouldn't it be a good idea to start treating each other a lot better than we do?

THE SUN IN SCORPIO

You're no stranger to sticks and stones or the names that will always hurt. For some reason you got picked on from an early age. Maybe you were weaker than the other kids, or fatter, or maybe you just didn't fit in. Something about you stood out. But where others were singled out for special praise and recognition, you were often targeted as prey. Cruelty is a predatory gene. It knows how to separate you from the others, make you the object of ridicule, and tighten the noose so that the more you cry out, the more others believe you asked for it. You learned all of this the hard way. Being ostracized is nothing new. Nor is being laughed at, bullied, or abused. But you've always had a defiant streak. Where other zodiac signs yield the field or lay low until the trouble passes, you will stand firm in your resistance. You know a wrong when you see it and you will never let the culprit off the hook. It's why you don't forget insults or forgive mean-spiritedness. And you hold on to that anger because anger makes you strong. It stokes your willpower and hardens your resolve. You know that you will never give up or give in as long as you are pissed off.

You got robbed. This feeling comes from being born in the heart of autumn, when everything has gone to seed. The garden days of summer are over and the promises of plenty have long since faded. It's not unlike arriving at a fancy party only to discover that the bottles are empty, nobody's around, and the only thing left is a crumpled bag of greasy potato chip crumbs. This feeling of being ditched pervades your entire life and it's not an easy thing to live with. Constantly being handed the short end of the stick doesn't exactly build confidence or lead you to believe that everything will turn out for the best. Is it any wonder that you might grow resentful of other people's successes? Jealous of their loves? Suspicious of their motives? Autumn was often associated with the Sun's descent into the underworld in ancient cultures as fields grew barren and trees redirected their energy from their branches down into their roots sunk beneath the soil. This is the realm of the dead, and it's no coincidence that Halloween and All Souls' Day are both celebrated when the Sun is in Scorpio. This is why you're so deadly serious, possess a grim sense of humor, and fight every fight as if your life depended on it.

Cancer, Virgo, and Scorpio are the three zodiac signs where the mother plays a prominent role in the horoscope. Scorpio is the sign of the Dark Mother. Now this doesn't mean that your mother was bad—"dark" refers to the time of year, not the person herself; however, your Sun being in Scorpio implies that your mother had a rough go of it and the battle scars remained like outdated tattoos. She may have experienced economic hardship growing up, struggled with bouts of depression, flown into fits of rage, or acted out in self-destructive ways. If she didn't dominate your life, then her inner demons did. And these demons didn't exactly lend themselves to being a loving and trustworthy parent. If anything, they created distance on both sides. But if there was a hardness to her, it wasn't borne from not caring; it was more like the hardness that comes from fighting so many uphill battles. And even if she lost more battles than she won, she would have still pulled herself up by her bootstraps and soldiered on. You learned that from her.

But what if your mother happens to be the most carefree person you know? It still doesn't matter because the times you remember will always be when that smile dropped. Maybe her marriage went through a rough patch, she got laid off from work, or she suffered the loss of a close friend or family member. Some might say you were traumatized when your mother failed to keep the bad things in life at bay, but actually it's the opposite. There's nothing like sharing the same foxhole to confirm that life really is an equal-opportunity offender. It's funny to say, but the times you miss most are the bad times. You never felt closer.

Scorpions are lethal creatures. They're frightening and venomous. That's why your zodiac sign is always being dressed up as a soaring eagle or a mythical phoenix rising from the ashes. Even the astrologers don't want to see you for who you are. You symbolize all the things people want to get away from, the parts of themselves that hide in dark places and only come out at night. As a Scorpio, you get the fantasies and the fetishes, the compulsions and obsessions, the hopelessness and despair. When you're born under the zodiac sign of sex and death, you have *verboten* written all over your horoscope. You're used to dealing with people's dark sides. And this is where you have to be careful or you will wind up being the person they sleep with one night and pretend not to know the next, or the friend they cling to in a crisis and then walk past when it's over. People are going to project the things that they're afraid of becoming onto you, like a dirty secret kept hidden in the back of a sock drawer. That's when you need to tell them, "Own your own shit."

Everyone knows better than to cross a Scorpio. You're often depicted as dangerous foes who come out stinging, and that makes perfect sense given that your ruling planet is Mars—named after the Roman god of war. You're nobody's victim and you'll return fire with fire. You don't start the fight, but you'll end it. You're the badass sign. However, you have another ruling planet: Pluto. Pluto was named after the Roman god of the dead. He ruled over everything buried beneath the earth. That refers to seeds and corpses, of course, but the god was said to also rule over riches. Gold, silver, precious metals, and oil all come from under the ground. Indeed, *pluto* means "wealth," which is why *plutocracy* refers to the moneyed class.

Scorpios are really good with other people's money. You're not always good with your own, but that changes when you're ready to take off the training wheels and start following your own advice. Permanent fixtures in the financial markets, wealth management, estate planning, and auction houses, you have a discerning eye and can spot the untapped potential in things most people overlook. Where others rely on trends and spreadsheets, you always trust your gut. You have a nose for riches. It comes from being born under the planet of buried treasure. You also have a love of fine things. People often think that Taurus and Libra are the luxury item signs because they're ruled by Venus, the planet of beauty, but it's really Scorpio. Scorpios are the ones sitting down to ponder the purchase of a gem kept in a high-security vault or examining a rare painting in a private showing. Scorpios aren't into labels. What you're after is always one of a kind.

But Pluto is also the planet of ordeals and the transformations that arise from them. What that means is you can't experience heaven without going through hell first. Crisis is your catharsis. That's why Scorpios are always descending into the underworld of themselves, and every time they do, they transmute a fallen angel into a rejoicing one. This is when you realize that you're bigger than your fears, more generous than your cynicism, and more loving than your hate. This is how you unlock your hidden talents, tap into strengths you never knew you had, and become the person you've been carrying inside. Scorpio is the zodiac sign of rebirth, but rebirths—like births—aren't easy. They're just as painful, bloody, and messy. Scorpios wind up in very different places in life from where they began. You always accomplish what you set out to do, but the result bears little resemblance to what you had in mind. You might have started out with an "I'll show them" chip on your shoulder, but what you wind up becoming is a better person than they will ever be, living a happier life than you ever imagined.

THE SUN IN SAGITTARIUS

Some people follow their passions. Others follow their heart. You answer to a higher authority: your life purpose. Now you may not have the clearest idea of what you're doing on this planet. Surely, you feel a connection to family and want to be there for friends, but there's always been a part of you that's itching to get away, to get lost, and to rediscover yourself. A part of you that believes that your *real* life is happening somewhere else. It's why you subscribe to Booking.com, listen to travel podcasts religiously, and may be the only person in the world who still reads *National Geographic* from cover to cover. But you're not doing this because of wanderlust or a need to go native. You're doing it because you know that there's a burning bush out there somewhere with a divine message meant for you. You may encounter it on a stopover, on a cross-country drive, or exploring the backstreets of some unfamiliar city. All you know is that whatever you're looking for, it's anywhere but here.

You've always had a spiritual bent. You've been asking the big questions since childhood. While other kids wanted to know if there was any more ice cream, you were contemplating the meaning of life, the existence of God, and why bad things happen to good people. But you weren't doing this flippantly or because you were especially precocious. You sensed early on that there are questions that can be answered and questions meant to remain unanswered. And that's the difference between curiosity and wonder. Some things are knowable and some things are not, and you're good with that.

You are ruled by your enthusiasms. They're the most honest thing about you. Something has to spark your interest to get you up and going; otherwise you remain inert. And it's not like you're being choosy or stubborn. If you're not into it, you're not into it, and all the coaxing and pleading, shaming and threatening in the world won't get you to budge. But if you're inspired? Well, then you're unstoppable. It's like you're possessed by something bigger and better than you.

Maybe it's a vision of the way things could be, a cause that promises to bring about real social justice, or a call to action to save the planet before it's too late. You always think in grand, sweeping terms. Nothing lowercase or italicized for you. It's ALL CAPS and exclamation points!!!

Your enthusiasm is so spirited it's infectious. It leaps from brow to brow like a tongue of flame. The way you talk about things is so lively and animated that people just want to rise to their feet. They feel like they "get it" for the first time, like they can see what you see, and they want to be a part of it. Sagittarius is the cheerleader of the zodiac. No one can pump up the volume and rally the forces like you can. The fact that you would never in a million years do what you'll happily urge others to do is beside the point. You get them to believe in the impossible, and once seized by that fervor they don't want to stop. They're happy to carry the ball from here.

But you're no snake oil seller. You're not out to fool people or profit at their expense. You believe in a moral universe. Right is interlaced with wrong, and it's up to each one of us to separate the wheat from the chaff. But how do we do this? For you, it's humor. Yours is the zodiac sign most likely to laugh at your own screw-ups. Your ruling planet is Jupiter, from which we get the word *jovial*, which means "good-humored." Sagittarians love a good laugh. That's why yours is so loud and boisterous. You disdain people who stifle their reactions, then turn around and shush others. They're pompous and stuffy and really know how to kill the moment. These are the enemies to your freedom of expression.

But on a deeper level it's really about your relationship to judgment. The autumn signs are the zodiac signs most concerned with justice. Libra is the letter of the law, Scorpio is an eye for an eye, and Sagittarius is the spirit of the law. You know there are people who are going to follow a rule word for word with no wiggle room, people who demand DEFCON 1 retaliation for any injury they've suffered, and then there's you—lenient and sparing. You believe in the spirit of the law—which relies a lot on its intent and naturally leaves things open to interpretation. Now this doesn't mean you'll go easy on people who mess up. You don't automatically take their side or become a bleeding heart. But you will ask: What purpose is being served? Is punishment the only way to send a message, or is there a teaching moment where this person might learn from their mistakes and go on to live a better life? You have a profound faith in humanity—despite its crimes and relapses—

which makes you the most humanitarian of all the zodiac signs. You feel people's sorrow, but you can get them to smile through the tears, too.

You will always be guilty of Pollyanna-ism—that gushing optimism that insists everything will turn out for the best in the end. And it's not an act—although many people think it is or wonder what kind of drugs you're on. Yours is the most vivacious and excitable of the fire signs. You can't help but believe that it only gets better. But you were also born in the autumn, that time of year when shadows grow longer and the Sun sets earlier. You could tell from the start that nothing lasts forever. Everything in this world has a shelf life. So what happens when things don't turn out as promised, your best shot falls short, and the Universe fumbles the ball? What do you have left to light your way in the dark? Faith. It's the light you carry inside when the Sun has gone down. It's the confidence that winter will pass and spring will bloom. People may call you gullible, poke fun at your naïveté, and chide you for the lengths you'll go to to find the upside in a debacle, but in truth your faith lights the way and they would miss it if that candle blew out.

But Sagittarians are rarely pious. If anything, you're the party animals of the zodiac. That's what centaurs were known for. Half man and half horse, they were always getting drunk at weddings, creating a ruckus, and galloping off with the bride and bridesmaids. You have an unbridled side that can get you into a lot of trouble. It's why your life reads like a morality tale. You often have to learn things the hard way. You have your prodigal binges when you spend everything you have, your Pinocchio folly where you keep making the same bad choices while lying to yourself about them, and long periods spent wandering in the wilderness. You can be stubborn like a horse that's led to water and still won't drink, and you spook easily—often stopping short of clearing an obstacle because you can't see what's on the other side. Yet through all of this is an unshakeable belief that whatever hardship you endure or setback you undergo there is a lesson to be learned. You believe that there's a moral to every story and a reason things happen the way they do. You know what it's like to have been lost and then found.

You also know that having been found doesn't mean you can't get lost again. Your life experience speaks to people more than rules and laws and creeds and scriptures do. And maybe that's your life purpose after all—to show us that follies aren't fruitless and mistakes aren't deal breakers. That when life throws us for a loop we all need to have the good humor and pluck to pick ourselves up, brush ourselves off, and start all over again. To err may be human, but without those fumbles and stumbles to learn from—how can we ever hope to be divine?

WINTER SUN SIGNS

THE SUN IN CAPRICORN

Winter is a gloomy season. Days are short, nights are long, and people huddle close together for warmth—which explains why more babies are born in September than at any other time of year. Yours is the season of scarcity when the ground is hard, branches are bare, and slopes are slippery. That dreaded rainy day that people are always being told to save for has been the story of your life since day one. And it doesn't matter if you live in a part of the country where the Sun always shines or if you came into the world sporting a silver spoon in your mouth, there's a chill to the soul that winter people never get over. You know that life isn't to be trusted, and when it disappoints (like it inevitably does) you want to be ready.

People might say that your pessimism acts like a self-fulfilling prophecy: that if you believe things will turn out badly, then they most certainly will. But what they don't realize is that separating you from your existential anxiety would be like trying to separate Linus from his security blanket. Worrying about life's pitfalls, agonizing over every step, and never forgetting that the higher you climb, the farther you fall, is your way of fending off disaster. Fear doesn't freeze you in your tracks. On the contrary, fear keeps you on your toes. It gets you to size up situations before entering into them, bird-dog developments as they unfold, and wait to secure your next foothold before proceeding any further. You have an instinctive feel for negotiating rough passages and treacherous terrain—just like a mountain goat scaling the face of a cliff. But there's more to your doom-and-gloom mind-set than fixating on all the things that could go wrong. You actually enjoy manufacturing worst-case scenarios and can get quite creative once you get going. You say it's your way of cushioning life's blows, but in truth it's more like a mind game you play with yourself. The more dire the forecast you paint in your mind's eye, the greater the relief you feel when things don't turn out so badly. In fact, you become so elated when you discover that the bill is much less than you expected to pay, or that the damage, though significant, is still reparable, that you can't help but go into your happy dance. You bounce off walls and race across the furniture like a kid on a sugar high—that is, until it's time to start fretting about all the new things that could possibly go wrong. Capricorns are a touch neurotic, but you also know from experience that showing any outward signs of contentment will surely jinx it. That's why you downplay your accomplishments and become seriously self-effacing when someone tries to compliment you. You don't want to tempt fate.

Aries, Leo, and Capricorn are the three zodiac signs where the father plays a prominent role in the horoscope. Capricorn is the sign of the Dark Father. Now this doesn't mean that your father was bad—"dark" refers to the time of year, not the person himself; however, your Sun being in Capricorn implies that some sort of crushing disappointment cast a very long shadow over his life. Everyone gets prescribed bitter pills, but some are harder to swallow than others. In your father's case he might have seen his dream career cut short when he was turned down for a position, became burdened with heavy financial obligations, or struggled with a physical or mental disability. Then again, he could have been hounded by a spate of bad luck that just followed him wherever he went. For some, their father's life may have been a lesson in what not to do, but for you it provided an instruction manual in exactly what *to* do when life keeps handing you one setback after the other. Some setbacks are non-negotiable. You just have to take it on the chin and live with them as best you can, while other setbacks can teach you resilience, perseverance, and how to work with what you have. Either by example or by know-how, your father would have shown you that it's the stone rejected by the builders that can wind up becoming the cornerstone of a whole new foundation if you have the vision to see it. But not all Dark Fathers are this dignified in the face of adversity. Some walk out on their families, some fade into the woodwork, and some take a perverse pleasure in withholding their love and approval because it makes them feel superior. Nevertheless, they still would have taught you the same lesson—it's up to you to be in your own corner.

That's a tall order for someone who can be so self-critical. Capricorns are often described as fault-finding and severe, but what the world sees is nothing compared to the number you do on yourself. Nobody can rake themselves over the coals and gleefully rub salt in their own wounds like you can. So why are you so hard on yourself and subsequently on other people? Is it because you're a perfectionist? A control freak? Or a frustrated Spanish Inquisitor in a past life? No. What it stems from is fear of that one misstep, that fatal error that sends you tumbling over the side of the cliff and down into the ravine. Did you take too long to text someone back after a first date? Did you overplay your hand with a client? Or get cold feet when you needed to be bold? You may never know. But getting down on yourself won't bring back a missed opportunity or salvage a failure; however, learning from your mistakes—and that means truly learning from them and not just rehashing that exhaustive list of what went wrong—ensures that next time you'll climb higher and go further. And being born under the sign of the mountain goat means you can't stop climbing. No grazing in grassy meadows or resting on laurels for you. You've always been attracted to the higher heights—even if that means climbing down off the mountaintop you're on so you can summit that taller peak you spy in the distance. This is why yours is the rags-to-riches sign.

Capricorns are scary ambitious. And that's not because you're power hungry or you need to have it all. All three earth signs are high achievers and work hard for their success. But at the end of the day a Taurus wants a good life. A Virgo wants to know they did a good job. And Capricorn? You want another day because there's always more to do. If you set your sights on something you will achieve it, but it won't be done overnight, nor will it go according to plan. You were born under Saturn, the planet of time, so nothing happens quickly with you. Things take twice as long to come together and twice as long to fall apart—which gives you plenty of time to mull over decisions, consider the consequences, and think about what you would do if you were finally dealt a winning hand. Saturn also teaches you patience, acceptance, and appreciation. And appreciation may be the most valuable of these—especially given all your years spent on the bench watching rivals get the easy breaks, squander their opportunities, and fall prey to those younger, leaner, and meaner than themselves. You've learned a lot by being made to go the long way. You know that a first success rarely lasts, that prosperity makes you forgetful, and that fear of losing what you have often creates the very circumstances that lead you to lose it. Saturn is in domicile in Capricorn, which is why in the seasonal cycle of life budding, flourishing, and fading, your connection to the planet of time makes you evergreen.

Goat used to refer to a loser. The idea comes from Leviticus, where a community would ritually unburden its sins onto a goat and then drive it out into the desert to perish. This is where the term *scapegoat* comes from, which probably explains all those times when you felt unjustly accused or blamed for somebody else's mistakes or inadequacies. Nowadays the acronym G.O.A.T. stands for "greatest of all time," which only goes to show that even with all the detours, delays, and setbacks, you—like your namesake—will always come out on top.

THE SUN IN AQUARIUS

You were born with a crazy genius. Now this doesn't make you Einstein. You're not like the Scarecrow in *The Wizard of Oz* who, after receiving a brain, is able to calculate all kinds of theorems and formulas on request. Our word *genius* comes from the ancient Roman idea that everyone born into this world arrives with a spirit in tow that watches over them throughout their entire lives. Part guide, part genie, this entity blesses you with a certain gift—maybe a genius for sports, picking up languages, or packing dishes in the dishwasher just right. Whatever it is, be it big or small, your genius makes you brilliant in your own distinct way. Most people might think of this as a talent or an aptitude, but your genius actually expresses itself through these. It's that invisible part of you that knows where to turn on a road you've never traveled, knows how to put together pieces that look like they shouldn't fit, and is certain that everything will work out just as long as you stick to the plan—even if said plan has never been tried before. Geminis have their alter egos, Libras have their other halves, and Aquarians have their higher consciousness.

But life with your crazy genius is a two-way street. It's not some gift you were blessed with that you get to walk away from. You have to honor this part of yourself or it will drive you nuts until you do. And it doesn't matter if you came from a disadvantaged background, were raised by wolves, or happened to have other plans in mind for your life. That crazy genius of yours would have found a way to put you in touch with that teacher who saw something special in you, the mentor who guided you, or the sponsor who was willing to take a chance. People speak of having a higher purpose, a raison d'être, or a destiny to fulfill. Your crazy genius is on the order of that. Many people talk about being true to who they are, but Aquarius is a futuristic sign. Your crazy genius's job is to ensure that you stay true to the person you've yet to become.

Everything with Aquarius is higher. You live according to a higher standard, commune on a higher plane, and always try to act from your higher self. And this makes perfect sense because one of your ruling planets is Uranus, named after the god of the heavens in Greek mythology. Uranus had no images made in his name. There were no pictures, statues, or temples built to commemorate him. What would be the point when all you had to do was look up? Nothing humankind made could ever compete with the shining majesty of the stars. The heavens, by their very nature, are uplifting and transcendent. It's to them that we ascribe our eternal truths, our purest values, and our radiant virtues. These ideals represent the highest in ourselves, the best lives that we could possibly live. It's why we set them like constellations in the nighttime sky to serve as guides for when we have lost our way.

But you're no airy fairy. Being idealistic doesn't mean you're naïve. It means you know better. You're all too familiar with people's downsides and shortcomings. You've watched them point fingers, pass the buck, bully those weaker than themselves, and cry foul when they in turn feel bullied. Everyone says this is the way of the world, but you don't buy it. There's got to be more to life than finding new ways to celebrate the lowest common denominator. Why are laziness, greed, lack of imagination, and willful ignorance acceptable while activism, social welfare, innovation, and education are not? Because it's easier to make fun, to roll your eyes, to say things can't be done and to get angry and defensive when you're called on it than it is to lift your head up and do something different. Yours is the woke sign of the zodiac. You don't slouch and you don't look the other way. You have always stood on principle—even if that means being shouted down, ostracized, or sabotaged. And you don't do this because you're especially brave or noble. You do it because you know it's right. Standing on principle reminds people of their faults and shortcomings, which is why they don't like it. It also reminds people that they can do better.

The Sun is in detriment in Aquarius. And that's not just because winter is when the Sun is coldest and weakest; it's because Aquarius, zodiac sign of the heavenly lights, is where the Sun feels like it's just another face in the crowd. When the Sun's out during the day you can't see the other stars. The Sun blocks their light and hogs all the attention for itself. But when the Sun sets and the stars come out again, we can all see that our sun is just one in a million. Actually, it's one in a billion trillion. And when faced with the sheer multitude of galaxies, solar systems, and planets that lie beyond our own, is it any wonder that you won't stay within the confines of conventional wisdom, that you will question authority in all its guises and march to the beat of a different drummer? And it doesn't matter if you've been fed a steady diet of facts, stats, and pat answers all your life, there's a part of you that knows that the truth is still out there.

Every Aquarius wants to change the world. That's why yours is the most radical sign of the zodiac. There are Aquarians who want to speed up the pace and change it into something better before it's too late, but there are also Aquarians who want to turn back the clock and restore it to the way it once was. These Aquarians don't get as much airplay as their more liberal-minded counterparts, but they're just as revolutionary. Yours is an extreme sign that won't think twice about burning down the house and starting again from scratch if that's what it takes to get things right. And that's an important distinction. Getting things right isn't the same as being right. You will be the first to admit to a mistake if you're wrong. You won't think twice about reversing your position if it's been disproved or removing yourself from the situation if your presence is causing more harm than good. The needs of the many will always outweigh the needs of the few as far as you're concerned. And that's what makes Aquarius the most selfless sign of the zodiac. If the Sun stands for the ego in an astrological chart and you regard the Sun as one of many stars in the firmament, then it makes perfect sense that you would treat others' opinions—as well as their hopes, dreams, feelings, and aspirations—as being just as important as your own.

You have another ruling planet: Saturn. The planet of tests, Saturn insists that you get your head out of the clouds and find a way to bring those precious ideals of yours down to earth. It's your job to make them real just like it's Saturn's job to thwart you at every turn. But Saturn doesn't do this to spoil your fun. It does it because you aren't going to become the person you're supposed to become by traveling a well-trodden path. You won't be inventive if you follow in others' footsteps, resourceful if you're given everything you want, or understanding if you've never been misunderstood. Enlightenment is hard to come by in a world where the lessons don't stick, dawning realizations fade, and progress is erased by a simple swing of the pendulum. The whole thing can feel like an exercise in futility. But Aquarius is a Utopian sign. You are committed to the world of tomorrow. You feel a responsibility to the people you'll never meet and the lives yet to be born. You know that society is only as good as the people who live in it. It is an obligation borne on all of our shoulders, and it only evolves if we evolve. Your commitment will always be to the better angels of our nature—which is why you will never stop pressing people to rise to the occasion of themselves.

THE SUN IN PISCES

Sometimes it feels like you're a sleepwalker in life—shuffling through the day, performing activities by rote, and winding up in places you can't remember setting out for. Loved ones and friends have grown accustomed to your dazed expression, that far-off look in your eyes signaling that the lights may be on, but nobody's home. And it's not like you're deliberately choosing to be preoccupied or absent. It's just that to be born under Pisces means that you're a fish out of water wherever you go, and the only time when you're truly yourself is when you can return to the undersea world of your imagination. You might do this in your dreams, with your VR headset, or through mind-altering drugs and alcohol. But you don't do this because you're an escapist who can't cope with the demands of everyday life. You do it because you feel like you've been marooned on a desert island and you're desperately searching for a way back home.

Nothing compares to what you see in your mind's eye. Here the painting you want to paint is beheld in masterful strokes. The song in your head is perfectly composed. How do you know? Because it sang to you every note. You can visit every room of the house you want to build, fine-tune every detail of your million-dollar idea, and lovingly scribble out mathematical equations that will radically alter our ideas of time and space. People might laugh at you and say this is nothing but wishful thinking, but it's not. You really can see, hear, and feel these things—so much so that they haunt you like a misplaced belonging or a lost limb. This is why you ache so deeply. How can you settle for this also-ran world when you've been to a place that's so full and so rich?

Pisces is probably the most soulful sign of the zodiac. It's certainly the most psychic. You have an ability to tap into that phantasmal world that surrounds us, a world that nobody sees but we all know is there. It's a place that mystics and saints visited all the time in earlier centuries, an ethereal plane where mysteries were revealed but never fully understood. These experiences couldn't be explained, but they could be described—and they filled the seer with such ecstasy that friends and neighbors couldn't help but respond. Some thought the person was crazy, but others were moved by their words and felt that this person had seen God. Some mystics held up the bleeding palms of their hands as evidence, unearthed hidden springs with healing waters for the sick to drink, or led armies to stunning victories against impossible odds. They were living proof of the miraculous at work in our world and that God had not abandoned us all together.

But what was revered in one century was burned at the stake in the next, and this explains the uneasy relationship between mystic and church—or you and your supervisor, for that matter. On one hand the church needed those mystic visions to refill its wineskins. It was thirsty for testimonials that would reintroduce the sacred back into the profane. Without it, the church would lose all relevance and ability to inspire. On the other hand the mystics could be a rowdy crowd with their radical reinterpretations of scripture, demands for reform, and clarion calls to repent. This is why they were quashed, and even put to death, when they got out of hand. It really was—and still is—a love/hate relationship that continues to this day. It's something you're keenly aware of when a supervisor praises you for your creativity in one breath and then asks you to rein it in with the next. Labels like *sensitive*, *artistic*, and *romantic* sound complimentary but they're actually condescending. And the mixed messages to be creative but not *too* creative can be dispiriting. This may explain the rageful feeling that wells up inside when people don't believe that you know what you're talking about. Why you react so heatedly when told to fall into line and not be such a martyr. Why you resent it when your voice is muzzled and your ideas are watered down.

To be soulful is to be sorrowful. Your ruling planet, Neptune, the planet of dreams and visions, is also the planet of unconditional love. When we think of unconditional love, we think of loving unselfishly without rules or expectations. We trust openly, sacrifice freely, and forgive repeatedly because we are so accepting that no matter what happens we will always be loving. Unconditional love asks for nothing in return.

That sounds like a pretty tall order. Most of us wouldn't even try to be that charitable, but for you it comes naturally. Of all the water signs, yours is the most fluid. You can plunge into the depths of depression and despair, glide through the whirlpools of jealousy and anger, ride the waves of happiness and delight, and languish in the pools of peace and tranquility. The fact that you can move from one emotional state to the next without getting snagged or pulled under is what makes you fluent in the universal language of feelings. Unconditional love isn't about attaining a state of bliss where you are removed and unmoving; unconditional love means experiencing the entire lexicon of love (which includes hate) constantly, and if you are capable of such a thing then you are truly soulful. There's a lot of pain in your life because you can't help feeling deeply. But there's a lot of joy, too.

One would think that this would make you super attentive to others, but actually it's the opposite. When you can stream your emotions as easily as you can, there's really no priority given to any single object of desire or moment of reverie. You'll gush on about a new love interest in the same way that you would about a favorite song, a new pair of shoes, or the play of light on the water. Every feeling carries the same emotional weight and is therefore generic. This can create the impression among loved ones and friends that they don't really matter—especially when you lament the human suffering happening halfway across the world while never once asking them about their own struggles and difficulties.

Pisces people tend to get apocalyptic. It comes from being born under the last sign of the zodiac. You often issue ultimatums, call down fiery curses, and paint doomsday scenarios if you're feeling persecuted. Apocalypses were a dime a dozen in the ancient world. The revenge fantasies of slaves, they fed the broken spirits of people who felt defeated in this world but knew that they would be redeemed in the next. This is the part of you that can be deeply pessimistic—annihilistic even. The part of you that just wants to throw in the towel.

Thankfully, you have another ruling planet, Jupiter. Jupiter is the planet of "what I believe," and it represents the God that we imagine. We can imagine a God outside ourselves—a Supreme Being that created the Universe in seven days but somehow remains conspicuously absent from our day-to-day life (and let's face it, if somebody initiated the nuclear launch codes tomorrow, it's unlikely that this God would intervene)—or we can imagine a God inside ourselves and ask the question: What would God do? Well, certainly not abandon this world and all of the beautiful things in it.

It's Jupiter that asks you to stop pinning your hopes on the life hereafter and to pin them on the one you're living today. You may never fully appreciate the ripple effect you have on others—the way your voice speaks to their sorrow, your insight unlocks a closed door, or how your refusal to give up on them provides the lifeline they need to pull themselves to safety—but you are their miracle worker! They don't need any convincing that you could get water out of a stone or translate your creative vision into reality if you wanted to. And if they believe that you can do such marvelous things, wouldn't it be nice if you believed it too?

THE PLANETS

In the beginning there were seven planets: the Sun, the Moon, Mercury, Venus, Mars, Jupiter, and Saturn. These are known as the ancient planets. The Sun and Moon are called the luminaries—"the lights"—because the Sun lights the day and the Moon lights the night. After them the planets are divided into two camps: Venus and Jupiter on one side and Mars and Saturn on the other. Venus and Jupiter are called the *benefics* because they bring good things, and Mars and Saturn are called the *malefics* because they bring bad things. The reason for this has to do with light. Although not as bright as the Sun and Moon, Venus and Jupiter are quite dazzling. You can't miss them when they're out at night. Mars and Saturn? Not so much. Mars has a glaring red glow, and Saturn is faded and slow-moving because it's the farthest away. You can think of these two camps as the jocks at one table and the goth kids at the other in the school cafeteria. And Mercury? It's neither malefic or benefic. But this doesn't make the planet neutral. If anything, Mercury plays both sides—it takes on the characteristics of whatever planet it's next to, hanging out with the benefics when they're in the ascendancy and buddying up to the malefics when they're not.

All of this changed in 1781 with the discovery of Uranus. Uranus upset the planetary order, and because it was the first planet that astrologers had to observe for themselves in order to grasp what its effects would be, it took about a hundred years before Uranus began appearing in astrological charts with any regularity.

Neptune's discovery in 1848 followed by Pluto's in 1930 added two more planets to the astrological pantheon in the late modern era, which is why these three are called the modern planets. Astrologers didn't know whether to label them benefic or malefic for the simple fact that their lights are not seen with the naked eye. They were discovered with observatory telescopes and guesswork.

The modern planets spend a long time in one zodiac sign because they're so distant. Remember that the Sun passes through twelve signs in a year—that works out to one sign per month. But Uranus takes eighty-four years to orbit the Sun, which means it will spend seven years in just one zodiac sign. Neptune spends fourteen years in a sign, and Pluto—because of its elliptical orbit—spends anywhere from twelve to thirty-two years in a sign. That's why in the section that follows you'll see twelve sign descriptions for Uranus but only seven for Neptune and Pluto. However, for Neptune and Pluto you will find listed the years that these planets were in a particular sign so that you can see how they impact the generation born under it. It's tempting to treat these like the astrological equivalent of boomers, Gen Xers, millennials, and iGens, but it's too soon to tell if there's any correlation—especially when the cut-off dates for the generations themselves are still being worked out. At the end of the day, the slower-moving planets need to be read in the same way that you would read the faster-moving ones.

THE MOON

The Moon is the planet of "what I feel about myself to be true." Everyone knows that feelings change—you can be happy one moment and sad the next—and this is reflected by the fastest-moving planet in the nighttime sky. No other planet changes its appearance as rapidly and dramatically as the Moon does. Yet even if its light isn't constant, its cycles are.

The Moon has always been connected to the soul. The Neoplatonists believed that at night when we slept, our souls left our bodies and traveled to the Moon, where they would bathe themselves in its cool waters after a hot and blistering day. Here they would reconnect and remember their true nature, which often got lost in the traffic of everyday worries and concerns. And when dawn's rosy strands unfurled across the sky, our souls would return to their bodies so that each person would awake feeling renewed and replenished. Morning dew on the grass and leaves was regarded as the wet footprints that souls left behind as they rushed back to be reunited with their slumbering selves. This is why the Moon has always been the planet of dreams.

Ruler of the unconscious, the Moon also houses our memories, needs, and habits. It's your private self that others don't see. You can think of the Moon as your emotional comfort zone. Your memories and how you recount them, your needs and how you fulfill them, and your habits and how you repeat them will all be described by the Moon's placement in your horoscope. As you can imagine, not everyone has the same emotional comfort zone. Some people need to sink their roots in deeply in order to feel secure while others are rolling stones who gather no moss.

A good way to think of the Moon is as the bed you sleep in. Maybe not your real one per se, but your metaphorical one. Are you a bed-of-nails person or do you hold court surrounded by fluffy pillows and bolster cushions? Do you long to sleep under the stars or are you happiest buried beneath a heap of blankets? Do you see yourself on a fold-out couch, spread across a king-size mattress, or is it strictly twin beds when it comes to relationships? Are you a cuddler or a splayer? Do you sleep naked?

The Moon is all about intimacy and that feeling of belonging. It determines how close we can get to another human being. As you might imagine, a lot of this depends on the nurturing and care we received in our childhood, which is why the Moon represents the mother in your astrological chart. Chances are the environment she provided for you will be the environment you provide for others. And this isn't the exclusive domain of loved ones and children. The Moon decides whether you're going to treat the team at work like family or if it's every person for themselves. Do you believe that good fences make good neighbors or will you invite them over for a barbecue? Trust issues, the way that you emotionally process things, and abandonment anxiety are all reflected by the Moon. The Moon is also where you go when you feel frightened or hurt. You may have the sort of Moon that takes you up into her arms and holds you close or a Moon that tells you to buck up, get back on out there, and give 'em hell. Not all Moons are nurturing. Some wax and some wane.

Finally, the Moon gives us our resilience. The fact that the Moon increases in light until it grows full only to lose its light until it disappears and then begins again reminds us of our psyche's innate ability to recover from hardship, to adapt with the times, and to love and trust and bond again when we thought our hearts would always remain broken. Yes, the Sun will always rise on a new day, but it's the Moon that provides the thread that runs through every one of our yesterdays, todays, and tomorrows.

The easiest way to gauge the Moon's strength in an astrological chart is to determine whether it's in domicile, detriment, exaltation, or fall. The Moon is at home in Cancer (domicile) because Cancer rules the summer solstice when the earth is bursting with life; it's out of season in Capricorn (detriment) because Capricorn rules the winter solstice when the earth is dark and dormant; it's most powerful in Taurus (exalted) because this is when spring has sprung (those flowers and roses will never look as green and resplendent as they do in May); and it's weakest in Scorpio (fall) because this is when the leaves drop and gardens have gone to seed.

It's important to remember that just because a Moon is exalted or in fall doesn't mean it's a good or bad Moon. Astrologers know full well that people blessed with good fortune from a planet can squander it, while those born with a less than stellar planetary placement often make more with less. It's something to keep in mind as you read about the Moon in the twelve signs.

MOON IN ARIES

An Aries Moon is fiery and combative. You don't walk on eggshells or tiptoe around sensitive topics. You stomp. You're bold, blunt, and in-your-face. The Moon struggles here because Aries's nature is heated and confrontational while the Moon's is calm and soothing. If you have an Aries Moon you can't relax until you get things off your chest. You hate holding anything in. Anyone who wants to get close to you needs to know that you will always say what you feel and feel what you say. They also have to be OK with sudden outbursts. Anger is your psyche's way of purging. Once you get things off your chest you'll quickly return to your good-natured self, but keep in mind that dishing it out means you're also going to have to take it. Yours may not be the most nurturing Moon, but it's certainly the most passionate. Aries Moon . . .

Does best with: Gemini and Aquarius Suns because it gives personal conviction to two signs that often lack it; Leo and Sagittarius Suns because it emboldens them to be the best that they can be.

Struggles with: Taurus and Pisces Suns because it's always trying to get these two low-key signs up and going. Virgo and Scorpio Suns because it makes them feel like somehow they should have done better.

Squares off with: Cancer and Capricorn Suns by holding their feet to the fire.

Is at odds with: Libra Suns. You were born under a full Moon if your Sun is in Libra. That makes your Sun and Moon equal partners. The struggle is between partnership (Libra) and acting on your own (Aries). This can give mixed signals in relationships and business associations because even though you say you're happy in the passenger seat, you really want to be behind the wheel. Make life easy and just take charge.

Is in the dark with: Aries Suns. You were born under a new Moon or very close to it. You have a blind spot when it comes to impulse control. There's no tempering mechanism. It's act first, ask questions later. This has landed you in many a briar patch and you have the lumps and bumps to show for it. But acting out also keeps you from questioning your impulses or taking responsibility for them. The best way to show people that you care is by caring.

MOON IN TAURUS

Your Moon is like Miracle-Gro. Not only do you have a green thumb for flowers and plants, but you have the same effect on raising a family, growing a business, or harvesting the fruits of a creative endeavor. Things flourish under your care. The Moon is exalted in Taurus. It's where it's the most fertile, productive, and abundant. You're very at home with your body and the bodies of others, which makes you a comfortable person to be around. Let others worry about squeezing into their skinny jeans. You're definitely Relaxed Fit. Besides, you couldn't care less—you've never had a problem attracting and keeping a lover. However, you do need to watch it with the conspicuous consumption. Taurus Moons eat, drink, and spend to excess. The downside to an exalted Moon is Fat Cat Syndrome. That's not a comment about weight but about complacency, because love and money will always come easy. This can lead you to take life for granted, and that's not good. Stay a little lean and mean, and you'll never be caught napping. Taurus Moon . . .

Does best with: Cancer and Pisces Suns because it makes them produce something instead of just dream about it. Virgo and Capricorn Suns because it gives them solid ground (materials, resources, money) to build on.

Struggles with: Aries and Gemini Suns because it puts the brakes on their impulses and plans by making them do the math first. Libra and Sagittarius Suns because it believes in taking what you can get, which often makes these signs feel like they're settling for less.

Squares off with: Leo and Aquarius Suns because it insists they stick to the bottom line.

Is at odds with: Scorpio Suns. You were born under a full Moon if your Sun is in Scorpio. That makes your Sun and Moon equal partners. The struggle is between scarcity (Scorpio) and plenty (Taurus). No matter what you do, you never feel like you make enough on your own. Maybe your partner earns more, your parents fund you, or your job is to oversee others' finances. This can make you feel beholden. Scorpio Suns hate depending on anyone, while Taurus Moons don't much care how the money shows up. This blessing needn't be a curse if you would only learn to trust.

Is in the dark with: Taurus Suns. You were born under a new Moon or very close to it. You have a blind spot when it comes to security. Making safe choices is great, but after a while they add up. You lower your sights, talk yourself out of opportunities, and make decisions based on convenience. Every plant needs repotting or else it gets rootbound. And likewise, from time to time, you need to move on to greener pastures. It promotes growth and keeps you from getting stuck in a rut.

MOON IN GEMINI

A Gemini Moon is like living with a three-year-old who's constantly tiptoeing into your room at night and asking if you're awake. When your conscious mind goes to sleep, your Gemini Moon comes out to play. Suddenly, unfinished ideas and half-baked schemes appear fully realized. You have all the words for things you should have said, explanations that leave nothing in doubt, and clever turns of phrase that would surely win any argument. The only problem is you're asleep. Like Mercury, the Moon is the planet of messages. Mercury rules tweets and the Moon rules dreams. A Gemini Moon means an active dream life. What's important is setting up office hours so it doesn't intrude on your sleep. You may be afraid of losing that mental thread, but remember that when you have a Gemini Moon, your unconscious is the co-pilot to your conscious, so those great thoughts aren't going away. They're in there somewhere. Meanwhile you need to rest and that nocturnal three-year-old needs to be told that anything worth saying can wait until morning. Gemini Moon . . .

Does best with: Leo and Aries Suns because it makes them approachable and easy to talk to. Libra and Aquarius Suns because it gets these two signs to talk to people "entre nous" instead of addressing them only in formal situations.

Struggles with: Taurus and Cancer Suns because it's restless and doesn't give these two signs any peace of mind. Scorpio and Capricorn Suns because it places a rationale where a naked feeling should be.

Squares off with: Virgo and Pisces Suns because it will always side with the head over the heart.

Is at odds with: Sagittarius Suns. You were born under a full Moon if your Sun is in Sagittarius. That makes your Sun and Moon equal partners. The struggle is between verve (Sagittarius) and intellect (Gemini). Your Sagittarius Sun wants to experience life full tilt while your Gemini Moon keeps one foot out the door. And it's not because you're cynical. You don't like it when your heart gets carried away. It means you have a lot to lose. That's why you always have an exit plan handy. You may never use it, but knowing it's there is tremendously reassuring.

Is in the dark with: Gemini Suns. You were born under a new Moon or very close to it. You have a blind spot when it comes to your mind. Sharp and alert, it doesn't like sharing space with your emotions. It's why you intellectualize when things get too heavy or intimate. But Geminis are often of two minds about things, not one. Make the switch from left-brain to right-brain thinking and let your emotions come out and do what they do best: feel. It's the most mindful thing you can do.

MOON IN CANCER

You are a creature of habit. And you're unapologetic about it. Whether it's preparing a meal, sitting down to work, or getting ready to exercise, everything has to be set up just right. It keeps you on track. Some people pursue goals, check off items on their to-do lists, or are slaves to their agendas, but your routine is organic. It centers and orients you. It's deeply ritualistic. The Moon is in domicile in Cancer, which allows you to maintain a consistent cycle in an off-kilter world. You believe in the past and you like that it repeats itself. The past isn't something you need to escape or reinvent. You love your family, traditions, and heritage. But something to keep in mind about the Moon is that it changes. It's consistent in its cycles but changes in its appearance. Loved ones change, and steering them back to the past—to something you find comfortable and familiar—isn't always the answer. It's something you need to be open to. Cancer Moon . . .

Does best with: Taurus and Virgo Suns because it gives them fertile bodies and equally fertile imaginations. Scorpio and Pisces Suns because it gives them some summertime joy to go along with all that Sturm und Drang.

Struggles with: Gemini and Leo Suns because it makes them needy at the most inopportune times. Sagittarius and Aquarius Suns because it's not as adventurous as these two signs would like to be, although once introduced to an exotic culture it finds appealing, it's quick to go "native."

Squares off with: Aries and Libra Suns because it cramps their style. Cancer Moons are homebodies whereas these two signs want to be out and about.

Is at odds with: Capricorn Suns. You were born under a full Moon if your Sun is in Capricorn. That makes your Sun and Moon equal partners. The struggle is between hard (Capricorn) and soft (Cancer). Your Capricorn Sun insists that hard work and discipline are the secrets to success. You're a climber, not a clinger. But your lunar side knows that scaling the highest heights can get exhausting. Sunny valleys lie between those forbidding peaks, verdant places where you can rest and recoup. There's nothing wrong with being "soft." Besides—all work and no play makes Capricorn a dull goat.

Is in the dark with: Cancer Suns. You were born under a new Moon or very close to it. You have a blind spot when it comes to the way things were. The Moon rules over memory, so it's easy to get nostalgic. A little nostalgia is sweet, but too much and you start glorifying the past. Open your world by sampling another culture's cuisine. Cancer rules the stomach and food is the great international language, after all—and as everyone knows, the best way to a person's heart is through their tummy.

MOON IN LEO

Your feelings are *very* important. There's nothing trivial or ridiculous about them. You take them seriously and expect everyone else to do the same. That's because what you feel matters. Your love matters. Your heartbreak matters. If you're angry, then you're right to be angry, because something pissed you off. It's not that you have a *right* to be angry, you *are* angry. Pure and simple. You were wronged and something needs to be done about it. Pronto. You own your emotions and insist that they be recognized and taken care of. People may question why your feelings should take prece-dence over others', but they do and you won't apologize for it. Leo Moons are lionhearted. Brave and determined, you always trust what's in your heart—and what you think is in the heart of others. Sometimes this can prove dangerously naïve—like when you extend the benefit of the doubt to someone who doesn't deserve it. Nevertheless, Leo Moons teach us all to have the strength of our emotional convictions. Leo Moon . . .

Does best with: Gemini and Libra Suns because it makes them be who they are rather than what others expect them to be. Aries and Sagittarius Suns because it gives them a heart to go along with those burning passions and runaway enthusiasms.

Struggles with: Cancer and Virgo Suns because it insists that they express their feelings when it would be safer not to. Capricorn and Pisces Suns because it makes them wrestle with the guilt trips they try to impose on themselves.

Squares off with: Taurus and Scorpio Suns by making it hard to be hard-hearted about matters where they have drawn the line.

Is at odds with: Aquarius Suns. You were born under a full Moon if your Sun is in Aquarius. That makes your Sun and Moon equal partners. The struggle is between the impersonal (Aquarius) and the personal (Leo). Aquarius Suns tend to infantilize emotions, to see them as reckless and irrational. The Leo Moon is here to remind you that emotions matter—no matter how you try to distance yourself from them.

Is in the dark with: Leo Suns. You were born under a new Moon or very close to it. You have a blind spot when it comes to your heart. You trust your heart absolutely, which is great, but then you also expect people to feel the same way as you and that's simply not going to happen. They have hearts of their own. Show the same respect you expect them to show you and you'll open your heart *and* your mind.

MOON IN VIRGO

Anything that stresses you out emotionally will have an immediate impact on your body. You might break out in rashes, wrestle with eating disorders, or experience sudden problems with your immune system. *Psychosomatic* is a word often used to describe physical ills being all in the head, but it's made up of two important words: *psyche* ("soul") and *soma* ("body"). The Moon rules both the soul and the body in astrology, and it's your soul's unsettledness in its body that expresses itself physically—not unlike like the way a sudden drop in the insect population signals that the planet Earth is feeling taxed. What's nice about having a Virgo Moon is that it alerts you in a timely manner so you can get to the bottom of whatever ails you. Your Virgo Moon keeps you emotionally honest about what you can—and cannot—take on. Virgo Moons are also extremely matter-of-fact when it comes to their bodies. They're the ones you can talk to about those sensitive health issues that you don't feel comfortable discussing with anyone else. Virgo Moon . . .

Does best with: Cancer and Scorpio Suns by preventing these two signs from getting too sentimental or sullen. It keeps the emotional temperature in the room just right. Taurus and Capricorn Suns because it treats the body like a temple and not a pup tent.

Struggles with: Leo and Libra Suns because it will always spot the fly in the ointment. Aries and Aquarius Suns because it's not afraid to pull the plug when it's reached its limit. And it will.

Squares off with: Gemini and Sagittarius Suns because it doesn't treat emotional truths like they're inconvenient.

Is at odds with: Pisces Suns. You were born under a full Moon if your Sun is in Pisces. That makes your Sun and Moon equal partners. The struggle is between letting go (Pisces) and holding back (Virgo). Your Pisces Sun believes in painting on the largest possible canvas. It's grand in scope and can be emotionally overwhelming. Your Virgo Moon, however, knows that less is more. It's kind of like the difference between epic poetry and haiku. Your Virgo Moon may not be big on dramatic sweeping gestures, but there's something to be said for leaving things up to the imagination.

Is in the dark with: Virgo Suns. You were born under a new Moon or very close to it. You have a blind spot when it comes to your body. But this isn't because you're a germophobe or vain. It's about apartness. You have a deep-rooted fear of becoming emotionally dependent on others. It's why you keep yourself able-bodied. This ensures that people will always depend on you rather than the other way around. Ironically, keeping your distance allows you to be intimate. It's when people say you should relax and unwind that you tense up.

MOON IN LIBRA

You don't like unpleasant emotions. You like nice ones. You know the world isn't always a pleasant place, which is why it's your job to help salvage something from the emotional wreckage that washes up on your shores. But you're not doing this because of some savior complex. It's to bring peace and order to your life. People produce when they're happy. They make trouble when they're not. And since you will always choose beauty and prosperity over discord and disarray, you will do whatever it takes to help loved ones, friends, and associates recover their emotional equilibrium and return to making something useful of their lives. You're a good listener. You have an extraordinary ability to remove yourself from the equation and just take in what the other person is saying. It's what makes you such good therapists, consultants, and mediators. Nevertheless, you're irresistibly drawn to bad boys, man-eaters, and hot messes. For some reason these red flags work more like aphrodisiacs than warning labels. Who knows? Maybe it's because they bring excitement and unpredictability to your sometimes overly well-balanced life. Libra Moon . . .

Does best with: Leo and Sagittarius Suns because it makes them polite. Gemini and Aquarius Suns because it makes them apologize instead of trying to explain things away.

Struggles with: Virgo and Scorpio Suns because it won't stop until they uncross those crossed arms. Taurus and Pisces Suns because it will always argue for quality over quantity.

Squares off with: Cancer and Capricorn Suns because it insists on hearing the other side of the story.

Is at odds with: Aries Suns. You were born under a full Moon if your Sun is in Aries. That makes your Sun and Moon equal partners. The struggle is between independence (Aries) and cooperation (Libra). Typically, Aries Suns tackle challenges alone; however, your Libra Moon learned a long time ago that it's better to lock in support beforehand. It extends your reach and strengthens your hold. So how do you win people over to your side? Nobody does charm offensive like you do. Your scintillating combination of passion and persuasion turns heads and changes minds.

Is in the dark with: Libra Suns. You were born under a new Moon or very close to it. You have a blind spot when it comes to relationships. You will take it upon yourself to do the relating for both sides, thereby unintentionally choking off the back-and-forth flow that needs to exist for any relationship to succeed. You are not in charge of making your relationship work. That rests on both parties' shoulders. The truer you are to yourself, the truer your partner will be to themselves, and that's what makes for a healthy bond.

MOON IN SCORPIO

You're not afraid of the dark. If anything, you're quite comfortable with it. You understand that there are lots of things that people feel deep down inside but don't want to talk about—much less own. And compiling an exhaustive list of triggers or reciting mantras every day won't keep those anxieties, fears, and panic attacks at bay. You believe in being brutally honest. Intense and fiercely devoted, you would love nothing more than to race to someone's emotional rescue, but you know this often makes matters worse. Life isn't pretty. And if loved ones don't learn how to pick themselves up after a spill, then they'll never stand on their own. The Moon is in fall in Scorpio. This doesn't make your Moon unloving, but it does give you a callused heart. Not a hard one. A gritty and experienced one. A lot of pain and suffering has gone into your emotional wisdom. Yours is a tough-love Moon, but just because it's seasoned doesn't make it any less nurturing. Scorpio Moon . . .

Does best with: Virgo and Capricorn Suns because it's not afraid to ask the uncomfortable questions. Cancer and Pisces Suns because it gives them co-jones.

Struggles with: Libra and Sagittarius Suns because it feels like it's always being prettified to fit in with their rose-colored view of life. Aries and Gemini Suns because it will always insist that they admit their feelings matter even when they say they don't.

Squares off with: Leo and Aquarius Suns by refusing to give up a grievance just to make people feel better.

Is at odds with: Taurus Suns. You were born under a full Moon if your Sun is in Taurus. That makes your Sun and Moon equal partners. The struggle is between having (Taurus) and not having (Scorpio). Taurus Suns take people at face value, while Scorpio Moons are convinced everyone's working an angle—one usually aimed at separating you from your money. Although it pains you to have such a suspicious side, your Scorpio Moon is often more right than wrong.

Is in the dark with: Scorpio Suns. You were born under a new Moon or very close to it. You have a blind spot when it comes to going negative. You assume that everyone wants to know the dirty truth, but actually they don't. Indeed, the glee you take in trumpeting your gotcha moments turns people off. It's easy to shame and blame, and much harder to help someone find their way back. Do this and you heal others as well as yourself.

MOON IN SAGITTARIUS

Your emotions are loud and your opinions colorful. And you believe in making them known right away—uncensored and without apology. People may not like it, but that's their problem. You are being true to what you feel. Sagittarius Moons are more expressive than receptive, which means that anyone who wants to talk about their feelings is going to have to crank up the volume. Yet there is no Moon more uplifting when spirits are down. Sagittarius Moons can spot the silver lining in a hurricane. The downside is you don't do downsides. If things don't turn out the way you had hoped, you'll just wave away the results. This abrupt dismissal can make you appear cavalier. What people don't realize is that you care deeply but are afraid that if you don't perk up immediately and climb back on that horse, then you never will. Sagittarius Moons need to learn to take the setbacks with the strides. Plus, letting someone else express what they're feeling from time to time is a good idea too. Sagittarius Moon . . .

Does best with: Libra and Aquarius Suns because it brings an emotional directness to two signs that often beat around the bush. Aries and Leo Suns because it raises their sights.

Struggles with: Scorpio and Capricorn Suns because it would rather take the stand than plead the Fifth. Taurus and Cancer Suns because it yearns for a more adventurous life.

Squares off with: Virgo and Pisces Suns by insisting they put their needs first.

Is at odds with: Gemini Suns. You were born under a full Moon if your Sun is in Gemini. That makes your Sun and Moon equal partners. The struggle is between the cerebral (Gemini) and the excitable (Sagittarius). Gemini Suns can sometimes feel stuck atop a runaway horse when their lunar side breaks into full gallop. There's no choice but to ride it out. Afterward, when you've regained control of the reins, a joke made at your own expense or a little self-deprecating humor is all it takes to remedy matters.

Is in the dark with: Sagittarius Suns. You were born under a new Moon or very close to it. You have a blind spot when it comes to fervor. Do you really believe in what you're feeling, or are you just getting off on the exhilaration? You feel like you have to keep things pumped in a relationship. This can get exhausting for both sides. If you don't want to wind up like an overstimulated child who runs around in circles before collapsing into a dead heap, dial it down. You shouldn't have to work so hard to keep someone around.

MOON IN CAPRICORN

You can get pretty heavy. That's because the Moon is in detriment in Capricorn. Being born with a wintry Moon makes you prone to dark moods. It's hard to see the bright side of things. Happy endings make you uneasy because you're too wary of the trip wires that lie underneath. Even growing up, you felt like a stranger in your household—like an orphan with misplaced papers or a changeling. But just because your imagination's gothic doesn't mean the rest of you is. You're actually wickedly funny. With a sardonic humor and a cryptic turn of phrase, you go to great lengths to create the impression that you just don't care. Yet your pained silences always give you away, which is why you should let yourself be who you are—someone who feels too deeply, thinks too seriously, and worries too much. You may not be everyone's cup of tea, but you're ambrosia to a select few. Impeccably responsible and preternaturally wise, you need a long time to warm up, but the wait is always worth it. Capricorn Moon . . .

Does best with: Scorpio and Pisces Suns because it makes them unashamedly melancholic. Taurus and Virgo Suns because it gets them to look beyond the grindstone they have their noses pressed to and to fix their sights on higher incomes.

Struggles with: Sagittarius and Aquarius Suns because it refuses to pay for the upkeep on all those castles in the air. Gemini and Leo Suns because there's nothing hypothetical about those worst-case scenarios.

Squares off with: Aries and Libra Suns by making them see things through to the end.

Is at odds with: Cancer Suns. You were born under a full Moon if your Sun is in Cancer. That makes your Sun and Moon equal partners. The struggle is between family (Cancer) and career (Capricorn). Your ruling planet is the Moon, so you'll always choose career over family. You'll work long hours to put food on the table. Yet by not making time for loved ones, you may discover they haven't much time for you later on. Reverse the trend while you can. A family is more than an obligation; it's your home.

Is in the dark with: Capricorn Suns. You were born under a new Moon or very close to it. You have a blind spot when it comes to guilt. You see all the things you should have done (but didn't), the obligations you failed to fulfill, and the emotional burdens that proved too heavy, and you wrap them around you like a security blanket. There's nothing wrong with a little guilt. It's healthy. But too much guilt leads to self-absorption. Self-debasement can be just as narcissistic as self-aggrandizement. Wean yourself off the guilt habit and you'll be there for people again.

MOON IN AQUARIUS

You are intensely interested in other people's well-being. Are they being treated fairly? Do they feel like they have a voice? Is there anything you can do to empower them? Yet when someone asks you how you're doing, you draw a blank. It's like you've just been asked a trick question. Aquarian Moons are surprisingly shy when it comes to discussing their feelings. That's because you see your feelings as selfish. It's why you constantly downplay them. But you should know by now that the more you try to repress any part of yourself, the more it will rise up against you. This can manifest as problems with addiction, self-medication, or compulsive perfectionism. How can you live a more emotionally intelligent life? Try giving your feelings more airplay—especially the dangerous ones like joy, pride, and satisfaction. The next time someone praises you, say "thank you" instead of looking awkward and embarrassed. It makes you own the moment and the feeling, which signals to your psyche that you're ready to own the rest of yourself as well. Aquarius Moon . . .

Does best with: Aries and Sagittarius Suns because it insists that they work for the greater good. Gemini and Libra Suns because it keeps them honest.

Struggles with: Capricorn and Pisces Suns because it's more stoic and self-sacrificing than either of these two signs want to be. Cancer and Virgo Suns because it will never water down truths to make them more appealing.

Squares off with: Taurus and Scorpio Suns because it will always underscore the *ours* in the struggle between *yours* and *mine*.

Is at odds with: Leo Suns. You were born under a full Moon if your Sun is in Leo. That makes your Sun and Moon equal partners. The struggle is between me (Leo) and everyone else (Aquarius). You are very much your own person, and your Aquarius Moon expects others to be their own persons too. But your idea of who people should be may not square with their own view of themselves, and that's when you need to respect differences. The point of individuality is that no two people are alike.

Is in the dark with: Aquarius Suns. You were born under a new Moon or very close to it. You have a blind spot when it comes to you. You're so focused on doing right by others that you often leave yourself out of the equation. You need to stop treating *self* like it's a four-letter word. You're a flesh-and-blood being with human wants and needs. Spend as much time looking after your own concerns as you do others'.

MOON IN PISCES

You have a psychic Moon. You may not be clairvoyant or able to channel past lives on request, but you do have a profound ability to pick up on what people feel. Images come easily, as do sensations—which sometimes take over your body. You may get choked up around someone who has difficulty expressing their feelings or short-tempered around somebody else who sits on their anger, but once you physically distance yourself your body returns to normal. Your chameleon Moon naturally takes on the colors of the person sitting next to you, creating an instant familiarity. It's great romantically or if you're working on a creative collaboration because you're totally in sync like jazz musicians jamming together, but it can work against you in more straightlaced environments. Not everyone wants to get soulful and deep, and your lunar x-ray vision makes them uncomfortable. The biggest lesson for a Pisces Moon to learn is that everyone has to do their own emotional homework. You may "see" the answers they seek, but they have to figure it out for themselves. Pisces Moon . . .

Does best with: Taurus and Capricorn Suns because it gives a soft side to two signs who often do things by the book. Cancer and Scorpio Suns because it makes them forgive.

Struggles with: Aries and Aquarius Suns because it makes them question if their heart is truly in the right place. Leo and Libra Suns because it insists that they actually walk a mile in somebody else's shoes instead of just talk about it.

Squares off with: Gemini and Sagittarius Suns by holding them emotionally responsible.

Is at odds with: Virgo Suns. You were born under a full Moon if your Sun is in Virgo. That makes your Sun and Moon equal partners. The struggle is between being of service (Virgo) and self-sacrifice (Pisces). Chances are you're always going to be self-sacrificing. You can't help but go the extra distance for someone in need. But put reasonable limits on what you can and cannot do. Somebody else's welfare shouldn't come at the expense of yours.

Is in the dark with: Pisces Suns. You were born under a new Moon or very close to it. You have a blind spot when it comes to empathy. You have such compassion for others that you wind up ignoring the people in your life. If you ever want true intimacy, then you need to make them your top priority. Take them for granted and they won't stick around. And you'll always feel at sea.

MERCURY

Do you do your best thinking when you're wired or in your sleep? Are you one of those people who have to plan everything out in advance, or is letting things go until the last moment your way of pulling the proverbial rabbit out of a hat? Mercury is the planet of "what I think" in astrology, and there are as many different kinds of intelligences as there are signs in the zodiac. We often think of intelligence as being cerebral and analytical, but over the years we've come to appreciate other states of mind as well, like emotional intelligence, body memory, intuitive flashes, and creative flow.

Mercury is the planet that connects our eyes to our hands. It could even be said that Mercury bestows our hands with an intelligence all their own. People with a pronounced Mercury in their charts excel at sports that require hand-eye coordination, but they can also be gifted musicians, detailed artisans, or wickedly quick gamers. Mercury bestows dexterity, inventiveness, and technique—the likes of which can move faster than conscious thought. Think of how we use hand imagery to describe mental activity. Don't we talk about juggling priorities, tossing ideas back and forth, trying to get a handle on a situation, or poking holes in somebody's argument? Isn't hands-on experience the secret ingredient that transforms book smarts into street smarts? But hands can also be deceptive, like when we talk of sleight-of-hand trickery, keeping our hands up in the air where they can be seen, or the right hand not knowing what the left hand is doing. Mercury reveals as much as it conceals.

Curiosity and play are key to understanding how Mercury works in our lives. Early childhood games like patty-cake, making faces, and singsong rhymes teach us how to interact, mimic, and memorize. Left to our own devices we'd probably just gurgle and burp, but Mercury is the planet that sees, learns, and applies. Inherently restless, it gets us to roll over onto our stomachs so we can crawl, sit up so that we can get a better view of things, and grab a table leg to help us stand until we're ready to walk on our own. Mercury gets us out of ourselves and into the world. It also teaches us how to navigate our way in a world that isn't always nice or trustworthy. How well we play with others—or play others—is best symbolized by the planet that believes that where there's a wile, there's a way.

You can have the most brilliant ideas ever conceived, but they won't mean a thing if you can't jot them down on paper or pitch them to a prospective buyer. Mercury is responsible for translating your idea from drawing board to reality. Mercury rules all the facilities that we use to write, speak, craft, and shape. Mercury also knows how to get your goods to market. The messenger of the gods, Mercury was the only one who could travel from heaven to earth to hell and back again. He knew all the ins and outs, all the names and passwords. He knew who to coax, who to butter up, who to threaten, and who to bribe. Mercury helps you find your way in life. It's the planet responsible for getting you from here to there.

Mercury is also the planet of buying and selling. Its name stems from the Latin root *merc*, which means "market" and appears in the words *merchant* and *merchandise*. Like all planets, Mercury has one face when it's direct and another when it's retrograde. Mercury direct was said to rule over shopkeepers, while Mercury retrograde ruled over shop*lifters*.

Mercury is the planet closest to the Sun. This is why we often don't see it in the nighttime sky, and when we do it's only three or four times a year for about ninety minutes before sunrise or ninety minutes after sunset. This is why in an astrological chart Mercury will only appear in the same zodiac sign as your Sun, the sign before, or the sign after. It will never be further away than that.

If your Mercury appears in the sign before your Sun sign (a "sunrise" Mercury), that means foresight. You live in the future, plan your moves accordingly, and are pretty good at anticipating how matters will play out. Some of this comes from being a quick study, and some of it comes from being three steps ahead of the game. You believe in getting out in front of a situation so nobody can get the drop on you. Proactive and prescient, you are rarely caught off guard. Nevertheless, you can still get too far ahead of yourself, and that's when you have to go back and correct—and even redo— what you've done.

If your Mercury appears in the same sign as your Sun, you feel like you know your mind. Whether you're logical, practical, intuitive, or creative, that's the lane you'll stay in. There's no real interest in trying on a different thinking cap. Obviously, this will allow you to excel in whatever mind-set you identify with, but the danger here is in exercising one set of mental muscles to the exclusion of everything else. Reinforcing what comes naturally can limit your curiosity, inhibit learning, and even create a blind spot where you're no longer receptive to anything new. Same Sun sign/Mercury signs need to work on keeping an open mind.

If your Mercury appears in the sign after your Sun sign (a "sunset" Mercury), that means hindsight. You never assume that you have all the information in front of you, which means you'll keep playing with the puzzle pieces long after everyone else has given up. This makes you an excellent problem solver. You're studied, deep thinking, and thorough. However, fear of getting things wrong can lead you to be too careful and to not weigh in when you need to. Sometimes it's best to go with what's in hand—especially since you're often right. And if not? Then you're not so far off the mark that a simple adjustment can't fix it.

What if you have Mercury retrograde? Mercury retrogrades are famous for tossing a monkey wrench into best-laid plans. That's why you always want to apply Murphy's law (whatever can go wrong will go wrong) to everything you do. It may sound unenviable, but a retrograde Mercury actually makes you better prepared for when things go south, because you expect them to. It forces you to think on your feet. The trick to working with Mercury retrograde is in finding a way to turn a liability into an asset. If one avenue is closed, nothing's stopping you from taking an alternate route. And who's to say that's not the better way to go?

The easiest way to gauge Mercury's strength in an astrological chart is to determine whether it's in domicile, detriment, exaltation, or fall. Mercury is at home (domicile) in two signs: Gemini and Virgo. Gemini and Virgo are the two signs that flank Cancer and Leo, which are ruled by the Moon and the Sun respectively. The Moon and the Sun are paired together because they rule night and day, and Mercury goes on both sides of them because Mercury orbits the Sun so closely that you can only see it just before sunrise when night is transitioning into day or just after sunset when day is transitioning into night.

Mercury is out of season (detriment) in Sagittarius and Pisces. These signs sit opposite Gemini and Virgo and they also bookend the winter—the time of year when the Sun is cold and distant—and wherever the Sun goes, Mercury goes, since Mercury is the Sun's closest companion. And in keeping with this idea, Mercury is most powerful (exalted) in Virgo because Virgo is the Mercury sign next to Leo in the zodiac, and Mercury is weakest (fall) in Pisces because Pisces is opposite Virgo. So basically if you have Mercury in Virgo you have a double bonus, and if you have Mercury in Pisces you have double the trouble. But it's important to remember that just because Mercury is exalted or in fall doesn't mean that it's a good or bad Mercury. Know-it-alls are often fooled while those who risk asking the "dumb" questions get the answers they seek.

MERCURY IN ARIES

You always speak your mind. You don't believe in hemming and hawing, cushioning the blow, or beating around the bush. You get straight to the point and insist that others do the same. If you like something, you'll say so. If you don't, you won't hold back. Yes, you're curt, you're blunt, and you can have the bedside manner of a jackhammer, but you've too much respect for people's intelligence to keep them in the dark. Everyone has the right to know the truth, and whether it hurts or sets them free is their own business. Aries is the zodiac sign that rules the head, which explains why you're so headstrong and often lock horns with others. However, Mercury in Aries people are also closet intellectuals. You're shy about your smarts and get easily embarrassed when someone points out how seriously you think about things. Aries may be a sign associated more with brawn than brain, but if you can acknowledge that the mind needs regular workouts—just like the body does in order to improve—then there's no limit to the hurdles you'll clear.

Aries Mercury/Pisces Sun:

Make sure you hear people out before answering, because you tend to jump the gun. Relax and breathe so you can really take in what they have to say. You don't want to assume the worst when you should be expecting the best.

Aries Mercury/Aries Sun:

Bold and incendiary, you have no problem expressing what you think. You believe in being honest. But being honest means others get to be honest back. Hopefully, you can take what you dish out—if not, then a little more discretion might be wise.

Aries Mercury/Taurus Sun:

Your first impulse is usually right. It's something you're constantly reminded of after taking the wrong turn or yielding to somebody else's judgment call.

One of these days you'll learn to follow it. Until then, try not to kick yourself when you're already down.

MERCURY IN TAURUS

You love the sound of your own voice. That's because Taurus is the zodiac sign that rules the throat. Many singers have Mercury in Taurus, making yours the sort of soothing tone that calms frazzled nerves, softens hardened hearts, and makes people trust you. You could probably charm the Cheshire Cat out of his tree. Nevertheless, like any good performer, you need to read your audience. You can't just prattle on, because people can tell when you're running on empty or papering over the cracks of a weak argument. Your voice gives you away. It's that telltale. Mercury in Taurus people also have a hard time yielding the floor. It's why you'll go on and on. You're desperately afraid of leaving something out or somebody coming along and stealing your thunder. That's why you should prepare your remarks ahead of time. It puts you in control of your message. Moreover, the less you say, the closer people listen. Trust in the power of your voice and you'll never have to raise it.

Taurus Mercury/Aries Sun:

You love the adventure of getting an enterprise up and going and making it a success. Nothing beats turning a dark horse into a photo-finish winner. However, you get restless once things are running smoothly. It's a surefire sign that it's time to move on.

Taurus Mercury/Taurus Sun:

Your mind-set is "if it ain't broke, don't fix it." Too many people want to change things for the sake of changing them, which results in more I-told-you-so's and cleanup work for you. You're open to new ideas if someone makes a compelling case. Otherwise you're not buying.

Taurus Mercury/Gemini Sun:

You're methodical in your thinking. You will break a problem down into its components and then address each in order of importance. This allows you to identify what's workable and what's not. Once the answer is clear, you'll cut to the chase and move purposefully toward your solution.

MERCURY IN GEMINI

You play with variables the way a child plays with their vegetables. Sometimes it's to pass the time until you're excused from the table, and sometimes it's because you're enamored with all the possibilities. You almost never have a plan. And if you do, you rarely stick to it. Your genius is in making things up as you go and convincing everyone else this was what you had in mind all along. Mercury is in domicile in Gemini. It's where it's the most spontaneous, inventive, and improvisational. Nobody can paint themselves into a corner or talk their way out of a jam like you. Life would be much easier if only you'd learn to leave well enough alone, but that's just not going to happen. You were born with a curious mind that can't resist a riddle, mystery, or "do not press" button. So what do you get for all your aggravation? The things that only experimentation can bring like a new twist on a familiar formula, a fresh approach to an obstinate problem, or a secret passage where a brick wall used to be.

Gemini Mercury/Taurus Sun:

You've got your hand on the buzzer and will press it even if you don't know the answer. You believe it's better to be in the game than warming up the bench. Thank heavens you're good at educated guesses, otherwise you'd be in a lot of trouble.

Gemini Mercury/Gemini Sun:

You have a quick mind and the short attention span to prove it. You thrive under constant deadlines. They make you think on your feet. You don't want to be with a project so long that you get bored. You do best with several balls in the air.

Gemini Mercury/Cancer Sun:

You're an expert collector. A frequenter of thrift stores, antique shops, and estate sales, you can spot the gold in the dross. Most people don't understand the value of what they have. And if they do, you can always talk them down. You drive a hard bargain.

MERCURY IN CANCER

You do your best thinking in your sleep. It's why you get drowsy when you're troubled. Your brain is searching for answers, but it has to turn off your conscious mind so that it can move about unfettered. Sleep allows you to revisit the sunken treasures of memory and imagination and to see the deep associations that lie beneath the stepping-stones of logic. When you wake up again (and this can even be after a few minutes of zoning out), the answer is there in front of you, as obvious as it is unquestionable. Your unconscious isn't your only information source; there's your body too. You can immediately feel when something's off. A person's presence makes you uncomfortable, a situation doesn't sit right, or your gut says there's more going on than meets the eye. But the gut is a funny thing. Sometimes you can trust it to warn and defend, and sometimes it's like a dog barking at squirrels. Heed your instincts, but include your critical faculties as well. A Cancer Mercury studies its target with all its senses and doesn't miss a trick.

Cancer Mercury/Gemini Sun:

You have a talent for turning a stranger into an accomplice. Maybe it's an inside joke, a shared glance, or a whispered secret. In any case, you enfold them in this invisible cloak of complicity so that even if this person didn't want to help before, they do now.

Cancer Mercury/Cancer Sun:

You have the rumpled folksiness of a Norman Rockwell painting. People feel comfortable with you and it's easy for them to open up and talk. You have a rich interior life. You should think about writing. You're an acute study and have a unique way of phrasing things.

Cancer Mercury/Leo Sun:

You are gushingly sentimental. The songs on your playlist read like the pages of your diary. You'd make a successful lyricist if you jotted your own thoughts down on paper. You have a way of speaking that makes people feel like you're expressing what's in their hearts.

MERCURY IN LEO

You take everything personally. You're thin-skinned and not very good at concealing your true feelings. That goes for your joy as well as your disappointment. The wonderful thing about having Mercury in Leo is that everyone listens. The not so wonderful thing about having Mercury in Leo is that everyone remembers, and this is where you need to be more mindful. What you say matters. People look up to you for approval, and when they get it they're happy, but when they don't? Well, they're likely to take it personally—just like you would. That's why it's always wise to ask yourself how you would want to hear a criticism or a reprimand if you were in the other person's shoes. Chances are you would want it to be honest (within reason) but also encouraging. Speaking to someone the way you would want to be spoken to creates a personal rapport that's heartfelt and resonant.

Leo Mercury/Cancer Sun:
Children gravitate to you, as do pets and small animals. It can get a little awkward when they ask you to take them home. What they all recognize is your kind and giving nature. You never lost touch with your inner child, and that makes you an endearing adult.

Leo Mercury/Leo Sun:
What you say goes. Being forthright and resolute makes people obey you. You can't abide wishy-washiness or ambivalence. You never want to create the impression of being weak. But adopting a what-I-say-goes policy means you also have to take responsibility for it. No passing the buck for you.

Leo Mercury/Virgo Sun:
You tend to apologize for what you say, but that won't keep you from saying it. That's because truth is the higher authority you answer to. Nevertheless, you won't just blurt out what you're thinking. You'll search for the right words and the right time to share them.

MERCURY IN VIRGO
Talent isn't everything. Gifted people are born every day, but it doesn't mean they'll do anything with it. Now this isn't to say you're without talent. You just don't trust it. You'd rather rely on skill. Skill can make a lot out of a little, it doesn't depend on your being "special," and it's an equal-opportunity improver because it builds on any aptitude you possess, turning it into a proficiency. Mercury is exalted in Virgo. It's where it's the most precise, hands-on, and instructive. Virgo Mercurys are drawn to practice. You don't

practice to make perfect (who wants a one-hit wonder?); you practice so you can produce the same desired result again and again. You like consistency. It's true that your formula for success can become formulaic, but that's when you know it's time to reinvent. A Virgo Mercury isn't afraid to go back to the drawing board. It's where you're free to tinker and fuss.

Virgo Mercury/Leo Sun:

This is an artistic combination. You have an ability to translate what you see in your heart or mind onto the page or performance space. You readily learn and absorb from others but then make it your own. Everything you create carries your unique signature.

Virgo Mercury/Virgo Sun:

You are the perennial student. You are always signing up for some new class, course, or field of study. People may think it's because you're a perfectionist or maybe even overcompensating, but the simple truth is you love to learn. You're the intellectual version of a foodie.

Virgo Mercury/Libra Sun:

You have a discerning eye and impeccable taste. But you can be too critical if you're not careful, and the result is you passing on jobs, relationships, and opportunities that you see as being beneath you. There's nothing wrong with test-driving things. You might surprise yourself.

MERCURY IN LIBRA

You have no problem letting the other person do all the talking. If anything, you encourage it. This way they divulge what's going on in their lives while you sit back and size up whether they would make a good partner, client, or ally. A Mercury in Libra has the art of the interview locked down to a science. You know where to smile and nod in all the right places. People often walk away feeling wonderful about their time with you while you walk away with all the information you need to make your decision while revealing little—if anything—about yourself. Etiquette and protocol are important. Etiquette ensures that everyone be on their best behavior (even if they don't feel like it), and protocol guarantees that things will proceed in an orderly manner. Your ability to deflect attention, graciously accept criticism, and redirect the conversation makes it hard for people to read you. And you wouldn't have it any other way.

Libra Mercury/Virgo Sun:
You want to do the right thing. Always careful to take the pulse of the room, you rarely stumble or misspeak. But sometimes doing the right thing flies in the face of what's socially acceptable. This is when you must choose between what's correct and what's just.

Libra Mercury/Libra Sun:
You are both conversational and well versed. People rarely catch on to how smart you are. You can talk to just about anyone about anything without making them feel condescended to. Equally comfortable in the 'hood as in the corridors of power, you care deeply about what matters to others.

Libra Mercury/Scorpio Sun:
This is the voice of conscience that gets you to rethink that counterproductive move you're about to make. You may resent being talked out of some of your more delicious vengeful scenarios, but there's no discounting the many times it's saved you from disaster. It's why you listen.

MERCURY IN SCORPIO
They say that the devil is in the details. It's why you have an exacting gaze when it comes to reviewing things that make other people's eyes glaze over,

like stats, graphs, and the fine print. You're constantly on the lookout for the one inconsistency that shows that somebody messed up or is trying to pull a fast one. You don't have trust issues because trust is a nonissue. Your working assumption is that everyone has something to hide and is guilty until proven otherwise. It may sound harsh and cynical, but it comes in handy for the type of work that you do, which is usually investigative in nature. Unafraid to ask the uncomfortable questions, you poke and probe. You listen with great intensity—focusing on what's said as much as what's unsaid. The devil is in the details, but the divine is too. That's why you also need to know when to extend the benefit of the doubt. You don't want to miss out on that key to salvation that could wind up saving the day.

Scorpio Mercury/Libra Sun:

You love double entendres and innuendos. Nothing delights you more than meeting someone who speaks the same code. Everything you say and do carries a veiled meaning. It's not like you've got something to hide. You just like creating the impression that you do.

Scorpio Mercury/Scorpio Sun:

You don't take anything at face value. You're always looking under the table, checking your boyfriend's texts, or rummaging through a friend's medicine cabinet. It comes from checking your closet at night for monsters when you were a kid. You believe it's better to be safe than sorry.

Scorpio Mercury/Sagittarius Sun:

The truth is still out there as far as you're concerned. You have a skeptic's smirk but a romantic's heart. You question everything not because you're a nonbeliever but because you never want to stop searching. You want to unlock the dirty secrets of the Universe.

MERCURY IN SAGITTARIUS

The truth is never as good as when you tell it. You know which facts to embellish, technical details to leave out, and emotional buttons to push to win over your audience. You want to create a narrative so compelling that even if it didn't happen, people will wish it had. Sagittarius Mercurys are the Pied Pipers of the zodiac. Everyone can't help but follow you around. You make things sound so colorful and adventurous! But it's not like you're trying to mislead anyone. Every story you tell or experience you share is meant to inspire. And the more excited people get about what you have to say, the more excited you get about their excitement until pretty soon you have a bonfire of enthusiasm bursting with revelation and wonder. Mercury is in detriment in Sagittarius, which explains your tendency to generalize, rhapsodize, and sermonize. You're not big on specifics or concerned about proof, but you won't let that detract from your message, which is always heartwarming, uplifting, and profound.

Sagittarius Mercury/Scorpio Sun:

You have a gift for zingers. They're always on target and your one-liners are often retweeted. But you must watch it with the stinging comments. Although they are great fun in the moment, you can rest assured they'll come back and bite you in the derrière.

Sagittarius Mercury/Sagittarius Sun:

You never met a high horse you couldn't mount. You'll gladly expound on a variety of moral, political, and philosophical topics. Unfortunately, you're a chronic malapropper—substituting one word for another at the most inopportune times. Thankfully, you've a sense of humor to go along with that self-righteousness.

Sagittarius Mercury/Capricorn Sun:

You are a born teacher, and your enthusiasm is infectious. But you're also a harsh taskmaster as you put pupils through their paces. You live for the moment when the lightbulb goes off. That's when you get to sing "the rain in Spain stays mainly in the plain" as you skip around the classroom.

MERCURY IN CAPRICORN

You can't help noticing what's wrong right off the bat. You're like a contestant on a game show itching to press the buzzer so you can call out the mistake, identify all the slip-ups, and detail each and every shortcoming. It feels great in the moment, but let's face it: nobody likes a killjoy. Poking holes in people's favorite assumptions isn't a ratings booster, but you also know that not speaking up isn't the answer either. It makes you complicit—especially if you know better. So what do you do? Push yourself to think deeper. Critics are a dime a dozen; a constructive thinker is a rare gem. If you're going to identify what's wrong, then be ready to show people how to make it right. You need to figure out what's salvageable about an unsalvageable situation, how to turn a near miss into a direct hit, or—if things truly are a disaster—how to begin again. Nobody's asking you to kiss their boo-boos and make them better. What they want is to make things better and for you to show them the way.

Capricorn Mercury/Sagittarius Sun:

You're not quick, but you're thorough. You rarely make a reference without citing sources, you use air quotes when unsure of your facts, and you footnote your texts with hyperlinks. All of this guardedness can sometimes result in endless disclaimers. Remember that the point is to get to the point.

Capricorn Mercury/Capricorn Sun:

You're like Hamlet on the parapets of Elsinore—absorbed with matters so weighty that they make "to be or not to be" sound like a trick question. But don't get so fixated on consequences that you never take action. The soul's joy is in the doing.

Capricorn Mercury/Aquarius Sun:

Worrying about what's left out leads you to neglect what's in hand. It's like discovering you haven't much time with someone. You're more focused on the clock than you are with enjoying the meeting or visit. Make the most of what you have and you'll find it's always enough.

MERCURY IN AQUARIUS

You're a great communicator. You can take an abstract concept or densely worded policy and break it down into easy-to-follow sentences. It's important that everyone in the room understands what's being talked about. You don't want anything going over anyone's head. Aquarius Mercurys are naturally inclusive. You want a safe space where people can say what needs to be heard. But you also insist on personal accountability. You have zero tolerance for anyone who skirts the issue, passes the buck, or plays the victim. And it doesn't matter if they say they don't remember things having been said a certain way, because you have this amazing ability to play back any conversation with the word-for-word accuracy of a court stenographer. Keep in mind that most people can't communicate as well as you can, and that can be a little intimidating. Learn to read their body language, their pregnant pauses, and between the lines of their *ums* and *ers*. They're telling you things about themselves that they can't easily put into words.

Aquarius Mercury/Capricorn Sun:

You choose your words carefully—like the mountain goat picking its way up a steep cliff. One false step is all it takes to send you tumbling. Strategic and politic, you have a way of making your case and with great success. It's all in the semantics.

Aquarius Mercury/Aquarius Sun:

Forward thinking and progressive, you can see farther down the road than most. The trick is in not running ahead but convincing others to follow you. This requires hand-holding and speaking in simple sentences. It's good exercise for someone who's often smarter than everyone else in the room.

Aquarius Mercury/Pisces Sun:

Everything is interconnected. You don't believe in accidents or coincidences. Whatever happens is a result of something done or undone. This can either give you a Zen approach to life or lead you in search of the butterfly whose flapping wings caused a hurricane half a world away.

MERCURY IN PISCES

You enjoy floating along the stream of consciousness—swirling and twirling around bubbling impressions and glistening insights, splashing over rocky realizations while chasing butterfly thoughts in your mind's eye. You might pause from time to time to reflect in the shaded corners of quiet waters before returning to your endless journey. Thoughts never really begin or end with you. They just keep flowing, like conversations that you can pick up and leave off again in midsentence. An underlying current runs through your conscious and unconscious minds, giving you unlimited access to these separate shores. This makes you equal friends with the rational and the irrational. It's how you can see the rhyme in the reason and divine the logic in the absurd. Yet Mercury is in detriment *and* fall in Pisces—making Pisces the most challenging placement for this analytical planet. But what you lose in methodology you gain in divine inspiration, which leaves others amazed. You'll want to explain how you came up with your unique conclusions, but don't. What makes perfect sense to you will only leave others totally mystified.

Pisces Mercury/Aquarius Sun:
Your mind never stops. You're constantly questioning, commenting, evaluating, and processing. This is what gives people the impression that you're not quite present—that you're distracted or preoccupied with something else. They often assume you're scattered, when in truth you operate on several platforms at once.

Pisces Mercury/Pisces Sun:
People treat you with the reverence of consulting an oracle. They hang on every turn of phrase or cryptic reference. You'd enjoy dishing out the sage advice if you weren't as mystified yourself. Like them, you're just as eager to see what you'll come up with next.

Pisces Mercury/Aries Sun:
You have an uncanny ability to say what's on people's minds. It's great if they want to talk; it's not so great if you're broaching topics they'd rather not discuss. Sometimes signaling that you know that they know that you know is all it takes to encourage them to speak up.

VENUS

Venus is the planet of "what I like" in astrology. Named after the Roman goddess of love and beauty, Venus rules over the power of attraction. What piques our interest, tickles our fancy, arouses our passion, or tempts us to do something we know we shouldn't is all tied up in this planet. Venus is responsible for drawing people into our lives. Like a male peacock fanning his tail or a flower opening its petals, Venus asks our prospective admirers, lovers, funders, and consumers: Do you like what you see?

Venus embodies the principle that like attracts like, and we signal this by our appearance. What you wear is more than just an expression of who you are. It broadcasts to other people if you are somebody they want to sit down next to or not. Too many pens in your shirt pocket makes as strong a statement as goth black, piercings, and tats. Changing your look every season to keep up with the latest trends is going to make you as recognizable to a fellow fashionista as a soldier in uniform would be to a comrade-in-arms. Shoes aren't just shoes any more than handbags are handbags or jewelry is jewelry. They tell us if you're flamboyant or looking to fit in, high maintenance or low profile, laid-back or crisp and particular. Fashion is just as codified nowadays as it was in the mirrored halls of Marie Antoinette's Versailles.

But there's more to Venus than just your "look." Venus's job is to hook, and she does this by acting on our pleasure centers. She shows up in a wink, a smile, a brushing of the sleeve, or a stolen glance that was never stolen. Think of her as astrology's version of perfume. Her scent is unique to your own personal horoscope, and it's specifically designed to attract those astrological charts that align with yours.

And that's the fundamental difference between the Sun and Venus in your astrological chart. The Sun's main concern is you. It insists that you be true to yourself, realize your potential, and grow into the person you were always meant to be. Venus's focus is on everyone else. Her mission is to find those people you click with. People who love the same music, hate the same politicians, know what you're thinking before you say it, and have your best interests at heart. Venus knows that in order to flourish you need to surround yourself with the right people, because nobody makes it on their own in this world. Every successful life is a cooperative effort.

Everyone likes to be liked. It brings out the best in people. And this is where things can get complicated, because Venus will do anything to be liked. Positive encouragement makes us funnier, prettier, smarter, or more enterprising as we seek to win favor with those whose "likes" matter most. But that same need to win favor can also lead us to edit out parts of ourselves we think others might find unacceptable, to defer, conform, and become mean-spirited toward those who don't belong in our circle. Venus may be the planet of love, but she's not especially discriminating. People are just as likely to rally around something they love as they are to rally against something they hate. And that's the funny thing about Venus—we have no control over how she works in our lives. The only way to know what kind of people we attract is to see who shows up.

Beauty is in the eye of the beholder—which means that with Venus it's the other person (and not you) who decides what it is about you that they find beautiful. Venus makes you want to be that person somebody else sees in you. Sometimes it's a disaster, like when you try to turn yourself into someone you're not, and sometimes it's the best thing that could possibly happen because that person's vision of you may be better than anything you could have imagined for yourself. Venus is a matchmaker, and where she appears in your astrological chart shows the type of person you will attract. Venus won't tell you what zodiac sign fits best with yours, but she will describe the personality traits and life circumstances under which you'll meet.

Like Mercury, Venus travels close to the Sun. It's why she will only appear in your own sign or in one of the two signs that precede or follow yours. She will never be farther away from the Sun in your chart than that. Unlike Mercury, she's much more visible in the nighttime sky in the hours before dawn or just after sunset. Venus is the third brightest light in the sky after the Sun and Moon, and when's she out (which is for about nine months at a time) you can't miss her!

Venus in one of the two signs preceding your Sun sign means she was rising before the Sun when you were born. This makes her a morning star. Morning star Venuses are the "that looks good" attractions. You fall in love quickly, romanticize rhapsodically, and can easily be led on or astray. Friends may chide you about your serial infatuations, but the truth is your romantic pursuits make you a better person. You become wiser, deeper, and better dressed. It takes you a while to get things right—you're not always clear on whether you're in love with the person or your idea of the person— but eventually you find your match. Your lover will always be your muse.

Venus in the same sign as your Sun means you're often blindsided by love. There's little distance between the Sun and Venus, so you may have no idea of the Venus signals you're sending. It's great if the person you're secretly crushing on surprises you by making the first move, but not so great if someone you never thought of in that way starts getting uncomfortably sexual. The other thing to watch out for is people projecting their personal issues onto you. Same Sun sign/Venus sign combinations makes you a natural hook, and since Venus rules mirrors, who knows what they see when they look at you? Learning how to defuse situations, redirect the conversation, and gently pass them back their own psychological baggage are valuable skills worth developing.

Venus in one of the two signs following your Sun sign means that she rose after sunset when you were born. This makes her an evening star. Evening star Venuses are the "good for you" attractions. You may not get what you want, but you'll get what you need. These are the attractions where it's hard to tell if the person you're drawn to is a soul mate or a life lesson. You'll face difficult situations that test your fidelity. If things don't work out you'll still grow as a person. And if they do? Then yours is the bond that once joined can never be put asunder.

What if Venus is retrograde in your chart? Venus retrogrades are famous for attracting what you don't like—like unwanted attention and unholy boors. Venus retrogrades often show up in the charts of people who experience bullying. The trick to working with Venus retrograde is not to withdraw into yourself. Venus's strength is in numbers. Even if you're a loner, there are millions of loners just like you. Venus retrograde means trouble fitting in. You may have to leave your home or travel outside your emotional comfort zone to find your "people," but once you do they'll stick by you through thick and thin.

You can gauge Venus's strength in an astrological chart by determining if it's in domicile, detriment, exaltation, or fall. Venus is at home (domicile) in Taurus and Libra. Roses bloom in Taurus's month and grapes are harvested in Libra's, so Venus literally rules over the days of wine and roses. Venus is out of season (detriment) in Aries and Scorpio. These are the two Mars-ruled signs, which means your Venus attracts trouble. Venus is exalted in Pisces, a sign famous for its compassion and empathy, and Venus is in fall in Virgo, a sign famous for looking after itself. Whether Venus is exalted or in fall doesn't mean it's a good or bad Venus. Yes, it's always nice when love comes easy, but that doesn't necessarily make it true love.

VENUS IN ARIES

You're a magnet for trouble. You don't go looking for it, but it sure knows where to find you. You've been caught in more compromising situations, tight corners, and emotional cliffhangers than a romantic lead on a soap opera. What can you say? You can't help playing with fire. Whether it's a passionate fling or a fabulous wipe-out, you never apologize for your feelings. The more heated the moment, the more real you become. But it's hard to keep those feelings stoked—which is why Venus is in detriment in Aries. You tend to lose interest once you get what you want. The longest-running relationships are usually the most dramatic—full of breakups and makeups or circumstances that prevent you from getting together. Being in a constant state of crisis keeps the blood pumped and the adrenaline rushing. The best mate is a comrade-in-arms. Someone who has been through the wringer, gets going when the going gets tough, and always has your back. It may not be warm and fuzzy, but tackling life's challenges together generates the fire that keeps your love alive.

Aries Venus/Aquarius Sun:

People really admire your independent thinking—until you disagree with them. That's when they discover just how much your head rules your heart. More relationships have ended over ideological differences than anything else. If you're not on the same page politics-wise, you might as well skip the meet-and-greet.

Aries Venus/Pisces Sun:

People think you're a fighter when actually you're a lover. Good luck convincing them otherwise. They'll only accuse you of playing the victim. You attract people who think you need toughening up. There's nothing wrong with developing a thick skin, but that shouldn't give anyone permission to bully you either.

Aries Venus/Aries Sun:

You're in love with the unobtainable. The colder they are, the hotter you get. Ironically, you lose all respect once someone falls in love with you. You see it as weakness. Stripping off your clothes doesn't make you naked. Being vulnerable does. Try getting naked with someone you like. You might enjoy it.

Aries Venus/Taurus Sun:

You may be peace loving, but your Venus isn't. It's why you attract people who rock the boat, boss you around, and hold your feet to the fire. They're the unstoppable force to your immovable object. Yes, they're a pain in the derrière, but there's no denying you get things done when they're around.

Aries Venus/Gemini Sun:

You attract either someone you can't keep your hands off but doesn't have much going on upstairs or an intellectual who's breathtakingly brilliant but needs help in the PE department. It's a good thing you're a natural coach. You know from firsthand experience that love is a work in progress.

VENUS IN TAURUS

You love slipping into something more comfortable. Other people might trot out thongs and bustiers, but with you it's likely going to be T-shirts and boxers. Who wants to play dress-up in the bedroom? You have to do enough of that at work. You want a relaxed private life and someone who's going to be just as laid-back as you are. Venus is in domicile in Taurus, which means that when it comes to beauty and the beholder, you are always beauty and the other person is always the beholder. You want people to want you. You're not bothered by possessive types. If anything, they make you feel valued. You know you will always be their top priority and that you'll never be kept waiting, told to fetch something yourself, or mistaken for a potted fern. Love and money come naturally for you. The best partner is someone who can keep you in the style to which you've become accustomed. You will never be high maintenance. But you don't come cheap either.

Taurus Venus/Pisces Sun:

You're really good at getting people to do things for you—like replace a halogen bulb, repair a leaky faucet, or foot the bill. And you don't mind sitting through lectures on self-sufficiency if it makes them feel smart. Nevertheless, opening up an owner's manual and fixing something yourself once in a while wouldn't be the worst thing.

Taurus Venus/Aries Sun:

You're often told to relax. Partners say you're too on edge and need to chill, but this only stresses you out more. It isn't comfortable partnering with people who have an easier time of it than you, but that may be why they're here. You don't always have to take the hard way.

Taurus Venus/Taurus Sun:

Get a prenup. That way you always know what's yours. It seems unromantic, but you're going to bring in a lot of money because of your relationship, and you need to know you've got your assets covered should things go south. You'll both sleep better at night.

Taurus Venus/Gemini Sun:

You like people who play hard to get. It makes you want them even more. You love finding ways to win them over. This impresses those who never thought you could and also lets you be the one who decides in the end if you want them or not.

Taurus Venus/Cancer Sun

Partners love to cook for you. You have this penchant for attracting foodies, gourmands, and the next up-and-coming top chef. The sex is great, but sometimes you have to admit the food is better. Hopefully, you're a light eater or else this combination will wreak havoc on your waistline.

VENUS IN GEMINI

You attract naughty children. Whether it's artful dodgers or girls with curls in the middle of their foreheads, you have a penchant for people who never lost touch with their inner rascal. They're the ones who shoot you the knowing glance, roll their eyes when the boss isn't looking, and include you in all of their private jokes. It's not always easy to tell if you're in love or in cahoots, but this idea that you're getting away with something you shouldn't creates a wonderfully dangerous sense of urgency and intimacy. This is the person you want behind the wheel of your getaway car. Unfortunately, it's also the person you're most likely to blame for bringing out sides of you that you would never have acted on had you been left alone. Sometimes relationships are mirrors and sometimes they're windows, but what's clear is that you have to take responsibility for your side of the looking glass.

Gemini Venus/Aries Sun:

You wind up with people you never really thought of in that way before. Maybe it's a critic, a rival, or someone who's always one-upping you at work. The sexual tension is more apparent to friends than to you, but eventually you clue in. Bickering is your way of flirting.

Gemini Venus/Taurus Sun:

Smart is sexy. But we're not talking academic accolades. That's too stuffy and boring. You like 'em when they mess with your head. You've always had a soft spot for the Bugs Bunnys of the world. You say you're not into playing games, but nothing wins you over like a good prankster.

Gemini Venus/Gemini Sun:

Things are so on-again, off-again that you have to check your partner's Facebook page to see what your relationship status is. You can't help attracting people who have one foot out the door. This mirrors your own ambivalence about committing to anything long-term. Miracle cure? Stick around and maybe they will too.

Gemini Venus/Cancer Sun:

Enfants terribles bound toward you like a litter of excited puppies. They recognize an indulgent parent when they see one. You love their swift minds and mischievous spirits. But what's precocious in childhood doesn't always age well. Champion their genius and nurture their talent, but make sure your protectiveness doesn't cross over into enabling.

Gemini Venus/Leo Sun:

You can always fill in the blanks. It's a special talent when dealing with someone who can run circles around you intellectually. All those big words and fancy concepts sound quite impressive, but you also see how your partner often overlooks very important details. You love being the one to point out the obvious.

VENUS IN CANCER

You're the person everyone takes home to Mother. You're family friendly, easy to get along with, and good with children and pets. You'll have no problem picking up the lingo, adopting the body language, and blending in. It's like you've been a part of the tribe all along. And this is where things can go wrong. The more loved ones and relatives ask after you, the less you'll see of the person you're dating. It can feel like you're being set up for failure—and you will fail if you don't smarten up. It's seductive hanging out with the folks, but stay focused on the person you came in with. Make this person feel like your allegiance is to them and you'll succeed. The best partner is someone you can be family with—whether that's starting a family of your own, stepping into the role of stepparent, or combining your two broods.

Cancer Venus/Taurus Sun:

Home is where the heart is, but you can wind up fading into the woodwork if you're not careful. That's because the everyday running of your household takes precedence over your personal wants and needs. Don't be such a beast of burden. Find ways to delegate responsibility and you'll never be taken for granted.

Cancer Venus/Gemini Sun:

No more carrying a torch for a secret crush or acting like you don't have feelings when you do. You're really good at deflecting attention and hiding in plain sight. You need to speak up—otherwise you'll be one of those BFFs who listens to everyone's love problems but never experiences them for yourself.

Cancer Venus/Cancer Sun:

You attract needy types—like *really* needy types. They're so needy they'll compete with your children and pets for your attention. If you don't want them to dominate your life, then you need to be the designated adult in the relationship. Take charge and they'll do what you say.

Cancer Venus/Leo Sun:

Partners will always support you in your endeavors—which is great!—but there's an unspoken expectation that you should support them in theirs.

This misunderstanding has torpedoed many a relationship. Praise your partner and ask them what's up once in a while and you'll never walk around on eggshells again.

Cancer Venus/Virgo Sun

You could grow old waiting for someone to make the first move. Between the other person's stealth approach and your analytical one, it would be a miracle if anything happened. Chances are you're friends and don't want your romantic feelings to upset that. News flash: if feelings are there, then the friendship's already changed.

VENUS IN LEO

Born under a golden Venus, you can't help attracting people who are a few rungs up on the social ladder. These may be friends in high places, people who can open doors for you, or the most eligible bachelor(ette) in the room. You don't have to campaign to get what you want, play hard to get, or prove yourself. Love just shows up. But this can get dicey if you don't "own" your Venus. In other words, people may see something special in you that you don't see yourself. Instead of saying "I don't see what you see in me," it may be wiser to play along until you can figure out what they're looking at. Maybe it's just romantic idealization or maybe it's something worth aspiring to. The best mate is someone who knows they're the greatest thing that ever happened to you and doesn't have to say it.

Leo Venus/Gemini Sun:

It's anxiety-provoking being around someone so good-looking and successful. How can you trust that their feelings are real? It's why you struggle to keep the upper hand with little put-downs or say you're not in a relationship (when you are). Over time your partner's confidence rubs off on you and you relax.

Leo Venus/Cancer Sun:

Your partner wouldn't be a success without you. You're always there with emotional support, savvy advice, and the swiftest means of disposing of the incriminating evidence. You like being the power behind the throne. You're never at risk and will always be the person that your partner turns to.

Leo Venus/Leo Sun:

You have your favorites. They're the people in your life who truly stand out. Romance-wise it's great, but favoritism can be problematic for the also-rans. Press yourself to go through the motions of treating everyone alike. It may feel dishonest, but it's the courteous thing to do.

Leo Venus/Virgo Sun:

You resent people who have it easy. It's a problem because they're the ones you wind up with. Can you ever feel equal to someone more affluent? You don't want to cut off your nose to spite your face, but you don't want to be a sellout either. Somewhere in all the politics are two identities trying to connect.

Leo Venus/Libra Sun:

You're surrounded by beautiful people. You can't help it. They flock to you like narcissists to a mirror. What's interesting is that you don't have to match them in the looks department. You've always been one of them—much to the envy and resentment of those who don't understand what they see in you.

VENUS IN VIRGO

You look after yourself. Nothing in life is free. Goodwill gestures come with strings attached, and accepting a favor means having to repay it one day. You learned a long time ago that it's better to partner with people who need you more than you need them. It ensures that you'll always have the upper hand. Yet Venus is in fall in Virgo. The assumption was that the planet of love and beauty would do poorly in the sign of the Virgin, but what it really comes down to is not wanting to feel beholden to anyone. Needs make us all beholden. And it's Venus's nature to be with people—not to serve them. This may run contrary to your thinking, but without a compelling need to be with someone else you'll always be on the outside looking in. Show your partner your needs and they'll show you theirs.

Virgo Venus/Cancer Sun:

You know you shouldn't mix work with pleasure, but somehow you wind up getting intimate with a colleague, client, or patient. It's understandable considering how much time we spend at work, but there's also no denying the taboo appeal. This is an HR disaster waiting to happen, so it's a good thing you're so adept at covering your traces.

Virgo Venus/Leo Sun:

A hundred people can applaud you, but you'll always focus on the one who didn't. Every performer needs a critic, but criticism is like cholesterol. There's good and there's bad. Partner with someone who's constructive and you'll grow; partner with someone who harps on every single defect and you'll wilt.

Virgo Venus/Virgo Sun:

People come to you with their problems. But not everyone you meet needs help. Some actually have their act together. However, they're not going to stick around if you only focus on what's wrong. Try focusing on what's right instead.

Virgo Venus/Libra Sun:

You drive each other crazy with all the back and forth. When one of you talks seriously about your future together, the other withdraws and vice versa. You may never get over the ambivalence, but do you really want to spend your life warming the bench? Love is like the lottery. You've got to be in it to win it.

Virgo Venus/Scorpio Sun:

There's no liaison too dangerous for you. People seek you out to talk about their marriage problems, sex secrets, or repressed feelings. These conversations can get erotic, and sometimes one thing leads to another. It's not always easy to tell when you're tempted by forbidden fruit or racing to the emotional rescue, but then that's what relationships are made of.

VENUS IN LIBRA

You're happiest in a relationship. You'll spend hours on dating apps or scheming to bump into that person you like at work, the dog park, or the yoga studio. You're aiming for a soul mate, but you'll settle for a work in progress as long as they're beautiful and smart and make more money than you. And that goes for men with Venus Libras as well. Ironically, you'll still act like you're single even when you're in a couple. You say you're just being flirty, but actually you're hedging your bets in case things don't work out. Venus is in domicile in Libra, which means you've no shortage of admirers and you like to keep them around. But this isn't about ego strokes. You're afraid of being left. The best mate is someone who has a strong ego and a good sense of humor and is always reassuring no matter how many times you ask if your jeans make your butt look fat.

Libra Venus/Leo Sun:

Love comes easy. Maybe too easy. Since you can have your pick of anyone in the room, your thinking is this: Why not have them all? At some point you'll meet the person who can stand shoulder to shoulder with you, and when you do—that's the one.

Libra Venus/Virgo Sun:

You attract sophisticated types. They're sharp dressers and penetrating thinkers. But what looks good on paper doesn't always translate to the bedroom. There can be an uptight quality that prevents the two of you from getting close. The first partner who farts under the sheets and giggles about it is the one for you.

Libra Venus/Libra Sun:

You're always torn between two lovers. One is the person you think will make you happy, the other is the one who will. On an instinctual level you can tell the difference, but you're too focused on things turning out the way you want. Only by taking your thumb off the scale will you see for yourself.

Libra Venus/Scorpio Sun:

People are intrigued by your mystery. But what's romantic for them is heartbreaking for you when they realize you're just too intense. It isn't easy being dark and moody, but if you can keep the faith, then you'll see the one who can't quit you circling back to be with you again.

Libra Venus/Sagittarius Sun:

"*L'amour, l'amour, toujours l'amour!*" is your battle cry. You've experienced more sharp turns, sudden drops, and loop-the-loops on your roller coaster of love than most people could stomach, but that won't stop you from wanting to ride again. What can you say? You're a thrill seeker. And for those who want things safe and secure? There's always the kiddie train.

VENUS IN SCORPIO

You like people with dark pasts. Yours is a film noir Venus. Hard-bitten guys and shady femmes fatales are your kryptonite. Nothing is more seductive than unraveling their web of lies, piecing together the inconsistencies in their stories, and falling for that same double-cross again and again. Why? Because you know they've got a dirty secret locked up inside and you want to find out what it is. And once it's unearthed, maybe you'll release them from their curse—or they'll release you from yours. Venus is in detriment in Scorpio. It means you're more into damaged goods than pretty faces and attract people who spell trouble. Some might say you're being self-sabotaging, but your perfect mate is someone who knows what it's like to have gone to hell and back. Someone who understands your regrets and your shames and doesn't have a problem with them. You can't ask for a sweeter obsession than that.

Scorpio Venus/Virgo Sun:

Saving people from themselves is what you do best, but not everybody wants to be saved. Given enough time and experience you'll weed out the ones who want to do better from those who just want to bring you down. Until then, don't wear your heart on your sleeve.

Scorpio Venus/Libra Sun:

Why do you keep attracting the wrong people? They're always so possessive, domineering, or heavy. Can't you go out with somebody who's easy to get along with? Bad relationships are like ghosts—they'll keep haunting you until you get to the bottom of what ails them. Own up to the parts of yourself you project onto others and your relationships improve immediately.

Scorpio Venus/Scorpio Sun:

Neither of you trusts the other. Surprisingly, this has nothing to do with lies or betrayals. It's all about gaining and keeping the upper hand. You two wield zingers, guilt trips, and psychological manipulation tactics like evenly matched opponents. One day you'll get to the place where you can lay down the weapons and just be together.

Scorpio Venus/Sagittarius Sun:

Hopefully, you're a cat person. It helps to explain how your lover can be affectionate one moment, then hissing and scratching the next. The mixed messages would drive anyone crazy, but you love it. The sooner you learn to let this person come to you, the better off you'll be.

Scorpio Venus/Capricorn Sun:

Sex is where you really open up. But pretending like nothing happened afterward isn't a healthy way to deal with abandonment issues. Rejecting someone before they reject you leads to a self-fulfilling prophecy of loneliness. There's nothing wrong with sex for sex's sake. But if there's more going on, then be honest with your partner. The love life you save may be your own.

VENUS IN SAGITTARIUS

You love a good laugh—anything from piercing satire to fart jokes. Nothing is too sacred or cheap as far as you're concerned. Laughter is the universal language, which is good because you often attract people from other countries or different backgrounds. What matters is being around someone who doesn't take life too seriously but can call out injustice or hypocrisy when they see it. Yours is a *Runaway Bride* Venus. Commitments make you skittish, and you'll bolt if you see the barn door closing. That's why you enjoy unavailable partners who are already spoken for, are married to their jobs, or live halfway across the world. Your best match is someone who makes you laugh (and cry), lives out of state, or works for an airline. You're looking for a fellow traveler—someone who can share your adventures but won't hold you back.

Sagittarius Venus/Libra Sun:

Your guilty secret is that you always think you can do better, and perhaps you can. But is that person you're aiming for really an improvement on what you have? You have a habit of circling back to relationships you just left. Make sure that when you break up again it's for real. No one likes being treated like a placeholder.

Sagittarius Venus/Scorpio Sun:
The other person was smitten immediately. You? Not so fast. That's because you'd rather pursue than be pursued. It isn't easy being targeted by people dead set on rocking your world. You're no fan of change, but you'll do it for love. It's the one thing you never want anyone to find out about you.

Sagittarius Venus/Sagittarius Sun:
You can get so carried away in the moment that you never bother getting to know the person you're climbing into bed with. And that can result in morning-after regret. If you're really serious about someone, then channel that passion into courtship. Not everything has to be taken at a full gallop.

Sagittarius Venus/Capricorn Sun:
You've always been into May–December romances. When you're younger you're drawn to mentoring types, and as you get older you'll attract the precocious ones. That said, try shooting for an age difference of seven to fourteen years instead of twenty or more. It's more manageable.

Sagittarius Venus/Aquarius Sun:
You're married to the cause, so any potential partner has to sign on for that. You're looking for someone who's just as impassioned about fighting social injustice and economic inequality. But you're no Trotskyite. After all the leafletting's done, you'll still want to dine out at a five-star restaurant.

VENUS IN CAPRICORN

You're only interested in people who mean business. Time is your most precious commodity, and you don't want anyone wasting it. Whether dating or mating, you expect the other person to be punctual, presentable, and ready to work. You're not into no-shows, slackers, or drama. You just want to see if you click or not, and the sooner you find out, the better. It sounds like a tall order. And it is—which explains why the tall orders are often drawn to you. Venus in Capricorn is as bougie as it gets. But it isn't easy to tell if that class act is worth the psychological baggage that comes along with it. Status anxiety, unresolved daddy issues, and emotional disconnects are just a few of the personal items you'll have to pick your way through as you try to determine if that person's baggage is carry-on or should be checked at the curb. The best partner is someone who has similar career ambitions. You want to be part of a power couple. Poseurs and wannabes need not apply.

Capricorn Venus/Scorpio Sun:

There's something about a tailored suit and a condescending air that makes you weak. It leaves so much to the imagination. And the slow unveiling of secrets, desires, and hidden foibles is a striptease you look forward to. You'd repeat it every night for the rest of your life if you could.

Capricorn Venus/Sagittarius Sun:

You like being disciplined. It's why you pull all those crazy stunts. You say you resent people spoiling your fun, but that won't stop you from doing things that make them come down on you like a ton of bricks. There are easier ways to get someone to show they care.

Capricorn Venus/Capricorn Sun:

You spend so much time fixating on why you can't be together that you risk never finding out if you should. Yours wouldn't be the first relationship to break up a marriage or cross the line. People often assume you make safe choices, but that's because they don't know about the one who got away. Don't let this happen again.

Capricorn Venus/Aquarius Sun:
You like 'em stodgy. And truth to tell, those stuffed shirts relish your unpredictability. It's not unlike bumping into each other only to discover that they got chocolate in your peanut butter and you got peanut butter in their chocolate. It may seem perplexing at first, but it's a winning combination.

Capricorn Venus/Pisces Sun:
Your partner may never see the world the way you do, but that doesn't mean they won't support you. The person who pokes holes in your dreams one moment is the same one who will help you find a way to make them happen the next.

VENUS IN AQUARIUS
You're usually the last to know when someone's interested in you romantically. You meet so many different people—and from a variety of backgrounds—that you accept everyone at face value. A friend is a friend, a colleague is a colleague, and so on. It never occurs to you that anyone might be interested in you in any other way. The reason you're so slow on the uptake is that you rarely hang out one on one. You're always in a group. Venus becomes the planet of cliques when she's in Aquarius. You don't want to upset the group dynamic, and that's what happens when love enters the picture. One might think your friends are hugely important, but actually being alone with someone is . . . awkward. The best partner is a people person like yourself. That way when you're both done socializing for the day, your private time together becomes something special. This allows you to open up in ways you wouldn't have otherwise.

Aquarius Venus/Sagittarius Sun:

Your partner makes you a better person: maybe by getting you to question beliefs you take for granted, throwing you a look when opinions get too colorful, or showing you that people aren't the enemy just because they disagree. And all of this is done by making you feel like it was your idea all along.

Aquarius Venus/Capricorn Sun:

It isn't easy competing with your work schedule. It's more demanding than a jealous ex. Thankfully, you attract partners who are equally intent on filling your life with friends and activities that bear little resemblance to what you do for a living. You may grumble about the distractions and interruptions, but you secretly love it.

Aquarius Venus/Aquarius Sun:

Friends first and always. The word *relationship* carries centuries of patriarchal baggage loaded with codified roles and reinforced expectations. Friendship is more forgiving. It will always bring you two back together no matter what. Knowing that you can talk to each other friend to friend is what keeps your relationship loving.

Aquarius Venus/Pisces Sun:

Your partner feels just as out of place as you do. You're both strangers in a strange land. It's your shared quirkiness—and refusal to apologize for it— that creates your special bond. But at some point you have to allow the outside world in. You can't live forever in your own private Idaho. Not when you have so much to give.

Aquarius Venus/Aries Sun:

You attract people who raise the bar or move the goalposts. You love it because you relish a good challenge. However, you can't help wondering if there really is a point to this or if they are just being evasive. You may never learn the answer—which is all part of the appeal, of course.

VENUS IN PISCES

You're the port in the storm for every lost soul, emotional wreck, or broken heart. They know that you understand them—and on a very deep and profound level. Obviously, they don't come into your life looking like something the cat dragged in. They may even be impeccably dressed, well-established, and financially successful. But behind closed doors they're an entirely different story—one full of complicated plot twists and strange interludes. Venus is exalted in Pisces, which means that she's at her most bewitching and seductive in this sign. And that goes both ways. The people drawn into your orbit may feel like you're their last chance at love, and you may feel like you're the only one who can save them. It's very romantic, but it can also be treacherous, like when you keep taking back—or returning to—someone who's no good. The best partner is someone who's there for you too. Let's face it: you don't attract these charity cases into your life unless you've also been there, done that too. It's nice to be with someone who gets it.

Pisces Venus/Capricorn Sun:

Nobody would ever suspect you had a soft side if it weren't for the company you keep. Your partner often expresses the sensitivity, compassion, and sentimentality you keep hidden. And it's OK because your partner's down with that. It's like your own special secret.

Pisces Venus/Aquarius Sun:

You attract people who defy logic. There's something about them that's unfathomable and enigmatic. Maybe it's their presence, worldview, or uncanny ability to be in the right place at the right time. In any case, they're wonderful reminders that love never loses its mystery no matter how familiar it becomes.

Pisces Venus/Pisces Sun:

"Don't speak" is your plaintive protest. Words only ruin the moment, and anything worth sharing is best expressed in the sacred silence that only the soul can understand. Hopefully, you and your romantic interest are on the same page with this, otherwise you're in danger of assuming a lot about a little.

Pisces Venus/Aries Sun:

You have a hard time keeping partners. Something always comes up to spirit them away—like a lover from the past, unforeseen complications, or bad timing. This doesn't mean your love life is star-crossed. You just have to work harder than most. Love doesn't come easy, but when it does, it will prove worth the struggle.

Pisces Venus/Taurus Sun:

Yours is an amorous, glamorous Venus. You're never alone for long, and if you are then there are plenty of other fish in the sea ready to jump into your boat. The downside is that people think you're flirting with them even when you're not. Watch it or you could get into a lot of trouble.

MARS

Mars is the planet of "what I want." If it sees something it wants, then it will go after it—no *ifs*, *and*s, or *but*s. Mars doesn't share, and Mars doesn't care if your gain results in somebody else's loss. Named after the Roman god of war, Mars expects to fight for it—and win. It's the most ruthless planet in your horoscope, which is good, because you need a planet like this to survive. If you don't come first, then everyone else does, and they're not going to look after you the way your Mars will.

Mars rules our desires, but it also stokes our ambitions. The big word with Mars is *push*. Mars pushes us to be the best that we can be. But that isn't going to happen by doing what comes easily, giving up when the going gets tough, or lounging around on the plump cushions of our comfort zones. Mars is by nature dissatisfied. Yes, it seeks instant gratification and immediate results—everything with Mars is fast and urgent—but the gratification isn't very fulfilling and the results are often short-lived. Where's the thrill in always getting what you want right when you want it? How do you improve, overcome, or master? But if something you want is kept out of reach, resists your best efforts to achieve it, or better yet, fights back—then that's exciting!

Passion is the fuel that drives Mars: a heady mix of love and fury, that drive to do whatever it takes creates a personal investment that can't be bought and a willpower that can never be watered down. We often think of passion as being too much. People who are passionate are too loud, too heated, too fixated on a single outcome. *Passion* is the word that employers use to praise you for your scary enthusiasm while they slowly inch their way toward the door and a quick escape. But *passion* actually means "suffering." It was originally coined in the sixteenth century to describe the sufferings of Christ that began with the night of the Last Supper and ended with his death on the cross. Betrayal. Despair. Torture. Humiliation. There's nothing meek about this kind of suffering. And for anyone with a strong Mars, these are also the very things that fuel the fire rather than extinguish it. Mars roars to life the more it is beaten down. It's the anger that rouses you from the heartbreak, the gumption that pulls you up by your bootstraps, the willpower that gets you through the chemo, and the revenge that really does want an eye for an eye and a tooth for a tooth. It isn't always pretty and it doesn't always win, but Mars won't go down without a fight. As the German philosopher Friedrich Nietzsche once said, "That which does not kill us, makes us stronger."

Make no mistake about it. Mars is a malefic planet. Mars rules over discord, and its presence in the world is hard to miss. One could say it's gone viral given our endless wars, the 24/7 news cycle of screaming heads, and dire warnings about the looming climate crisis. Mars will appear prominently in the horoscopes of people who have experienced violence and abuse regardless of whether they're predator or prey. It will also appear prominently in the horoscopes of athletes, dancers, and soldiers—people whose bodies take a lot of punishment in order to do what they do.

But malefic planets have their bright sides, just like the benefic ones (Venus and Jupiter) have their dark ones. Malefic planets are in the horoscope to provide you with the means necessary to get through the tough times. You may like a fight in your video games or boxing matches but not when it's happening to you personally. Yet Mars is the planet that teaches us how to fight and that not all fights are the same.

Not all fights are pointless barroom brawls. You can fight the good fight—like when you stand up for what's right at a time when everyone else has disappeared down their rabbit holes. There's the creative struggle to get things perfect. Competition pushes you to perform better than you would on your own, and collaborations—although fiery—leave little doubt that both parties are fighting for what they think is best. Mars shows up in all of these heated exchanges. The secret to any relationship's success is in knowing how to fight. Not fighting to win, but fighting for the relationship in times of crisis, getting a partner to face something you know they don't want to face, or showing restraint when all you want to do is make someone hurt in the way that they hurt you. Mars gives strength in the face of adversity. It's the guts that gets us to stand tall in the face of an outrageous fortune hell-bent on laying us low.

Mars isn't always in your corner. That's because the planet travels outside the Earth's orbit around the Sun, which means that it can appear anywhere in your astrological chart. It might be in the same sign as yours or a sign that's completely opposite.

Mars in the same sign as your Sun bolsters **confidence**. It makes you aggressive and affirmative.

Mars in the sign before or after your Sun sign is an **irritant**. This Mars just doesn't sit well with you no matter how hard you try to make it right.

Mars in the sign two signs before or after your Sun sign is an **ally**. This Mars is always there to lend a helping hand.

Mars in the sign three signs before or after your Sun sign is an **adversary**. Sometimes competitive, sometimes combative, this Mars asks whether you're up to the task at hand.

Mars in the sign four signs before or after your Sun sign is a **supporter**. You can always rely on this Mars for backup and follow-through.

Mars in the sign five signs before or after your Sun sign is **anyone's guess**. It hurts as much as it helps, and it's hard to tell if it makes things better or worse.

Mars in the sign six signs away from your Sun sign is a **total disconnect**. You don't identify with this Mars in any way, so that what happens is it gets projected onto others—particularly in relationships or with close business associates. You may feel like it's the other person who always gets their way, wins, or has the final say.

What if you have Mars retrograde? Mars retrogrades choose flight over fight. That's why you go out of your way to avoid conflict, but it's not something that sits easily with you. Haunted by the feeling that you missed your chance to have it out—and filled with dread that one day you'll have to—you can wind up becoming a fuming presence of resentment. It's always a good idea to bite the bullet when you're born with Mars retrograde. Your voice may crack and your palms may grow sweaty, but you'll feel much better getting things off your chest.

You can gauge Mars's strength in an astrological chart by determining if it's in domicile, detriment, exaltation, or fall. Mars is at home (domicile) in Aries and Scorpio. In medieval Europe, spring and autumn were the ideal seasons for battle. You didn't want to fight in the summer when the temperature inside that armor could become stiflingly hot, and you didn't want to fight in the winter when mountain passes were snowed in, making the transport of artillery impossible. Mars is out of season (detriment) in Taurus and Libra. These are the two Venus-ruled signs, which means that Mars has to be on good behavior when it's in them. Mars isn't known for playing well with others. Mars is exalted in Capricorn, a sign famous for austerity and discipline, and Mars is in fall in Cancer, a sign famous for its gushing sentimentality. Whether Mars is exalted or in fall doesn't mean it's a good or bad Mars. A "strong" Mars may not care whose toes get stepped on as long as it gets what it wants, while a "weak" Mars may be self-sacrificing and protective of those unable to fend for themselves.

MARS IN ARIES

You're a fighter, not a lover. You don't like it when life gets too cushy. Your Mars feeds on conflict. You love a good argument when voices are raised and tempers flare. It shows that people care. It's why you make provocative statements aimed at getting a rise out of them. But this doesn't necessarily mean you're a troublemaker. It could even make you heroic. Mars is in domicile in Aries, which means you say what nobody else has the courage to say, do what everyone wishes they had done in the moment, and keep on pushing for what's right long after others have given up. Obviously, you're no stranger to pushback. But there's a difference between getting an opponent's attention and kicking the hornet's nest. Do you have a vision of how you want things to work out in the end? Hopefully, you do. If not, then try being less scorched-earth in your policy and find a way for conflicting interests to dovetail. Not only will you succeed in constructing something positive—you may even turn an enemy into a friend. Aries Mars . . .

Fires up: Aries Suns by making them lock horns with the opposition.

Irritates: Taurus and Pisces Suns because it makes these two laid-back signs nervous and edgy.

Allies with: Gemini and Aquarius Suns by instilling self-confidence in two signs that question themselves too much.

Squares off against: Cancer and Capricorn Suns by forcing them to be straightforward and assertive.

Supports: Leo and Sagittarius Suns by encouraging them to take on those impossible challenges.

Is anyone's guess with: Virgo and Scorpio Suns because it won't quit while it's ahead. Sometimes that finishing touch really does bring it all together and sometimes it winds up spoiling everything.

Opposes: Libra Suns. You see other people as bullying, bossy, and intent on getting their way. When Mars is opposite your Sun sign, you don't connect to its energy naturally, which means you will always find yourself in challenging situations where you have to assert yourself until you do. The best way to assert yourself is to use your diplomatic skills. Find ways to turn a confrontation into a conversation. You'll reduce the tension and bring light rather than heat to your interactions.

MARS IN TAURUS

If you could rope off your corner of the world and hang a *No Trespassing* sign, you would. You've been telling people to stay out of your room, keep their hands off your stuff, and stop interfering with your life since you were a teenager. Nobody owns you, but you can own people if you make enough money to pay for it. Money talks and you'll use it to get your way. Now that might seem reasonable. After all, you bought their services, own the space, and put food on the table, so why can't people work faster, pay their rent on time, or show some gratitude? Money may not be the root of all evil, but it's certainly going to be the source of all conflict in your life, and that's because nobody likes being told what to do any more than you do. Mars is in detriment in Taurus, a Venus-ruled sign, because it believes that the more you acquire, the more what you say goes. But money can't buy you love, and the sooner you learn that, the better. Taurus Mars . . .

Fires up: Taurus Suns by making them protect their interests.

Irritates: Aries and Gemini Suns because it makes them bullheaded. It doesn't always recognize how forcing someone into a corner gives them no choice but to lash out.

Allies with: Cancer and Pisces Suns by giving these two fluid signs a stick-to-it-iveness.

Squares off against: Leo and Aquarius Suns by involving them in endless turf wars at work and pitched battles over parking spaces.

Supports: Virgo and Capricorn Suns by urging them to take as much ground as they can when they can.

Is anyone's guess with: Libra and Sagittarius Suns because it makes them uncertain. Asking for reassurance once or twice is fine, but asking again and again becomes tedious and counterproductive.

Opposes: Scorpio Suns. You see other people as bullish, grabby, and horning in on your turf. When Mars is opposite your Sun sign, you don't connect to its energy naturally, which means you will always find yourself in challenging situations where you have to assert yourself until you do. The best way to assert yourself is to stake your claim. This keeps people from poaching your ideas or walking off with your love interest.

MARS IN GEMINI

The only reason you want something is because somebody else wanted it first. It's been going on since childhood. Maybe it began with beating your brother out for that spot on the team, competing with your sister for the same boyfriend, or accompanying a friend to an audition only to land the role yourself. You just have this knack for emerging with other people's prizes in hand. And the funny thing is—winning it is almost always a disappointment. If anything, you'd hand it back if you could, but by that time the damage has been done. Taking the things that other people want isn't really a good way to go through life even if you are better at the job or more deserving of the relationship. However, if you were to set your sights on taking the things that the people you don't like want—such as outsmarting a competitor, foiling a rival, or running circles around an opponent—then you'd be a lot happier. This is bound to invite retaliation, and that's the point. It's what keeps the game going. Gemini Mars . . .

Fires up: Gemini Suns by making them best their rivals.

Irritates: Taurus and Cancer Suns because it likes to pick fights.

Allies with: Aries and Leo Suns by outtalking instead of outmuscling.

Squares off against: Virgo and Pisces Suns by forcing them to engage rather than duck out the back door.

Supports: Libra and Aquarius Suns by winning people over to its side.

Is anyone's guess with: Scorpio and Capricorn Suns because it won't leave well enough alone. Sometimes this pushes them to ask questions that need to be asked, and sometimes this exacerbates things.

Opposes: Sagittarius Suns. You see other people as duplicitous, sneaky, and looking to pull a fast one. When Mars is opposite your Sun sign, you don't connect to its energy naturally, which means you will always find yourself in challenging situations where you have to assert yourself until you do. The best way to assert yourself is to call them out on it. No one's saying you have to sound the alarm, but letting them know that you know what they're up to gets them to stop in their tracks and even wins their respect.

MARS IN CANCER

The first words out of your mouth are almost always "I can't." You're so convinced that you're not good enough, that you'll be rejected, or that you haven't a snowball's chance in hell that you'd rather not try. Picking up your things and leaving the scene is easier than facing disappointment. Mars is in fall in Cancer because the Crab is famous for beating a hasty retreat. Self-preservation trumps risk every time. But just because you left doesn't mean you won't be back. You're not very successful at talking yourself out of things you truly want. In fact, the more you try to talk yourself out of something, the more you'll wind up going for it—which explains why after piling all the cheaper items on the counter, you'll inevitably purchase the most expensive one. Bass-ackward, but it works. Walking away from challenges has taught you a lot about how to approach them. Preparation is one. The element of surprise is another. You only act when you're ready, and when you do it's with the expectation of success. Cancer Mars . . .

Fires up: Cancer Suns by making them hold on to what they've got.

Irritates: Gemini and Leo Suns by making them ornery and cranky.

Allies with: Taurus and Virgo Suns because it really knows how to drive a hard bargain.

Squares off against: Aries and Libra Suns by forcing them to address what lies beneath the surface.

Supports: Scorpio and Pisces Suns by making them express their needs unapologetically.

Is anyone's guess with: Sagittarius and Aquarius Suns because it instinctively avoids confrontation. Sometimes this buys precious time and sometimes it just draws things out unnecessarily.

Opposes: Capricorn Suns. You see other people as defeatist crybabies who play the victim card the first chance they get. When Mars is opposite your Sun sign, you don't connect to its energy naturally, which means you will always find yourself in challenging situations where you have to assert yourself until you do. The best way to assert yourself is to be bold but sensitive. You can't let others guilt-trip you any more than you can tell them to butch it up. Acknowledging that they're having a tough time and taking their needs into consideration will do a lot to win their trust and earn their cooperation.

MARS IN LEO

What you want has your name on it. It's so obvious that you expect people to hand it over to you without a fight. And often they do. They'll offer up the last slice of cake, let you cut ahead in line, or pass you a piece of clothing saying it looks better on you anyway. You don't really have to push, shove, or elbow. Your regal bearing says it all. Mars in the sign of kings means you're not shy about exercising your divine right, but you can create unnecessary trouble for yourself if you don't build support. Generously reward those who supported you, and while you're at it, toss a few scraps to your rivals as well. It's the law of the jungle: nobody's going to mess with you on a full stomach—plus it keeps the hyenas at bay. Leo Mars . . .

Fires up: Leo Suns by making them extraordinary.

Irritates: Cancer and Virgo Suns because it will pick up its things and leave in a huff if it doesn't get its way.

Allies with: Gemini and Libra Suns by increasing their personal investment.

Squares off against: Taurus and Scorpio Suns by making them prideful at the most inopportune times.

Supports: Aries and Sagittarius Suns by making them truly exceptional.

Is anyone's guess with: Capricorn and Pisces Suns because it pushes them to be more self-promoting. Sometimes this showcases talents never seen before and sometimes it comes across as desperate for attention.

Opposes: Aquarius Suns. You see other people as self-absorbed, proud, and entitled. When Mars is opposite your Sun sign, you don't connect to its energy naturally, which means you will always find yourself in challenging situations where you have to assert yourself until you do. The best way to assert yourself is to puff up your chest. *Ego* is such a loaded word, which is why you keep yours under lock and key. There's nothing wrong with showing off what you can do. After all, if you don't blow your own horn, who will?

MARS IN VIRGO

You follow orders and execute them to the best of your ability. That's saying a lot, since your personal standards exceed most people's expectations. What you deliver in the end is such an improvement that those who made the original request may not even recognize it. Your perfectionism is impressive. It's also unsettling. It reminds the powers that be that you have a better understanding of what needs to be done than they do. They're lucky your Mars is so obedient. Virgo is the sign of service, which means you can only perform if someone else gives the orders. Left to your own devices, you'd wander around in a swirl of competing priorities—unable to choose one over the other. You need a strict routine to stay on point. Mars is at its most soldierly in Virgo. It's frustrating working for people who don't always know what they want, but it's also a godsend. You're so ahead of the game that you can make changes to the overall plan without anyone catching on. Virgo Mars . . .

Fires up: Virgo Suns by making them ready, willing, and able.

Irritates: Leo and Libra Suns because it can't say no to a request or order.

Allies with: Cancer and Scorpio Suns with its matter-of-fact approach.

Squares off against: Gemini and Sagittarius Suns because it's not afraid to go back to square one to get things right.

Supports: Taurus and Capricorn Suns by making them finish what they started.

Is anyone's guess with: Aries and Aquarius Suns because it's committed to doing the right thing. Sometimes this corrects a terrible wrong, and sometimes it's the right thing but at the wrong time.

Opposes: Pisces Suns. You see other people as nitpicky, nagging, and out to spoil your fun. When Mars is opposite your Sun sign, you don't connect to its energy naturally, which means you will always find yourself in challenging situations where you have to assert yourself until you do. The best way to assert yourself is to thank them for their input. People like to be heard, and when you acknowledge what they said they usually back off. But listening doesn't mean that you agree. It's up to you to decide if their criticisms are worthwhile, and that's best done alone and in private.

MARS IN LIBRA

The only way to get what you want is to combine forces. And it doesn't help that the person whose assistance you need most is often a flake, someone you detest or alienated in the past. This doesn't sit well with a planet famous for going it alone and spitting in its opponent's eye. Mars is in detriment in Libra. It's as comfortable in this sign as a tomboy in a Disney princess dress. Nevertheless, you have to find a way to make it work. What you feel may be spite at first sight, but ask yourself: How much of this has to do with the other party or the fact that you're stuck in a situation where you're always beholden to someone else? This pattern is never going to change, so it would be a good idea to figure out how to start building bridges and playing nicely with others. And who knows? You may wind up developing a begrudging respect after all and grow to see this person in a more favorable light. Libra Mars . . .

Fires up: Libra Suns by making them keep the peace.

Irritates: Virgo and Scorpio Suns by redrawing those lines in the sand.

Allies with: Leo and Sagittarius Suns by making them coordinate efforts instead of flying solo.

Squares off against: Cancer and Capricorn Suns when it asks them to throw a battle to win the war.

Supports: Gemini and Aquarius Suns by insisting that cool heads prevail in heated situations.

Is anyone's guess with: Taurus and Pisces Suns because it will please and appease. Sometimes this allows these two signs to work their magic of persuasion, and sometimes it reinforces their don't-rock-the-boat tendencies to a disastrous effect.

Opposes: Aries Suns. You see other people as indirect, pussyfooting, and passive-aggressive. When Mars is opposite your Sun sign, you don't connect to its energy naturally, which means you will always find yourself in challenging situations where you have to assert yourself until you do. The best way to assert yourself in the face of others' passive-aggressiveness is by exercising some inertness of your own. Play clueless, be equally noncommittal, and eventually they'll have to come forward with what they want out of sheer frustration.

MARS IN SCORPIO

You never blink first. The other side does. Whether it's pushing the limit, raising the stakes, or refusing to back down, you have an extraordinary ability to keep your cool under pressure. Most people go out of their way to avoid tense standoffs. You relish them. But you're not into power grabs or throwing your weight around. Everything you do is well thought out, deliberate, and under the radar. When you set out to win, it's a win that's meant to last. It needs to be clear, indisputable, and final. Mars in Scorpio is a fait accompli Mars. By the time others hear about what you've done, they have no choice but to accept it—or leave. Yet nobody can trip you up like you can trip yourself. Mars is in domicile in Scorpio, which means you don't know when to stop. You pursue what you want relentlessly, and this can lead you to spoil your victory by going too far. In those moments when you feel like you should push for more, it's always a good idea to quit while you're ahead. Scorpio Mars . . .

Fires up: Scorpio Suns by making them strike while the iron's hot.

Irritates: Libra and Sagittarius Suns by always focusing on the negative.

Allies with: Virgo and Capricorn Suns by getting them to skip the formalities and cut to the chase.

Squares off against: Leo and Aquarius Suns because it likes to fight dirty.

Supports: Cancer and Pisces Suns by making people think twice about playing with their hearts.

Is anyone's guess with: Aries and Gemini Suns because it will tell it like it is. Sometimes people appreciate the honesty, and sometimes they'd be grateful if you'd just give it a rest.

Opposes: Taurus Suns. You see other people as psychic minefields— oversensitive, unforgiving, and riddled with trip wires. When Mars is opposite your Sun sign, you don't connect to its energy naturally, which means you will always find yourself in challenging situations where you have to assert yourself until you do. The best way to assert yourself is to take responsibility for your part in what went wrong. This lowers the defenses on both sides. Copping to your bad gets the other person to cop to theirs.

MARS IN SAGITTARIUS

You always take sides. There's no such thing as Switzerland. People are either on board or not, and if not, then they need to be sent packing ASAP. You have zero tolerance for wafflers, appeasers, or those looking to hedge their bets. You firmly believe that right will triumph over wrong and that the two should duke it out in the arena. Any cause worth fighting for has to prove itself, and if it's just, then it will prevail. But what if your side loses? That's when you cry foul, call for a rematch, and start pouring gasoline on the fire with taunts, insults, and cutting statements. You're an unapologetic zealot. Mars in Sagittarius can be divisive, but there's good sportsmanship too. You know the other side is fighting just as vigorously as you are, which is why—win or lose—you make a point of shaking hands afterward to show that there are no hard feelings. Hopefully, the other side will shake back. Sagittarius Mars . . .

Fires up: Sagittarius Suns by getting them to paint on the largest possible canvas.

Irritates: Scorpio and Capricorn Suns when it telegraphs what it's going to do ahead of time.

Allies with: Libra and Aquarius Suns by championing their ideals.

Squares off against: Virgo and Pisces Suns when it refuses to acquiesce.

Supports: Aries and Leo Suns by urging them to go high when others go low.

Is anyone's guess with: Taurus and Cancer Suns because it acts so recklessly. Both signs tend to ride the brakes, while Sagittarius pushes the pedal to the metal. Sometimes gunning it is good, and sometimes you just hit a brick wall.

Opposes: Gemini Suns. You see other people as sanctimonious, boastful, and quick to point out the fault in others while ignoring their own. When Mars is opposite your Sun sign, you don't connect to its energy naturally, which means you will always find yourself in challenging situations where you have to assert yourself until you do. The best way to assert yourself is to poke fun. Lightly. It's not your job to call out hypocrisy, but pointing out the inconsistencies and getting people to laugh at themselves does a lot to introduce self-awareness.

MARS IN CAPRICORN

You will climb every mountain and summit every peak, but it's not a dream you're chasing—it's your next crowning achievement. Mars is exalted in Capricorn because it combines discipline with drive. You don't just reach out and grab anything in sight. You put in the time and effort to master the things that lie *beyond* reach. And you'll do this over and over. Mars in Capricorn means nothing comes easy, and you have the rejection letters, failures, and humiliating defeats to prove it. Most people wouldn't have taken the kind of punishment or made the heavy sacrifices you made to get you to where you are today, yet you'd risk it all again in a heartbeat if it meant climbing even higher. The downside is you're scary competitive. Shooting down people's opinions because they disagree with yours or reacting to innovation as an attempt to undermine your authority isn't good. Support new voices and nurture growing talent. They won't take away from what you've done. They'll memorialize it. Capricorn Mars . . .

Fires up: Capricorn Suns by pushing them to push themselves.

Irritates: Sagittarius and Aquarius Suns because it will fixate on a problem until it's solved. It doesn't believe in leaving it for now and revisiting it later.

Allies with: Scorpio and Pisces Suns by giving them true grit.

Squares off against: Aries and Libra Suns by raising the bar as soon as it's in reach.

Supports: Taurus and Virgo Suns by toughing it out when the going gets tough.

Is anyone's guess with: Gemini and Leo Suns because it won't take the easy way out. Sometimes this is laudable, and sometimes it makes life unnecessarily difficult.

Opposes: Cancer Suns. You see other people as stern, judgmental, and impossible to please. When Mars is opposite your Sun sign, you don't connect to its energy naturally, which means you will always find yourself in challenging situations where you have to assert yourself until you do. The best way to assert yourself is to put yourself out there. Fear of rejection often leads you to quit the game before you even play it. Try giving a competition, contest, or audition your best shot. You may do better than you think.

MARS IN AQUARIUS

You like to have a lot of things going on at once. It's hard to think straight if you don't. People say you've got too many irons in the fire, but you have your eye on every single one of them. You pride yourself on showing up in the nick of time to salvage a situation and disappearing the moment the job is done. An Aquarius Mars loves to be in demand, to race from spinning plate to spinning plate. Hopefully, you can keep up. If not, this Mars can run you ragged. You're a team player and enjoy being part of a group; however, you have a deep mistrust of authority and question whether the people in charge are living up to their obligations. This is why you constantly challenge them and press for change. Sometimes you're accused of being a rabble-rouser, but the truth is you often wind up being on the right side of history—especially when those farfetched ideas that people scoff at today wind up becoming mainstays that everyone takes for granted tomorrow. You're that foresighted. Aquarius Mars . . .

Fires up: Aquarius Suns by pushing the envelope.

Irritates: Capricorn and Pisces Suns because it assumes responsibility—even if it doesn't have to.

Allies with: Sagittarius and Aries Suns by making them coolly objective.

Squares off against: Taurus and Scorpio Suns because it will always put others' interests before its own.

Supports: Gemini and Libra Suns by making them stick to the game plan.

Is anyone's guess with: Cancer and Virgo Suns because it's always on call. Sometimes this is good because both signs want to be there, and sometimes it's not because they don't get any downtime.

Opposes: Leo Suns. You see other people as impatient, radical, and looking to upset the apple cart. When Mars is opposite your Sun sign, you don't connect to its energy naturally, which means you will always find yourself in challenging situations where you have to assert yourself until you do. The best way to assert yourself is to keep an open mind. Differences of opinion shouldn't shut down the conversation—they should enrich it. If you truly possess the courage of your convictions, then you should have no problem listening to someone else's.

MARS IN PISCES

Maybe you wanted something else. That may explain the sinking feeling you experience after landing the job, upgrading your relationship status, or seeing a dream come true. So what's your problem? Is it fear of success? Cold feet? You've asked yourself this hundreds of times and discussed it with every befuddled boss and brokenhearted lover. Sometimes it's gotten so bad that you won't even pursue your desires for fear of letting others down. Mars in Pisces yearns for the things it cannot have. Constant craving keeps it active and engaged. But the moment it gets what it wants, it's like waking from a dream. You can't remember what you saw in the first place and want to move on. Now you may not be the committing type. Going from job to job or relationship to relationship may be what keeps those creative juices flowing. Then again, try sticking around past the disappointment phase. You could discover it's better to have than have not. Pisces Mars . . .

Fires up: Pisces Suns by coming to the emotional rescue.

Irritates: Aquarius and Aries Suns because it's always going off on a tangent.

Allies with: Taurus and Capricorn Suns by factoring in other people's concerns.

Squares off against: Gemini and Sagittarius Suns by being confused and confusing.

Supports: Cancer and Scorpio Suns by finding a way for everyone to benefit.

Is anyone's guess with: Leo and Libra Suns because it's always searching. Discovery is good, but sometimes too much searching and not enough finding can leave you feeling lost at sea.

Opposes: Virgo Suns. You see other people as unreliable, spacey, and looking to you for help. When Mars is opposite your Sun sign, you don't connect to its energy naturally, which means you will always find yourself in challenging situations where you have to assert yourself until you do. The best way to assert yourself is to stay on your side of the fence. Other people's business is their business, and it's up to them to sort things out. If they want advice? Great. If they want a helping hand? Sit on it. You've cleaned up too many messes to be suckered into doing it again.

JUPITER

4

Do you believe in a higher power that looks out after us, or is it up to each person to make the world a better place? When good things happen to you in life, does that mean you're good or just lucky? And when bad things happen, is that mischance or did you ask for it? Jupiter is the planet of "what I believe" in astrology. If we were made in God's image, then Jupiter represents the God that we imagine. Is He a She or a They? Are you theistic, pantheistic, or atheistic? Is your God loving? Stern? All-knowing? Or is God math? Wherever the divine is enshrined in your life, it will be flanked by the Jupiterian values of good fortune and higher purpose.

In mythology the Sun brought the day, but it was Jupiter that brought blue skies. Now this may seem like hairsplitting until you think of a candle. Light a candle and you have a spot of light in the dark, but put that candle in a hurricane lamp and its light fills the room. And that's the way that Jupiter works. The Sun lights and Jupiter illuminates. Its blue sky masks the heavens during the day so that we can see the world we live in. We can spot what lies underfoot, search long distances, and admire the clouds floating overhead. This is why Jupiter is the planet of your worldview.

We make moral judgments based on Jupiter. Success is our reward for talent and hard work. Love is our reward for being likable. Plenty is our reward for being devout. The more good things happen to you, the more you'll believe that the Universe is a fair and just place. But what if things aren't going well for you? What if—despite your best efforts—good fortune just doesn't smile on you? Well, bad luck can't just be bad luck. It has to be rationalized in some way. Maybe things aren't going well because you kicked a Buddha in the pants in a past life, you have a negative outlook, or you don't try hard enough and are in desperate need of character building. It's extraordinary, the lengths to which we will go to avert our gaze from the unblinking stares of mishap and misery. We make up reasons to explain away the bad because we don't want it to upset our belief in the good and just world that is lit by Jupiter's rays. Better to demonize the less fortunate than to believe that there could be gaps in Jupiter's providence.

One would think that Jupiter's rewards system is pretty straightforward, but it's not. Like Venus, Jupiter is a benefic planet. That means it brings good things into your life for the express purpose of begetting more good things. If Venus brings people together to create more people, then Jupiter brings all those different groups of people together to create a better society. But Jupiter isn't about filling up your coffers. It's about paying it forward. This is why Jupiter is the planet of philanthropy. Its roots lie in the Greek tradition of guest-friendship.

Hospitality (guest-friendship) was a cardinal virtue in the ancient Greek world. The idea was that if a stranger from another land was shipwrecked on your shores, you wouldn't turn him away, enslave him, or serve him up as a human sacrifice to the gods. You would welcome him into your home and feed and clothe him. The stranger, in turn, wouldn't take advantage of your hospitality by stealing your silverware, seducing your wife, or overstaying his welcome. Indeed, he was expected to reciprocate by making himself useful, showing you a better way to do things, or perhaps returning the favor of hospitality one day. This idea of forging ties that go beyond one's borders has always been connected to Jupiter.

Jupiter is often described as the planet of expansion in astrology. Astrologers say he makes things bigger—whether it's your fortunes, your expectations, your ego, or your thighs. But Jupiter doesn't expand just to expend, Jupiter expands in order to incorporate—like an empire. Empires have a nasty reputation nowadays because of their bloody history of military conquest and colonization, but they weren't all bad. Instead of razing the societies they conquered, they took them under their wing and incorporated them into a wider network of kingdoms and territories. Trade routes allowed for the intermixing of cultures, exposure to foreign ways of life, and the adoption of exotic beliefs that produced new religions, new ways of learning, and new ways of being. In many ways, your Jupiter encourages you to do the same thing. By getting you to embrace the world rather than judge it, Jupiter expands your horizons, diversifies your community, and broadens your outlook so that you become a more humane human being.

Jupiter isn't always by your side. That's because the planet travels outside the Earth's orbit around the Sun, which means that it can appear anywhere in your astrological chart. It might be in the same sign as yours or a sign that's completely opposite.

Jupiter in the same sign as your Sun **enriches**. Gifts and blessings are showered on you as long as you are true to yourself.

Jupiter in the sign before or after your Sun sign **misses the boat**. This is the area of life where you have good fortune but may be slow to recognize it.

Jupiter in the sign two signs before or after your Sun sign **benefits**. This Jupiter wants to see you succeed and has a lot of ideas about how to make that happen.

Jupiter in the sign three signs before or after your Sun sign is your **conscience**. Sometimes goading, sometimes shaming, this Jupiter struggles to make you do the right thing.

Jupiter in the sign four signs before or after your Sun sign **blesses**. This Jupiter provides the opportunities you need to go further than you would on your own.

Jupiter in the sign five signs before or after your Sun sign is **anyone's**

guess. Good fortune hurts as much as it helps and it's hard to tell if it makes things better or worse.

Jupiter in the sign six signs away from your Sun sign is a **total disconnect**. You don't identify with this Jupiter in any way, so that what happens is it gets projected onto others—particularly in relationships or with close business associates. You may feel like it's the other person who's lucky, gets all the breaks, or steals your thunder.

What if you have Jupiter retrograde? Jupiter retrogrades are famous for pulling the plug right when you're ready to make that big leap. It's not unlike the *Millennium Falcon* busting a gasket when trying to make its escape into light speed. You may not have Imperial fighters on your tail, but reversals in fortune are nothing new and often leave you scrambling for last-minute solutions to salvage the situation. You've gotten quite good at pulling rabbits out of a hat. Fortune is fickle, but you're not ready to forswear it. It has a funny way of coming back online in times when it's needed most.

You can gauge Jupiter's strength in an astrological chart by determining if it's in domicile, detriment, exaltation, or fall. Jupiter is at home (domicile) in Sagittarius and Pisces. These are the signs associated with Advent and Lent in the Christian liturgical calendar. The first looks forward to Christ's birth (Christmas), while the second looks forward to Christ's resurrection (Easter). Jupiter rules the times of year when we move closer to God in our hearts. Jupiter is out of season (detriment) in Gemini and Virgo. These are the two Mercury-ruled signs—fact-based and intellectual. Jupiter doesn't do well in signs that poke holes in its spiritual faith. Jupiter is exalted in Cancer—a sign famous for its well-stocked shelves and hospitality—and Jupiter is in fall in Capricorn—a sign famous for its tight grip on the purse strings. Whether Jupiter is exalted or in fall doesn't make it a good or bad Jupiter. A "strong" Jupiter may be generous to a fault (thereby imperiling its fortunes), while a "weak" Jupiter is sure to have savings tucked away for a rainy day.

JUPITER IN ARIES

You preach the gospel of self-reliance. You don't depend on others and therefore don't owe anyone anything. You are completely self-made and answer only to yourself. When you follow your own path, then you discover what you are truly capable of. Your wins are your wins; your failures are your failures. Nobody can buy you. Nobody can silence you. You have a hero's valor, which means you're no stranger to fighting the good fight. If you believe in a cause, then you are all in. But you don't sign petitions or quietly give money to a GoFundMe account. You put yourself on the line. You believe in raising people's consciousnesses, and sometimes the only way to do that is to prick their conscience—like when athletes go down on one knee to protest the playing of America's national anthem. What looks like disrespect is actually an expression of deep respect for forgotten battles and liberties that are taken for granted. You will always strive to do your personal best, but personal best isn't just about peak performance. It means doing your moral best as well. Aries Jupiter . . .

Enriches: Aries Suns by getting them to practice what they preach.

Misses the boat with: Taurus and Pisces Suns by pushing them to take leaps of faith before they're ready. The result can be a chilly case of cold feet.

Benefits: Gemini and Aquarius Suns by rallying the troops.

Squares off against: Cancer and Capricorn Suns by taking unnecessary risks.

Blesses: Leo and Sagittarius Suns with a spirit of adventure.

Is anyone's guess with: Virgo and Scorpio Suns because it brings surprise breakthroughs. Sometimes this results in an overnight success and sometimes it's just a one-hit wonder.

Opposes: Libra Suns. You see others as always getting what they want. When Jupiter is opposite your Sun sign, you don't connect to its energy naturally, which means you will always find yourself at a disadvantage until you do. The best way to tap into your fortune is to hang out with people who aren't afraid to take what's theirs. Opportunities are meant to be seized, not hemmed and hawed over. Fortune favors the bold.

JUPITER IN TAURUS

Prosperity likes you. But you don't see it as playing favorites. You see it as a reward for all the hard work you put in. You know that life isn't fair. You could have been one of those seeds from the parable that fell by the wayside where the birds ate it, on rocky ground with no soil, or lost in the weeds. This makes you even more grateful that your life took root on fertile ground and you've been flowering ever since. Now this isn't to say that you're exempt from life's ups and downs. You aren't. You've experienced numerous setbacks and debacles, but through it all you've always maintained a deep and abiding faith that the Universe will provide. You don't see the Universe as doling out handouts; you see the Universe as a benefactor who invests in your interests and to whom you have to answer. Everybody gets a patch of land to work. And it's up to each one of us to make the most of our resources, talents, and opportunities. Fortune is what you make of it. Taurus Jupiter . . .

Enriches: Taurus Suns by making them prolific.

Misses the boat with: Aries and Gemini Suns because it wants something in return. Fixating on results before investing the time and money is like putting the cart before the horse.

Benefits: Cancer and Pisces Suns by making them produce actual things.

Squares off against: Leo and Aquarius Suns by making money an object.

Blesses: Virgo and Capricorn Suns with funding.

Is anyone's guess with: Libra and Sagittarius Suns with its "what's in it for me" attitude. Sometimes good because these two signs can be too generous; sometimes bad because putting self-interest ahead of everyone else is a real buzzkill.

Opposes: Scorpio Suns. Other people possess the golden touch. They make making money look so easy. When Jupiter is opposite your Sun sign, you don't connect to its energy naturally, which means that you will always find yourself at a disadvantage until you do. The best way to tap into your fortune is to stop begrudging people their successes. Jealousy is a weed, not a flower. Invest energy in the things that are working in your life—even if they're just seedlings—and you'll see them blossom and grow.

JUPITER IN GEMINI

For every answer there's a question. You just can't help it. You don't take anything on faith and have a mistrust of platitudes and profound-sounding sayings aimed at shutting down intellectual conversation. People often think you're being flippant or argumentative, but you're not. You're genuinely interested in why they believe in the things that they do. What do they get that you don't? Jupiter is in detriment in Gemini. It's as comfortable in this sign as a squirmy kid in a church pew. When it comes to your spiritual questing, you don't like being told to be quiet and sit still. You'd love nothing more than to engage your teacher, guru, or yoga instructor in electrifying debates as to their particular word choices, their primary source materials, and the ethno-anthropological history of the crow pose. It's immensely fascinating to you but won't win you friends in yoga class. Questions are great, but ask yourself: Are you really interested in the answer? Or is it your cue to just come up with another question aimed at keeping one foot outside the spiritual experience you seek? Gemini Jupiter . . .

Enriches: Gemini Suns by expanding their social network.

Misses the boat with: Taurus and Cancer Suns because it doesn't stick to the point.

Benefits: Aries and Leo Suns by teaming up with like-minded people.

Squares off against: Virgo and Pisces Suns by losing the forest for the trees.

Blesses: Libra and Aquarius Suns with likes, clicks, and followers.

Is anyone's guess with: Scorpio and Capricorn Suns because it's always chasing the next golden apple. That's good because it gets these two staid signs to pursue things they normally wouldn't, but it's self-defeating if the only thing they wind up with is an armload of rotten fruit.

Opposes: Sagittarius Suns. You see other people getting away with murder. The rules that apply to everyone else don't apply to them. When Jupiter is opposite your Sun sign, you don't connect to its energy naturally, which means that you will always find yourself at a disadvantage until you do. The best way to tap into your fortune is to ask yourself what these people know that you don't. What looks like cheating may actually be a talent for working the system. You could benefit by taking a page from their playbook.

JUPITER IN CANCER

You are blessed with abundance. Even if it doesn't look like a lot to others, it's more than enough for you. It's like that Roman myth where in a town of closed doors, it's the elderly couple with the least to offer who open their home to Jupiter disguised as a beggar. They haven't much fruit and they haven't much wine, but somehow the bowl never empties and the cups refill themselves. Eventually, the couple realizes that they are in the presence of a god. You may have noticed that a similar thing happens to you in your life when money for an unexpected emergency materializes out of nowhere or someone you barely know comes through in your hour of need. That's because Jupiter is exalted in Cancer. It's because you won't think twice about taking someone in and offering them a place at your table that the good you do will always circle back and sustain you. Jupiter, the planet of sanctuaries, smiles on those who provide a safe space— whether it's a shoulder to lean on or shelter from the storm. Cancer Jupiter . . .

Enriches: Cancer Suns through real estate and property.

Misses the boat with: Gemini and Leo Suns by making them complacent. This leads them to assume everything's in the bag when it may not be.

Benefits: Taurus and Virgo Suns by making them shrewd investors.

Squares off against: Aries and Libra Suns by making their eyes bigger than their stomachs.

Blesses: Scorpio and Pisces with creativity and artistic inspiration.

Is anyone's guess with: Sagittarius and Aquarius Suns because it keeps them close to home. Sometimes this is good because both signs enjoy raising big broods, but sometimes it's not because it keeps them from spreading their wings.

Opposes: Capricorn Suns. You see others as blessed. When Jupiter is opposite your Sun sign, you don't connect to its energy naturally, which means that you will always find yourself at a disadvantage until you do. The best way to tap into your fortune is to do something for someone else. You can intercede on their behalf, make resources available, or mentor them. Jupiter is the planet of paying it forward. Do a good turn for somebody else and you won't be left out in the cold.

JUPITER IN LEO

For some people it's being in the right place at the right time. For others it's reaping the rewards after years of hard work. But for you? It's you being you. Your fortune smiles when you're true to who you are. And that's a tall order because those qualities that make you stand out are often the same qualities that make you stand apart, which doesn't always rub people the right way. And this is where you must have faith in yourself if you're going to make the leap to where you want to be. You need audacity to dare, pride to jump high, and a glorious sense of entitlement that knows you were meant for great things. And your Leo Jupiter gets it. Like a good patron it will open doors and introduce you to golden opportunities, but it's not enough for you to just *feel* special; you have to *be* special. Develop your talent, flesh out those ideas, and test-drive your message so that you can give the world something exceptional. You want to make a big splash, not a big splat. Leo Jupiter . . .

Enriches: Leo Suns through sports, arts, and entertainment.

Misses the boat with: Cancer and Virgo Suns because it loves the spotlight and these two signs are stage shy.

Benefits: Gemini and Libra Suns with its good humor and bonhomie.

Squares off against: Taurus and Scorpio Suns by getting imperious.

Blesses: Aries and Sagittarius Suns with a joie de vivre.

Is anyone's guess with: Capricorn and Pisces Suns because it's extravagant. Sometimes good because these two signs can be a little tight-fisted; sometimes bad because once they start bingeing, it's hard to stop.

Opposes: Aquarius Suns. You see others as born lucky. When Jupiter is opposite your Sun sign, you don't connect to its energy naturally, which means that you will always find yourself at a disadvantage until you do. The best way to tap into your good fortune is to say that you deserve it. Saying you can get by on your own or that you don't need a helping hand signals to your Jupiter that you don't want it. Say it enough times and your good fortune will move on to somebody else who appreciates it.

JUPITER IN VIRGO

You understand that people need something to believe in. It's a necessary evil. People need something larger than life to inspire them, to lift their spirits and get them to see, walk, and live again. But for all the show and promises, you can't help fixating on the feet of clay. How did this belief arrive at this position of veneration? What makes it credible? Why should it be followed? Jupiter is in detriment in Virgo. Where others marvel at the wonderous wizard, you're looking for the man behind the curtain. You know that every miracle has an explanation, and it's going to be either mundane or up to no good. It's no fun being the spoiler. You get no joy from poking holes in people's wonderment, but you feel it's your duty. Otherwise they'll wind up buying a false bill of goods. Virgo Jupiters are often inspectors, debunkers, and whistle-blowers. Everyone's grateful that you exposed what you did, but they also miss the magic. Nevertheless, there's still a secret part of you that wishes one day you really will encounter something miraculous that can't be explained. Virgo Jupiter . . .

Enriches: Virgo Suns through its work ethic.

Misses the boat with: Leo and Libra Suns because it doesn't take things on faith.

Benefits: Cancer and Scorpio Suns by being conscientious.

Squares off against: Gemini and Sagittarius Suns by forcing them to do things right the first time.

Blesses: Taurus and Capricorn Suns with the means to an end.

Is anyone's guess with: Aries and Aquarius Suns because it will always come up with a solution in a pinch. Good for getting them out of tight corners; bad if they go from quick fix to quick fix and never think ahead.

Opposes: Pisces Suns. You see other people as opportunistic. When Jupiter is opposite your Sun sign, you don't connect to its energy naturally, which means you will always find yourself at a disadvantage until you do. The best way to tap into your good fortune is to take advantage of what comes your way. An offer, favor, or opening doesn't do you any good collecting dust on the shelf. You need to answer them immediately. Otherwise you'll be left with a string of *woulda, coulda, shoulda*s—and that's no way to live.

JUPITER IN LIBRA

You've always paired well. When it comes to choosing partners you inevitably end up with the smartest person on the project, the most beautiful person in the room, or the wealthiest donor at the fund-raiser. And whether your associations are long or brief, you invariably walk away with something positive to show from the experience. Now this isn't to say that all pairings are ideal. Sometimes you can feel like fugitives from justice handcuffed to each other as you scramble over the rocks and riverbeds in pursuit of the key that will free you. But even in these unlikely alliances there's a higher purpose being served. They get you to put aside your differences and work together. Sometimes these adventures are the very thing that makes you see people in ways you wouldn't have before. They inspire you to revisit your beliefs and drop your prejudices. Many people think that Jupiter in Libra makes you lucky in love, and it does insofar as your partner brings good things. But it's not about finding the perfect mate, it's about finding the right person to open your world. Libra Jupiter . . .

Enriches: Libra Suns by the lives it touches.

Misses the boat with: Virgo and Scorpio Suns when it insists on always doing things by the book.

Benefits: Leo and Sagittarius Suns by getting them to reach across the aisle.

Squares off against: Cancer and Capricorn Suns by being too impartial.

Blesses: Gemini and Aquarius Suns with good taste.

Is anyone's guess with: Taurus and Pisces Suns because it loves the finer things in life. Sometimes this is good because it gives these two signs something to aspire to, sometimes it's bad—like when they go into credit card debt because of it.

Opposes: Aries Suns. You see other people as having it easy. When Jupiter is opposite your Sun sign, you don't connect to its energy naturally, which means you will always find yourself at a disadvantage until you do. The best way to tap into your good fortune is to enjoy it. Treating life like a never-ending obstacle course gets old if you don't celebrate your victories. Rewarding yourself with something nice won't spoil you. It takes the chip off your shoulder and may even make you a more agreeable person to live with.

JUPITER IN SCORPIO

Life isn't always kind, but your fortune is. It's what keeps you going when the outlook appears grim. You learned a long time ago that your good fortune isn't the kind that arrives in the nick of time; it's the kind that gets you through. You don't really discuss your spiritual life. It's private. And it's your silence—combined with everything you've endured—that creates the aura of being profoundly religious. It's why people come to you in their time of need. They feel like you get it. And you do. You can speak to what they're going through and provide guidance by asking the right questions, but in truth, you and faith parted company a long time ago. Ironically, this hasn't made you cynical; it's made you deeper. You don't attach words or expectations to what you believe. You just let that part of yourself be. It's how you can sit in a pew and listen to sermons that don't really speak to you, but enjoy them just the same. It's the dark nights of the soul that have made you who you are today. Scorpio Jupiter . . .

Enriches: Scorpio Suns through inheritances and investments.

Misses the boat with: Libra and Sagittarius Suns because it never really banishes the dark.

Benefits: Virgo and Capricorn Suns by putting them in charge of other people's money.

Squares off against: Leo and Aquarius Suns by staying in its gilded cage.

Blesses: Cancer and Pisces Suns with the strength to get through anything.

Is anyone's guess with: Aries and Gemini Suns because their gains stem from others' losses. Sometimes good, like when they inherit the position from someone unfit for the job; sometimes bad when they profit from someone else's misfortune.

Opposes: Taurus Suns. You see other people as coming by their gains illicitly. When Jupiter is opposite your Sun sign, you don't connect to its energy naturally, which means you will always find yourself at a disadvantage until you do. The best way to tap into your good fortune is to do a better job of safeguarding it. You can't blame a credit card company for charging late fees or the IRS for collecting on back taxes. Honor your debts and obligations and you'll never owe anyone a cent.

JUPITER IN SAGITTARIUS

Somebody upstairs likes you. What else can explain all the close calls and eleventh-hour saves? One might think that this kind of bailout would make you foolhardy and profligate—and you probably once were—but over time you've grown deeply reverential. Jupiter is in domicile in Sagittarius. It won't make you lucky, but it does make you fortunate. It's got your back. And this stems from the fact that Jupiter is the largest planet in our solar system. It has the strongest gravitational pull, so asteroids and comets are drawn right to it. Scientists speculate that an asteroid crashes into Jupiter at least once a week, so we have Jupiter to thank for planet Earth still being around. Jupiter in Sagittarius also gives you a "big tent" philosophy. There's no such thing as one way of doing things or a single belief that outranks them all. The fate of the planet—for better or worse—lies with humanity. We've got the whole world in our hands. Sagittarius Jupiter . . .

Enriches: Sagittarius Suns by being welcoming.

Misses the boat with: Scorpio and Capricorn Suns when it gives away more than it takes in.

Benefits: Libra and Aquarius Suns because it won't stop believing.

Squares off against: Virgo and Pisces Suns when it makes promises it can't keep.

Blesses: Aries and Leo with fun and laughter.

Is anyone's guess with: Taurus and Cancer Suns because it's a big spender. Both signs like to live well, but there's a difference between living well and living beyond your means.

Opposes: Gemini Suns. You see other people as getting all the breaks. When Jupiter is opposite your Sun sign, you don't connect to its energy naturally, which means you will always find yourself at a disadvantage until you do. The best way to tap into your good fortune is to not give up. Yes, it's true that other people get all the breaks at all the right times while you have to make the most of what you have—which often isn't much. Nevertheless, this makes you inventive and resourceful so that when it's your turn to profit from Jupiter's largesse, you'll know exactly what to do with it.

JUPITER IN CAPRICORN

Yours is a hard-knock life. Sometimes it feels like circumstances get together somewhere over coffee just to conspire against you. You're used to disappointment and setbacks. They're to be expected. But yours inevitably follow on the footsteps of a big breakthrough or stunning success. No sooner do you find your place in the Sun than the skies cloud over and you discover that your prize comes at a price or becomes a Pandora's box of complications. Jupiter is in fall in Capricorn so fortune is hard to come by, but as with all things Jupiter, there's a higher purpose. Yours is a rags-to-riches life, which means that you have the greatest distance to travel beset by obstacles and tests. You could throw up your hands in defeat and say "Story of my life" whenever you encounter a new roadblock, or you could roll up your sleeves and get back to the work of making something of yourself. It's up to you. Good fortune comes later in life after everyone else's fortunes have run their course. It may be tardy to the party, but better late than never. Capricorn Jupiter . . .

Enriches: Capricorn Suns with the wealth of experience.

Misses the boat with: Sagittarius and Aquarius Suns by siding with conventional wisdom.

Benefits: Scorpio and Pisces Suns with its business acumen.

Squares off against: Aries and Libra Suns by underplaying its accomplishments.

Blesses: Taurus and Virgo Suns with perseverance.

Is anyone's guess with: Gemini and Leo Suns because it insists that anything worth having is worth waiting for. Sometimes good because it teaches these two signs patience, sometimes bad because they can't help feeling like they're waiting on a no-show.

Opposes: Cancer Suns. You see others as holding the purse strings. When Jupiter is opposite your Sun sign, you don't connect to its energy naturally, which means that you will always find yourself at a disadvantage until you do. The best way to tap into your good fortune is to stop being so obliging. People with money use it to bully, so you never want to appear servile. Showing that you don't care may get you fired (in which case you didn't want to work for this person anyway), but in the long run it demonstrates that you're there to do business and not to play games. An I-can't-be-bought attitude wins respect and backing.

JUPITER IN AQUARIUS

Your good fortune is tied to the fortunes of others. The realization of your hopes and dreams and the success of all your ventures depends on your friends in high places. These are the people who can make things happen. Benefactors are drawn to you like fairies to a princess's christening. They want to imbue you with their wealth, wisdom, and grace. They're more than happy to introduce you to their friends and friends of friends. They see something in you—which means that you need to be something worth seeing, and this is where life gets tricky. How can you be true to yourself and to them at the same time? It's the predicament that every politician faces. You have to have a mission statement and a genuine love of people when you have Jupiter in Aquarius. Otherwise it will backfire. Jupiter isn't kind to us-ers and social climbers. Monies are at your disposal to serve the common good. Serve them well and the tide of fortune will lift all boats—serve only yourself and you'll be left high and dry. Aquarius Jupiter . . .

Enriches: Aquarius Suns through cooperative effort.

Misses the boat with: Capricorns and Pisces Suns by being uncompromising. Both signs want the best but also recognize the need for give and take.

Benefits: Aries and Sagittarius by giving them a social conscience.

Squares off against: Taurus and Scorpio Suns when it gets too idealistic.

Blesses: Gemini and Libra with community spirit.

Is anyone's guess with: Cancer and Virgo Suns because if you don't schmooze, you lose. Sometimes good because it gets them out of their shells; sometimes bad because trying to remember all the names and who owes who lunch, a favor, or a thank-you card is a job in and of itself.

Opposes: Leo Suns. You see other people as holier-than-thou. When Jupiter is opposite your Sun sign, you don't connect to its energy naturally, which means you will always find yourself at a disadvantage until you do. The best way to tap into your good fortune is to look past the messenger and embrace the message. Maybe it's about economic equality, reducing your carbon footprint, or being more progressive. It's grating that it's coming through someone so sanctimonious, but it's a small price to pay for being on the right side of history.

JUPITER IN PISCES

You have always depended on the kindness of strangers, and they've never let you down. It doesn't matter what your gender, skin color, or income is. You can be traveling far from home and people you've never met before (and may never see again) will naturally open their hearts and hearths to you. That's because they recognize you as brethren. You are—soulfully speaking—their brother or sister. This is why you can walk down streets in neighborhoods others wouldn't go near, chum around with those who live on the other side of the political divide, and why hardened types always show you their softer side. There is no lion's den where you aren't welcome. Jupiter is in domicile in Pisces. It brings good fortune and protection in those places where you feel most like you don't belong. It's why you won't think twice about befriending the friendless, visiting the abandoned, and consoling the hopeless. Yours is an invisible church. It has no walls, altar, or creed because it lives in your heart. Your Jupiter comes alive when you work to make the world a better place. Pisces Jupiter . . .

Enriches: Pisces Suns through grants, sponsorships, and seed money.

Misses the boat with: Aquarius and Aries Suns when it gives up its autonomy.

Benefits: Taurus and Capricorn Suns by developing its resources.

Squares off against: Gemini and Sagittarius Suns when it gives away the store.

Blesses: Cancer and Scorpio Suns with emotional resilience.

Is anyone's guess with: Leo and Libra Suns because it's so lenient. Sometimes good because these two signs always mean well, sometimes bad because good intentions can pave the way to hellish situations.

Opposes: Virgo Suns. You see other people as spoiled. They don't know how good they've got it, and that irks you. When Jupiter is opposite your Sun sign, you don't connect to its energy naturally, which means you will always find yourself at a disadvantage until you do. The best way to tap into your good fortune is to value what you have. It may not be as much as others have, but it makes you happy and that's the rarest blessing of all.

SATURN

♄

Saturn is the planet of "what I fear." The last of the ancient planets, Saturn was the slowest and dimmest of the lights, so he was seen as elderly, burdensome, and melancholic. Saturn's association with the infirmities of old age makes him the planet of fear—fear of being destitute, unloved, abandoned, or incapacitated. Saturn's fears aren't horror-movie fears. Nor are they catastrophic or apocalyptic. Those troubles belong to other planets. Saturn's reality—grief, pain, and decay—waits for us patiently at the end of our lives, and the knowledge of its inevitability makes us want to do everything we can to avoid going there.

Everyone is afraid of fear. We're so afraid that we don't talk about it. It's why we treat misfortune like a contagion. We don't want to be infected, so we blame poor people for being poor and sick people for being sick. Fear is why we ostracize, demonize, and shame. It hardens our hearts, points fingers, and takes things away from people who didn't have much to begin with. Saturn often gets vilified in astrology, but Saturn's not the one that brings misfortune. On the contrary, Saturn reveals how each of us becomes the author of our own misfortune by showing what fear can make us do.

We do cruel things when we're afraid. We also do stupid things. *Oedipus Rex* is the story of a prince who was told that one day he would grow up to kill his father and marry his mother. Horrified by this prophecy, Oedipus hits the road, where he encounters an angry charioteer who threatens to run him down if he doesn't get out of the way and whom Oedipus kills in self-defense. Oedipus then goes on to defeat the Sphynx, a monstrous creature terrorizing the city of Thebes, and to marry the recently widowed queen, who's grateful for the assist. It's only after he becomes king that Oedipus learns that he was adopted—that the parents who raised him weren't his biological parents, that the charioteer he killed was his father and the widowed queen is his mother. Unable to cope, Oedipus gouges out his eyes and wanders the streets as a blind beggar. The story of Oedipus Rex sounds cruel, but it's actually the story of what happens when we let fear seize control of our lives, because when we run away from the things we dread most, we wind up tripping headlong into the very outcome we were seeking to avoid.

Saturn is the planet of tests. It tests us by playing on our fears. And Saturn in your horoscope shows you exactly where you'll encounter them. Maybe it's fear of loss that leads you to keep people at arm's length, fear of poverty that keeps you working a job you hate, or fear of disappointment that compels you to choose the hell you know over the heaven you don't. These are the self-fulfilling prophecies that keep you locked in an endless loop. But a test isn't the same as a challenge. A challenge provokes you to act; it shoves you in the chest and dares you to shove it back. A test, on the other hand, judges whether you are truly capable or not.

Saturn is a malefic planet. It's famous for stacking the deck against you and snatching away the football right when you're ready to kick it. Saturn doesn't make things easy, and that's the point. When you come up against an obstacle to happiness and immediately admit defeat, Saturn shows you that you must not have wanted it that much in the first place because you gave up so easily. Saturn tested your resolve, and your resolve was found wanting. Saturn always tests you in the area of life you care the *most* about, which is why it's a constant source of anxiety and pain. It's the one problem that you just can't beat.

Saturn teaches through the tedium of repetition. And by making you face the same obstacle time and time again, Saturn wears you down until you get to the place where you are so sick and tired of feeling sick and tired that you will try just about anything as long as it's different. And this is Saturn's miracle moment. By withholding the rewards you seek, Saturn teaches you to draw on resources you never dreamed you had and to make the most of your limitations instead of succumbing to them. This is what makes Saturn a teacher and not a tyrant, a builder and not a destroyer. We learn from our mistakes, not from our perfect test scores.

Saturn isn't always on your case. That's because the planet travels outside the Earth's orbit around the Sun, which means that it can appear anywhere in your astrological chart. It may be in the same sign as yours or a sign that's completely opposite.

Saturn in the same sign as your Sun sign **burdens**. The weight that's too much to carry is also the very thing that builds strength.

Saturn in the sign before or after your Sun sign is **exasperating**. This is the area of life where it's hard to absorb the lessons you're being taught.

Saturn in the sign two signs before or after your Sun sign is an **ally**. This Saturn wants to see you succeed and will provide the learning opportunities that can help make that happen.

Saturn in the sign three signs before or after your Sun sign **thwarts**. It frustrates and bedevils you. Unable to get what you want or to walk away, Saturn here creates a never-ending struggle.

Saturn in the sign four signs before or after your Sun sign is a **mentor**. This Saturn connects you to people who have been down the same road you're on and who want to help.

Saturn in the sign five signs before or after your Sun sign is **anyone's guess**. You feel blocked and wonder if redoubling efforts is really the answer, or are you better off just calling it quits?

Saturn in the sign six signs away from your Sun sign is a **total disconnect**. You don't identify with this Saturn in any way, so that what happens is it gets projected onto others—particularly in relationships or with close business associates. You may feel like it's the other person who's too taxing, limited, or a real downer.

What if you have Saturn retrograde? Saturn retrogrades are famous for things taking longer than they should. If Saturn is the tortoise in the race between the tortoise and the hare, then Saturn retrograde is like that tortoise on Valium. It wanders, meanders, and sometimes just stands there staring. Yet somehow Saturn retrograde delivers. You may find your calling late in life, experience an unexpected second act, or go back and pick up something you shelved years ago. Time is always on your side, which only goes to show that delayed gratification is better than no gratification at all.

You can gauge Saturn's strength in an astrological chart by determining if it's in domicile, detriment, exaltation, or fall. Saturn is at home (domicile) in Capricorn and Aquarius. These are the dark months when life is dormant. Think of midnight when the Sun crosses the threshold from one day into the next. Saturn rules that period in the calendar when the old year ends and the new one begins. Saturn is out of season (detriment) in Cancer and Leo. These are the summer signs, and Saturn isn't exactly known for being warm and sunny. Saturn is exalted in Libra, the harvesting sign when you find out if it's a bumper crop or slim pickings, and Saturn is in fall in Aries, the sowing sign where you're planting seeds and encouraging new growth. Frosty Saturn is a closer, not an opener, so it's not welcome in spring. Whether Saturn is exalted or in fall doesn't make it a good or bad Saturn. A "strong" Saturn may be severe while a "weak" Saturn is always tough, but fair.

SATURN IN ARIES

You're slow out of the starting gate. And that's not by choice. Unexpected delays have hobbled you since childhood. Maybe it took a long time to speak as a toddler, you were beset with health issues early on, or you were held back a grade. Whatever the initial stumbling blocks, you've been playing catch-up ever since. Watching the light turn red when everyone else gets the go-ahead is discouraging. What's the point of competing if you're always being tripped up? Saturn is in fall in Aries, which means that your biggest fear is things being over before they've begun. And if you take yourself out of the running, that's exactly what will happen. The solution is to choose your races wisely. You know you weren't built for speed, so skip the sprints and sign up for the marathons. Saturn in Aries gives you endurance, stamina, and that ability to pour it on when the finish line's in sight. It's ideal for pulling all-nighters, powering through obstacles, and delivering in the end. Aries Saturn . . .

Burdens: Aries Suns with false starts and premature endings.

Exacerbates: Taurus and Pisces Suns because it won't let them walk away from a fight.

Allies with: Gemini and Aquarius Suns by making them go the distance.

Thwarts: Cancer and Capricorn Suns when it doesn't step up to the plate.

Mentors: Leo and Sagittarius Suns by getting them back on their feet again when they've been laid low.

Is anyone's guess with: Virgo and Scorpio Suns because they can't win for losing. Sometimes good because they do make headway, sometimes bad because for every three steps forward there are two steps back.

Opposes: Libra Suns. You see others as closed doors. When Saturn is opposite your Sun sign, you don't connect to its energy naturally, and you'll find yourself being tested until you do. Your big test is to knock. Libras hate making the first move, but you could grow old waiting on others. If someone answers: great! You know you're in. If not? Then move on, because you don't want to be left standing outside a closed door with no one on the other side.

SATURN IN TAURUS

Denial is a survival mechanism. We couldn't function without it. We need to forget that every day brings us closer to the end or else we'd be paralyzed by fear. For most people, anxieties rule their waking hours, but not you. The fact that you can put all of this out of your mind and go about your business is a testament to your ability to wall off your own little corner of the world and keep it safe. It's what makes you everyone's favorite Rock of Gibraltar. It also makes you impossibly exasperating when your default response to a crisis is to act like nothing happened. Admittedly, you have a problem acknowledging when you're out of your depth, but you do this because you believe in normalizing out-of-control situations. Wait long enough and that mountain will surely revert to its former status as molehill. People like to say, "Denial ain't just a river in Egypt," but the part they leave out—and that you know to be true—is that Egypt would never have flourished without "de" Nile. Taurus Saturn . . .

Burdens: Taurus Suns with financial anxiety.

Exacerbates: Aries and Gemini Suns because it's penny wise and pound foolish.

Allies with: Cancer and Pisces Suns when it takes stock of the situation.

Thwarts: Leo and Aquarius Suns by getting stuck on a sticking point and refusing to move past it.

Mentors: Virgo and Capricorn Suns when it gets back to basics.

Is anyone's guess with: Libra and Sagittarius Suns because it wants guarantees up front. Sometimes good because these signs tend to take too much on faith, sometimes bad because not every situation comes with a guarantee.

Opposes: Scorpio Suns. You see others as financial burdens. When Saturn is opposite your Sun sign, you don't connect to its energy naturally, which means you will always find yourself being tested until you do. Your big test is to examine your motives. Why are you bankrolling someone who makes less money than you? Is it because you want to help out, or are you fostering dependency so they will never leave? If you're going to support someone financially, then it's got to be with no strings attached. And if not? The sooner you cut the purse strings, the better.

SATURN IN GEMINI

Saturn is the planet of detours and delays, and nowhere is it more confounding than in Gemini. Think of it as a cosmic version of Siri on the fritz—repeatedly misunderstanding your commands and rerouting you whenever you get close to your destination. Saturn is the sworn enemy of easy answers. It knows that the more hastily solutions are patched together, the faster they will fall apart—and usually with disastrous consequences. You may be afraid of opportunities slipping through your fingers if you don't grab them right away, but are they really worth it if they wind up costing you in the end? Yes, it's tedious how your Saturn insists on always taking the long way, but it's better to be safe than sorry. Gemini Saturn . . .

Burdens: Gemini Suns with second thoughts and second-guessing.

Exacerbates: Taurus and Cancer Suns by making them overthink it.

Allies with: Aries and Leo Suns by mapping out plans one step at a time.

Thwarts: Virgo and Pisces Suns when it's being contrary for contrariness's sake.

Mentors: Libra and Aquarius Suns by getting them to talk to—and not at—people.

Is anyone's guess with: Scorpio and Capricorn Suns because it makes them painstakingly precise. Sometimes good because they will never be disputed, sometimes bad because there's no tolerance for error.

Opposes: Sagittarius Suns. You see others as hard-nosed skeptics. When Saturn is opposite your Sun sign, you don't connect to its energy naturally, and you'll find yourself being tested until you do. Your big test is to win them over. Being a Sagittarius, you'll want to wow your critics, but that's not the way to go. You'll only make them more standoffish. Be inquisitive and conversational instead. Not only will you come to appreciate their point of view, but you may even discover that some of their reservations are valid.

SATURN IN CANCER

People can be *so* needy. Constantly asking for love and reassurance, and whining or acting out when they don't get it. It's tough being the only adult in a room full of yowling brats. People trust you to be their emotional anchor. As long as you're centered and unfazed they know everything will be all right. But who looks after you? Who reaches out and holds your hand in the dark? Needs are frightening—not because you don't like feeling vulnerable, but because needs mean relying on someone else, and you don't believe anyone's going to be there for you. Saturn is in detriment in Cancer, which means you clam up when it comes to expressing your needs. You're so afraid of being let down that you'd rather not put anyone on the spot. But how can people know what's going on if you don't speak up? Give them a chance to come through and you may discover they're more willing and able than you gave them credit for. Cancer Saturn . . .

Burdens: Cancer Suns with weighty responsibilities.

Exacerbates: Gemini and Leo Suns because it won't let them blow off an obligation.

Allies with: Taurus and Virgo Suns by bringing a personal touch to what they do.

Thwarts: Aries and Libra Suns when it holds back.

Mentors: Scorpio and Pisces Suns by doing what needs to be done despite past history and bad blood.

Is anyone's guess with: Sagittarius and Aquarius Suns by making them hands-off. Sometimes good because they support people in making their own decisions, sometimes bad when they're too absentee.

Opposes: Capricorn Suns. You see others as emotionally unavailable. When Saturn is opposite your Sun sign, you don't connect to its energy naturally, and you'll find yourself being tested until you do. Your big test is to be present. And that doesn't mean being someone's emotional support animal. Just be who you are—be affectionate when you're loving, be angry when you're mad, and cry when you're sad. The more comfortable you are in your own emotional skin—which is already a stretch for a Capricorn—the more the other person will open up.

SATURN IN LEO

You're afraid that you'll never become the person you were meant to be. Maybe the hopes are too high, the expectations too heavy, or your personal history too replete with broken promises and no-shows. Life has dealt you a series of crippling blows, and the fact that you're still standing is a testament to your strength and endurance. You wear it like a badge of honor. But "still standing" is no substitute for a stolen life. It's tempting to let your regrets define you and to blame circumstances for blocking you at every turn, but this would only allow you to walk away from who you are, and that's a shame you just can't live with. You may feel like it's too late to pick up a talent again or revisit a choice, but that doesn't mean you can't cultivate talent in someone else or help them make the most of choices that were unavailable to you. You may not become that person you feel you were meant to be, but nothing's stopping you from becoming that person for someone else. Leo Saturn . . .

Burdens: Leo Suns by being painfully self-conscious.

Exacerbates: Cancer and Virgo Suns by making them feel like people are talking about them behind their backs.

Allies with: Gemini and Libra Suns by setting a personal example.

Thwarts: Taurus and Scorpio Suns when it undermines their confidence.

Mentors: Aries and Sagittarius Suns by getting them to take the high road.

Is anyone's guess with: Capricorn and Pisces Suns because it makes them jealous of others' accomplishments. Sometimes good because studying a competitor's performance helps to improve their own, sometimes bad because they lose touch with what makes them special.

Opposes: Aquarius Suns. You see others as wounded children. When Saturn is opposite your Sun sign, you don't connect to its energy naturally, and you'll find yourself being tested until you do. Your big test is to honor their pain. Help them understand that every disagreement isn't about them, that every *no* doesn't mean rejection, and disappointments don't have to trigger early traumas. But don't be too rigid in your approach. You don't want to ignore their legitimate struggles.

SATURN IN VIRGO

You're not good at good-byes. Even if you know you're going to see someone soon, you keep coming up with last-minute things to say, a burning question that just can't wait, or a part of the story you left out. You know you should just say "Later" and be done with it, but instead you go on and on as if you were being led away from the courtroom in chains. Good-byes trigger your abandonment anxiety on a very deep level. They also make you clingy. And the most painful part is that that's exactly how you *don't* want to come across. What this stems from is a fear of disappearing. It's why you schedule every minute of every day. You're afraid that if you didn't have another meeting to attend or deadline to meet, you would vanish from people's lives altogether. The easiest remedy is to focus on your hellos instead. It makes you more welcoming and genuinely pleased to get together again. It also invites you to relax and enjoy the moments that you're so worried are passing you by. Virgo Saturn . . .

Burdens: Virgo Suns by being difficult to please.

Exacerbates: Leo and Libra Suns by focusing on what's not working rather than on what is.

Allies with: Cancer and Scorpio Suns by paying attention to the little details that matter.

Thwarts: Gemini and Sagittarius Suns by getting stuck on specifics.

Mentors: Taurus and Capricorn Suns by building an airtight case.

Is anyone's guess with: Aries and Aquarius Suns because it's always coming up with contingency plans. Sometimes good because they're never caught off guard, sometimes bad because they make things unnecessarily complicated—like when their contingency plans have contingency plans.

Opposes: Pisces Suns. You see others as having exacting standards. When Saturn is opposite your Sun sign, you don't connect to its energy naturally, and you find yourself being tested until you do. Your big test is to work with them. Yes, they may be impossibly demanding and are probably the bane of everyone's existence but that doesn't mean they don't have valuable knowledge to impart. Don't let the teacher get in the way of what's being taught.

SATURN IN LIBRA

You test people. You have a clever mind, you're a keen observer, and you can always invent new ways to put them through their paces. You don't do this to make their lives miserable. If anything, you feel for them and wish them all the best. But you're committed to the process, which is why you pit one person against another, study their performance under pressure, and wait for the shortcomings—or merits—to reveal themselves. Saturn is exalted in Libra, which means that it's at its most prudent and impartial in your horoscope. You can be sure your final judgment will be clear-eyed and definitive. The only problem is that you may never render it. You're so afraid of making the wrong choice that you could wind up making no choice at all. Testing is good if you know what the answers are, but if you don't you'll only follow up one test with another. Choices are like cards dealt in a card game. Whether good or bad, it's best to play what's in hand rather than wait for something better to come along. Libra Saturn . . .

Burdens: Libra Suns by being too choosy.

Exacerbates: Virgo and Scorpio Suns when it stops short of making a final decision.

Allies with: Leo and Sagittarius Suns by being fair.

Thwarts: Cancer and Capricorn Suns when it insists on total transparency.

Mentors: Gemini and Aquarius Suns by sticking to the rules no matter how much they want to bend them.

Is anyone's guess with: Taurus and Pisces Suns because they mate for life. Sometimes good when they pick the right partner, sometimes bad when they don't.

Opposes: Aries Suns. You see others as condescending. When Saturn is opposite your Sun sign, you don't connect to its energy naturally, and you find yourself being tested until you do. Your big test is to better yourself. Your first reaction may be to deride their elitism. But there's no disputing that for all their affectations they're cultured and sophisticated. It takes a special kind of courage to put aside insecurities and aspire to their level, but who knows? You might like the view from up there.

SATURN IN SCORPIO

There's nothing wrong with life in a gilded cage if it comes with everything money can buy. People talk about what they'll do for love and how they'll never stop pursuing their dreams, but what does it get them in the end? A broken heart and credit card debt. How do you know this? Because you've been there, done that. But disappointment doesn't have to make you bitter. It can make you smart. Life becomes so much easier once you learn to take *no* for an answer. It readjusts your gaze so that you make more enlightened choices—like targeting those gatekeeper positions that decide who gets in and who stays out. Isn't it better to be the person people are trying to impress than the person who has to do the impressing? You may not be the star, but there's nothing wrong with repping him. Your guilty secret is fear of being destitute, and you sometimes wonder if you're selling out—that is, until you see one of those guitar-playing boomers with CDs for sale at the local coffeehouse. Then you know you did good. Scorpio Saturn . . .

Burdens: Scorpio Suns with a hardened cynicism.

Exacerbates: Libra and Sagittarius Suns because it doesn't believe in happily-ever-afters.

Allies with: Virgo and Capricorn Suns by keeping facts and feelings separate.

Thwarts: Leo and Aquarius Suns when it makes them hold back.

Mentors: Cancer and Pisces Suns by speaking the emotional truth—no matter how dark or painful.

Is anyone's guess with: Aries and Gemini Suns by making them sticklers. Sometimes good because they don't let anyone get away with anything, sometimes bad because too much exactitude becomes stifling.

Opposes: Taurus Suns. You see others as emotionally manipulative. When Saturn is opposite your Sun sign, you don't connect to its energy naturally, and you find yourself being tested until you do. Your big test is to call them out on it. You need to be up front when you feel they're being withholding or disingenuous or guilt-tripping you into doing things their way. It sounds combative, but chances are they're covering up some deep psychological wounds. The sooner you get to the bottom of what ails them, the sooner you'll see if you want these people in your life or not.

SATURN IN SAGITTARIUS

You can't have faith without doubt. Faith is that unsubstantiated trust that someone will ultimately make the right decision, justice will prevail, or things will work out in the end. When you have Saturn in Sagittarius your faith is tested constantly. The planet of predicaments and dilemmas, Saturn places you in situations where there are no easy answers and forces you to decide for yourself if the next step is right or not. Beliefs, on the other hand, are foregone conclusions. They don't like to be shaken. And it doesn't matter how often they're disproved or exposed, they'll just keep sprouting new justifications and rationales. Beliefs are meant to be reinforced. They want to banish doubt. Yet doubt is the kindling to faith. Without those situations that bring us to the brink, we'd never take the leap into the arms of a Universe that moves in strange and mysterious ways. Testing awakens faith and stokes it into a flame. Sagittarius Saturn . . .

Burdens: Sagittarius Suns with a rigid belief system.

Exacerbates: Scorpio and Capricorn Suns because it makes them more judgmental than they already are.

Allies with: Libra and Aquarius Suns by giving them a philosophical bent.

Thwarts: Virgo and Pisces Suns when it introduces moral quandaries.

Mentors: Aries and Leo Suns by making them well read and learned.

Is anyone's guess with: Taurus and Cancer Suns because it makes them devout. Sometimes good because they're devoted to the cause, sometimes bad when they're intolerant of views that differ from their own.

Opposes: Gemini Suns. You see others as dogmatic. When Saturn is opposite your Sun sign, you don't connect to its energy naturally, and you find yourself being tested until you do. Your big test is to redirect the conversation. Fraternizing with people whose political and/or religious views are diametrically opposed to yours isn't easy, but it's doable. Focus on the things you have in common and you'll build trust, respect, and camaraderie. Everyone has their differences, but your gift is in finding constructive ways to bridge them.

SATURN IN CAPRICORN

Nothing freezes the blood like being told the boss wants to see you. It immediately reminds you of being summoned to the principal's office. And it doesn't matter how much money you make or how successful you become—that feeling of dread never goes away. Yet how many times have you truly been in trouble? You can probably count them on one hand. Saturn is in domicile in Capricorn, which means that you're about as law-abiding as they come. So why the cold sweat? Guilt. Plain and simple. Guilt is so woven into the fabric of the Capricorn hair shirt that you don't even have to do anything bad. You just know you're in the wrong. Yet paradoxically it's that fear of being in trouble that drives you to ascend the corporate ladder so that you never have to answer to anyone again. One day you'll be sitting in the boss's office that people get called to, and hopefully on that day you'll treat them with the same respect and sensitivity that you wish someone had shown you. Capricorn Saturn . . .

Burdens: Capricorn Suns with self-doubt.

Exacerbates: Sagittarius and Aquarius Suns when it's being snide.

Allies with: Scorpio and Pisces Suns by giving them discriminating taste.

Thwarts: Aries and Libra Suns with an overwhelming fear of failure.

Mentors: Taurus and Virgo Suns by streamlining their approach.

Is anyone's guess with: Gemini and Leo Suns because it makes them caustic. Sometimes good because these two signs know how to deliver a well-timed quip, sometimes bad when they don't take responsibility for the feelings they hurt.

Opposes: Cancer Suns. You see others as mean-spirited. When Saturn is opposite your Sun sign, you don't connect to its energy naturally, and you find yourself being tested until you do. Your big test is to be kind. This isn't going to go over well with people who delight in bursting others' bubbles. Ironically, they will see you as spoiling their fun. Nevertheless, your good example prevails upon them to behave more compassionately—or at least feel a little ashamed when they gloat over somebody else's misfortunes.

SATURN IN AQUARIUS

People never seem to think you care. It's bewildering, considering all the causes you sign up for and the hours you put in. Nobody works as tirelessly as you to effect real and meaningful social change. Yet somehow they remain unconvinced that you mean it, and suspicious that you're not truly one of them. Saturn is in domicile in Aquarius, an extremely intellectual sign. You are systematic and unerringly logical, and your matter-of-fact way of putting things gives you the bedside manner of a Vulcan. You have this way of coming across as . . . superior. This may have made you the object of ridicule when you were young, and that feeling of not belonging has trailed you ever since. People often mistake Aquarius for a rebellious sign. It's not. It's actually quite focused on building consensus—it's just that the "consensus" doesn't fully embrace Aquarius back. There's just something about the Aquarian energy that rubs them the wrong way. Thankfully, time is kind to you. You may start out feeling like you'll never fit in only to discover over the years that your outsider status becomes the very thing people treasure and respect most. Aquarius Saturn . . .

Burdens: Aquarius Suns by making them too abstract.

Exacerbates: Capricorn and Pisces Suns when it does a disconnect.

Allies with: Aries and Sagittarius Suns by making them au courant.

Thwarts: Taurus and Scorpio Suns when it's too austere.

Mentors: Gemini and Libra Suns by getting them to take care of unfinished business and tie up loose ends.

Is anyone's guess with: Cancer and Virgo Suns because it believes that all people are created equal. Sometimes good because it won't let the egomaniacs hog all the attention, sometimes bad because it won't praise anyone for being outstanding for fear of others being overlooked. The result is that nobody feels special.

Opposes: Leo Suns. You see others as indifferent. When Saturn is opposite your Sun sign, you don't connect to its energy naturally, and you find yourself being tested until you do. Your big test is to warm them up. Nobody's better at owning their feelings and expressing them than a Leo. You're like an inviting campfire that others want to sit close to. Your easygoing nature gets those who live in their heads to spend some time in their hearts instead.

SATURN IN PISCES

You may not have been left at the church door when you were an infant, but it sure feels like it. And it doesn't matter if you were showered with hugs and kisses all your life, you've always felt unwanted. Maybe you came into the world when your parents were going through a rough time or were raised by grandparents. That feeling of being a burden has never left, which is why you make a point of not becoming one. You pay your way—as well as the way of others—because you don't want to be seen as ungrateful or taking advantage. Unfortunately, that doesn't prevent others from taking advantage of you. You've never been one to wallow in self-pity, although you've experienced hardships that would warrant it. Nothing makes you see red like someone playing the victim card. You go on the attack—ridiculing them and poking holes in their story. It strikes a nerve because their pain is fake while yours is real. However, they are doing something you should be doing, which is speaking up. No one's going to know you're hurting inside if you don't show it. Pisces Saturn . . .

Burdens: Pisces Suns with too much self-denial.

Exacerbates: Aries and Aquarius Suns when it makes them self-sabotaging.

Allies with: Taurus and Capricorn Suns because it can take a licking and keep on ticking.

Thwarts: Gemini and Sagittarius Suns when it's too unassuming.

Mentors: Cancer and Scorpio Suns because it will always care.

Is anyone's guess with: Leo and Libra Suns because it makes them long-suffering. Sometimes good because they have the patience of Job, sometimes bad because they can't always tell the difference between humility and humiliation.

Opposes: Virgo Suns. You see others as masochists. When Saturn is opposite your Sun sign, you don't connect to its energy naturally, and you find yourself being tested until you do. Your big test is to be more understanding. Virgos are afraid of being used and abused and believe that anyone who doesn't set personal boundaries is a sap. However, life doesn't always respect boundaries and sometimes even overflows our banks. You may not like it when a loved one stands by someone who doesn't deserve it or a friend takes back an ex, but they do it because they know that there for but the grace of God goes any of us.

URANUS

Uranus is the planet of "what I don't expect." And it certainly took everyone by surprise when it was discovered by the British astronomer Sir William Herschel in March 1781. The first planet to be found since ancient times, Uranus upset the status quo of our solar system, which is why it was deemed the planet of revolution and change by astrologers. To be clear, the changes that Uranus brings aren't slight adjustments or cosmetic alterations. It doesn't busy itself arranging and then rearranging things like flowers in a vase. Uranus is famous for kicking over the game board and sending all the pieces flying. Wherever it resides in your horoscope is an area of volatility and disruption.

Overthrowing the old in order to make way for the new is the perfect mission statement for a planet that was discovered at the midpoint between the American War of Independence and the French Revolution. Both conflicts were fueled by the Enlightenment, a philosophical movement that began in the salons of the intelligentsia and wound up bloodied in the streets. The Enlightenment held that freedom, democracy, and science—and not the absolute authority of kings, the church, or the rich—should determine the way a society is governed. And if a government doesn't recognize the inalienable rights of life, liberty, and the pursuit of happiness, then, as Thomas Jefferson, author of the Declaration of Independence, put it, "it is the Right of the People to alter or abolish it." These were inflammatory words then and they're just as inflammatory now, as mass protests worldwide demonstrate. But Uranus in your horoscope doesn't mean that you're going to don a Guy Fawkes mask at some point and start tossing Molotov cocktails. Uranus is the planet of revolution and change, and revolutions aren't choosy about political sides. You can be just as revolutionary in your pursuit of progressive reforms as you can be in your efforts to restore things to what they once were.

Uranus is a peculiar planet. It's the only one to orbit the Sun on its side, which means that its north and south poles are where other planets' equators would be. This gives the appearance of Uranus rotating on its axis like a big wheel in the sky. It also has rings, like Saturn.

The Wheel of Fortune is a good image to keep in mind when thinking of Uranus. What's up one day can be down the next, and what was down could come flying up. Uranus is a hurly-burly, topsy-turvy energy: an enemy to everything that is fixed and nailed to the floor. It traffics in surprise upsets, unexpected twists, and rude awakenings. It's the reason people suddenly walk out on everything they built, espouse beliefs they once derided, or change their sexual orientation later in life. Uranus will always turn your life upside down, but it also asks: How do you know that the side you're used to is any better than the one to come?

Uranus, Neptune, and Pluto are known as the "modern" planets because they were discovered after 1781. Planets known before then—the Sun, Moon, Mercury, Venus, Mars, Jupiter, and Saturn—are the ancient planets, while Uranus, Neptune and Pluto are the modern ones.

The modern planets were named after deities who epitomized realms removed from our human experience. Uranus was named after the heavens, Neptune the seas, and Pluto the underworld—"the undiscovered country," as Shakespeare put it. The Sun, the Moon, Mercury, and the other ancients are called the personal planets because they describe psychological traits we can relate to, like our identity, our feelings, our thought processes, and so on, while the modern planets are referred to as *trans*personal planets because there is a distinctly impersonal quality to them. They connect us to worlds beyond our scope. Some astrologers see these planets as playing a key role in our evolution as a species while others regard them as a hot mess—radical elements thrown into the horoscope for the express purpose of wreaking havoc in our lives.

The heavens are democratic. Our Sun, which we honor and obey, is just one of many stars in the nighttime sky. Eclectic and multifaceted, the heavens have always been the vault where higher ideals and eternal truths are stored—forever out of reach, but always enlightening. These truths make themselves known through revelation. Sometimes they arrive with a parting of the clouds and sometimes they're the result of critical thinking, exploration, experimentation, and invention. Nevertheless, a higher truth is a square peg that we often try to squeeze into a round hole, so is it any wonder that it would revolt? That it would knock us upside our heads in order to get us to see the light? And that's Uranus's job in your chart: to wake you up to the fact that the abstract painting you admire on the wall is actually hung upside down, and now that you know better you need to do everything you can to get it right side up. It may not always be comprehensible, but Uranus ensures that there really is a grand design to the Universe—even if we can seldom make sense of it.

Uranus isn't always upsetting the apple cart. That's because the planet travels outside the Earth's orbit around the Sun, which means that it can appear anywhere in your astrological chart. It might be in the same sign as yours or a sign that's completely opposite.

Uranus in the same sign as your Sun sign **electrifies**. It awakens and excites.

Uranus in the sign before or after your Sun sign is a **gadfly**. It never stops buzzing in your ear, challenging the decisions you make and positions you take.

Uranus in the sign two signs before or after your Sun sign **enlightens**.

By continually removing blinders, it increases your awareness of the world you live in.

Uranus in the sign three signs before or after your Sun sign **overthrows**. Sometimes rebellious, sometimes liberating, this Uranus will never be oppressed or repressed.

Uranus in the sign four signs before or after your Sun sign **galvanizes**. It invigorates and enlivens.

Uranus in the sign five signs before or after your Sun sign is **anyone's guess**. You get thrown a lot of curves, and you're not always sure if they're happy accidents or catastrophic ones.

Uranus in the sign six signs away from your Sun sign is a **total disconnect**. You don't identify with this Uranus in any way, so that what happens is it gets projected onto others—particularly in relationships or with close business associates. You may feel like it's the other person who's too wild, erratic, and "out there."

What if you have Uranus retrograde? Uranus retrogrades are famous for pendulum swings. They're not as abrupt in their about-faces, but they can be just as absolute and uncompromising. Let's say you've spent years rallying against a cause, refusing to yield an inch or see things from a different perspective. Well, when that pendulum swings you may find yourself embracing—if not championing—the very things you found objectionable. But instead of it hitting you like a bolt out of the blue, this realization gradually dawns on you so that the changes you make are more gradual and long-lasting.

Although considered to be the co-ruler of Aquarius, the traditional rules of domicile, detriment, exaltation, and fall do not apply to Uranus and the other modern planets.

URANUS IN ARIES

You have this knack for showing up in places where angels fear to tread. It's like you're irresistibly drawn to conflicts where the people in charge have their foot on the neck of those helpless to oppose them. Maybe it's executives who abuse their authority, a system that's been rigged for years, or a cultural mind-set in need of some serious updating. In any case, you are here to do something about it. The irony is that you didn't go looking for a fight. There's no code of honor that you subscribe to, no glistening set of principles. You just know a wrong when you see it—which is why even if you're the soft-spoken, button-down type, you still roll up your sleeves and jump into the fray. And this struggle wakes you up to the things you've been missing. It feeds you, motivates you, and educates you. And once activated, you don't ever want to go back. You're like the rebel who's finally found the right cause. Aries Uranus . . .

Electrifies: Aries Suns with thrills and spills.

Gadflies: Taurus and Pisces Suns because it won't let them remain silent.

Enlightens: Gemini and Aquarius Suns by making friends and working with people they wouldn't typically meet.

Overthrows: Cancer and Capricorn Suns when it tosses caution to the wind.

Galvanizes: Leo and Sagittarius Suns by getting them to shake things up.

Is anyone's guess with: Virgo and Scorpio Suns by making them agents for change. Sometimes good because once they get started they won't stop, sometimes bad because they don't know when to quit.

Opposes: Libra Suns. You see others as pissed off and unreasonable. When Uranus is opposite your Sun sign, you don't connect to its energy naturally, so you always get thrown for a loop until you do. The best way to harness this energy is to hear what people have to say. You may not agree with all of their gripes, but there's bound to be one or two points worth considering.

URANUS IN TAURUS

It never fails, the way that life keeps shifting the goalposts. It doesn't matter how hard you work to get things right; something always happens to change the rules of the game. You gave up trying to reason with the unreasonable long ago, but what you have come to rely on is your persistence. It doesn't matter how many times you've been cheated or seen high hopes leveled— you always go back to the beginning and start again. And the funny thing is that you invariably discover some way to improve on what you did before. Most people would feel defeated being repeatedly forced to go back to square one, but it makes you more inventive. It gets you to study what went wrong, explore your alternatives, and test-drive a different approach—all things you wouldn't have done had everything gone according to plan. There's no saying that you will ever make peace with Uranus in Taurus, but there's also no denying that the ball moves farther down the field with every go. Taurus Uranus . . .

Electrifies: Taurus Suns by keeping them on their toes.

Gadflies: Aries and Gemini Suns because it upsets their best-laid plans.

Enlightens: Cancer and Pisces Suns by introducing a new twist on a familiar situation.

Overthrows: Leo and Aquarius Suns when the bottom drops out.

Galvanizes: Virgo and Capricorn Suns by never letting them get set in their ways.

Is anyone's guess with: Libra and Sagittarius Suns by turning situations on their head. Sometimes good because it gets them to see the world differently, sometimes bad because they can't always tell which end is up.

Opposes: Scorpio Suns. You see others as bitchy and high-strung. When Uranus is opposite your Sun sign, you don't connect to its energy naturally, so you always get thrown for a loop until you do. The best way to harness this energy is to stop trying to engage someone who doesn't want to be engaged. You're like the dog to their cat, so don't give chase, put your nose in their business, or bark at them. Follow these simple steps and they'll cozy up to you in their own good time.

URANUS IN GEMINI

You believe in free speech and exercise it vigorously on a daily basis. You're just as likely to burn a flag as erect a cross on public property. You might even do both at the same time just to make a point. Some might say you do this just to get a rise out of everyone, but your intent is sincere. You want to get people talking. You believe that a society is only as healthy as the free flow of ideas circulating within it—and that includes ideas that people don't like. You may not agree with what's being said, but you will defend a person's right to say it, because you know that if it's blocked, there's no telling what other "unacceptable" ideas will be blocked as well. It's a fight without friends that's often landed you in verbal barroom brawls, but it's a struggle you won't give up. Controversy and convention always sit opposite each other on the seesaw, but you need both. Gemini Uranus . . .

Electrifies: Gemini Suns with eye-opening experiences.

Gadflies: Taurus and Cancer Suns by broaching the one subject that shouldn't be broached.

Enlightens: Aries and Leo Suns by connecting the dots.

Overthrows: Virgo and Pisces Suns when it pulls the rug out from under them.

Galvanizes: Libra and Aquarius Suns by getting them to see the writing on the wall.

Is anyone's guess with: Scorpio and Capricorn Suns because it encourages them to play devil's advocate. Sometimes good because they're experts at exposing flaws in people's thinking, sometimes bad because argument for argument's sake might destroy something valuable in the process.

Opposes: Sagittarius Suns. You see others as stirring the pot. When Uranus is opposite your Sun sign, you don't connect to its energy naturally, so you always get thrown for a loop until you do. The best way to harness this energy is to take what they're saying seriously. They may not share your moral concerns—indeed, some of their arguments sound like putting firearms into the hands of children—but things are better thought out than you give them credit for.

URANUS IN CANCER

Not all revelations are based on discoveries. Some are sinking feelings you get when you learn that you've made a terrible mistake. Wheels spin forward just as easily as they spin backward, and when you have Uranus in Cancer you're driven by this need to get things back to the way they were before. It's the premise of countless time travel shows, and if you've watched any one of them, you know that do-overs only make matters worse. So how can you fix what went wrong? Put your trust in the Universe and let developments unfold on their own. *Revolution* doesn't just mean overthrowing governments. *Revolution* also refers to the orbit a planet makes around the Sun, to things coming full circle. Where you wind up is often back where you began when you have Uranus in Cancer, but the difference is you're wiser for the experience. Cancer Uranus . . .

Electrifies: Cancer Suns with wake-up calls.

Gadflies: Gemini and Leo Suns because there's no going back the way they came.

Enlightens: Taurus and Virgo Suns by showing them how to make what's old new again.

Overthrows: Aries and Libra Suns when it uproots.

Galvanizes: Scorpio and Pisces Suns by pushing them out of the nest so they can fly on their own.

Is anyone's guess with: Sagittarius and Aquarius Suns because they can't go home again. Sometimes good because home might not have been so great, sometimes bad because it can turn them into rolling stones that gather no moss.

Opposes: Capricorn Suns. You see others as walking out on you. When Uranus is opposite your Sun sign, you don't connect to its energy naturally, so you always get thrown for a loop until you do. The best way to harness this energy is not to squeeze too tightly. Give people their space. It may be frightening letting people come and go as they please, but instead of leaving you'll see them want to sit down and make themselves comfortable instead.

URANUS IN LEO

You don't know who—or what—you are and sometimes wonder if you ever will. Now, this doesn't mean you are confused, are in the dark, or have low self-esteem. On the contrary, you can be quite forceful and opinionated.

What it means is that there's a wide-open space where an ego should be, and you like it like that. Egos are so limited. You are so much more than labels and expectations. You are pure energy! And you are here to wake people up to the power within. Uranus in Leo makes you a catalyst for change. Nobody can enliven, inspire, and motivate like you. The not-so-good thing about Uranus in Leo is that you don't own your bad calls and even get mad at people when the great transfigurations you promised fail to materialize in their lives. It's almost like *they* somehow let *you* down. You blame it on their lack of faith, passion, or oomph. You may be pure energy, but until you shuffle off this mortal coil you're still a human being like the rest of us. And maybe that's what you've been searching for all along. Leo Uranus . . .

Electrifies: Leo Suns with flashes of insight.

Gadflies: Cancer and Virgo Suns by being peevish and on edge.

Enlightens: Gemini and Libra Suns with coincidences that aren't just coincidences.

Overthrows: Taurus and Scorpio Suns when it won't suffer fools gladly.

Galvanizes: Aries and Sagittarius Suns by making them a force to be reckoned with.

Is anyone's guess with: Capricorn and Pisces Suns by making them a bit of a wild card. Sometimes good because it keeps others guessing, sometimes bad because even they don't know what they're going to do next.

Opposes: Aquarius Suns. You see others as spinning out of control. When Uranus is opposite your Sun sign, you don't connect to its energy naturally, so you always get thrown for a loop until you do. The best way to harness this energy is to slow it down. You were born under Aquarius. You can move at a glacial pace when you want to. This dials down the craziness, lowers the temperature in the room, and gets others to step back and take a breath. Once calmed, you can go ahead and have a constructive conversation.

URANUS IN VIRGO

You help people help themselves. And the people you're looking to help are the ones who have been ostracized, neglected, or left behind. But your mission isn't to make them feel acceptable, shower them with love and attention, or bring them up to speed with the way things are done. Your mission is to support them in who they are. Maybe you're the teacher students come to when they can't talk to anyone else, the nurse who shows their patients how to work the system, or the judge who helps an immigrant evade detention. You intervene in people's lives because it's the right thing to do—even if that means putting your job on the line. Uranus in Virgo is a common astrological placement for civil disobedience. However, Virgo is still an earth sign, which means you believe things work best when there's a system in place. Your aim is to reform, not revolt. You connect people in need with the support, tools, and resources to stand on their own two feet so their voices will be heard. The establishment will have no choice but to listen. Virgo Uranus . . .

Electrifies: Virgo Suns when it speaks truth to power.

Gadflies: Leo and Libra Suns because it takes on lost causes.

Enlightens: Cancer and Scorpio Suns by changing it up.

Overthrows: Gemini and Sagittarius Suns when it pulls at the one loose thread that makes the whole thing unravel.

Galvanizes: Taurus and Capricorn Suns by speeding up the process.

Is anyone's guess with: Aries and Aquarius Suns by making them dot every *i* and cross every *t*. Sometimes good because it makes these fast-moving signs double-check their work, sometimes bad because it also makes them anal.

Opposes: Pisces Suns. You see others as having no time for you. When Uranus is opposite your Sun sign, you don't connect to its energy naturally, so you always get thrown for a loop until you do. The best way to harness this energy is to work yourself into their busy schedule. They're not going to stop for you. You're going to have to keep up with them. Volunteer to help out, tag along, or collaborate on a project. Make yourself useful and people will wonder how they ever lived without you.

URANUS IN LIBRA

For someone who refuses to be tied down, it's amazing how much time you spend in relationships. If you're not on the phone consoling a plaintive ex, then you're touching base with your spouse or thinking up new ways to make the person you're currently seeing feel special and included. It's a never-ending balancing act, but it's better to have too many people in your life than too few. Uranus in Libra mates for life, but nowhere is it written how many mates you'll share your life with. It takes a lot of stars to make up your constellation, and you're true to every single one of them—albeit in your fashion. Interestingly, you need a lot of space but not a lot of freedom—as evidenced by your jam-packed schedule. In fact, you don't do well when you have too much time on your hands. Some may wonder how you can juggle so many relationships all at once, but your question is how would you ever get along without them? Libra Uranus . . .

Electrifies: Libra Suns when it's consciousness raising.

Gadflies: Virgo and Scorpio Suns because it never can say good-bye.

Enlightens: Leo and Sagittarius Suns by making the scales fall from their eyes.

Overthrows: Cancer and Capricorn Suns when it meets a new face.

Galvanizes: Gemini and Aquarius Suns by getting them to re-evaluate.

Is anyone's guess with: Taurus and Pisces Suns because relationships are a revolving door. Sometimes good because there are plenty of fish in the sea, sometimes bad because they often wind up with the same type of fish.

Opposes: Aries Suns. You see others as commitment-phobes. When Uranus is opposite your Sun sign, you don't connect to its energy naturally, so you always get thrown for a loop until you do. The best way to harness this energy is to make people feel valuable, but show them that they are also replaceable. It will take a while to build up this kind of entourage, but once you do you'll have a pool of talent to choose from so that if things don't work out with one person, you can always move on to the next.

URANUS IN SCORPIO

You don't want there to be any secrets. Everything needs to be out in the open. It's your way of launching a preemptive strike against being taken by surprise. This is why you disclose much more than you should and invite others to do the same. Indeed the more embarrassed, squeamish, or shut down people get, the more you will pursue the point. You have no problem sharing the DVD of your colonoscopy or recommending your three favorite debt management programs. It all comes from a good place, but sometimes you can be so insistent on total transparency that people may respond by hiding things from you even more just to protect their privacy. There is such a thing as waiting for people to come to you when they're ready. It builds trust and rapport. Do that and you'll never be caught off guard again. Scorpio Uranus . . .

Electrifies: Scorpio Suns when it exposes.

Gadflies: Libra and Sagittarius Suns because it will never believe its eyes.

Enlightens: Virgo and Capricorn Suns when it tips sacred cows.

Overthrows: Leo and Aquarius Suns when it stirs up a hornet's nest.

Galvanizes: Cancer and Pisces Suns by being fearless.

Is anyone's guess with: Aries and Gemini Suns because it makes them unashamed. Sometimes good—like when they've done nothing to apologize for, sometimes bad for when they have.

Opposes: Taurus Suns. You see others as accidents waiting to happen. When Uranus is opposite your Sun sign, you don't connect to its energy naturally, so you always get thrown for a loop until you do. The best way to harness this energy is to take the bull by the horns. You know it's unpleasant, but someone's got to talk to that co-worker about their personal hygiene or spearhead an intervention for a loved one who's hooked on drugs. Better to alert someone to what's at risk than to stand by and do nothing.

URANUS IN SAGITTARIUS

You still believe in a global village. Yes, walls have gone up and borders are closed, but you're convinced we're all in it together and that your universal outlook will ultimately win out. You believe that if people got a chance to truly engage one another they would discover, learn, and thrive. Each of us carries a piece of the puzzle. Maybe it's tucked inside a point of view, sealed in a reverie, or passed down through a people. The answers we're looking for aren't shut away in vaults or towers or industrial complexes. They are in each of us. Sagittarius Uranus . . .

Electrifies: Sagittarius Suns when it frees the mind.

Gadflies: Scorpio and Capricorn Suns because it won't write people off.

Enlightens: Libra and Aquarius Suns through alternative beliefs and eso-teric practices.

Overthrows: Virgo and Pisces Suns when it gets militant.

Galvanizes: Aries and Leo Suns by educating them about the issues of the day.

Is anyone's guess with: Taurus and Cancer Suns by making them spiritual, but not religious. Sometimes good because they're responsible for their own belief system, sometimes bad when there's no real group or community to share these experiences with.

Opposes: Gemini Suns. You see others as wanting to change you. When Uranus is opposite your Sun sign, you don't connect to its energy naturally, so you always get thrown for a loop until you do. The best way to harness this energy is to see what they have to say. Some zodiac signs get bent out of shape when people try to change their lives, while others feel controlled or manipulated. You're pretty relaxed. As a Gemini you know you can always change things back. Meanwhile: Who knows? They might have a better idea of what would make you happy than you do.

URANUS IN CAPRICORN

Nothing lasts forever. And you don't say this because you're being jaded or blasé. It comes from firsthand experience. You're so used to the things you've worked hard to build collapsing inexplicably that you've come to expect it. One would think you'd be shell-shocked walking among the rubble of your hopes and expectations—and you were when you were younger—but over time you've gotten used to it. In fact, it's even become a barometer as to whether you're making the right decisions in your life. Security is a double-edged sword with you. On one hand it's the holy grail for anyone with planets in Capricorn—security is much more important than love or fame—but you also know that the very thing that protects you can also imprison you. And it's right when you're wondering if this might be the case that you experience the inevitable shake-up. If what you've built still stands, then you know it passed muster. And if it doesn't? Then it was keeping you down and it's time to move on and rebuild somewhere else. Capricorn Uranus . . .

Electrifies: Capricorn Suns when it liberates.

Gadflies: Sagittarius and Aquarius Suns because it's like *Groundhog Day*—always repeating the same life pattern until they get things right.

Enlightens: Scorpio and Pisces Suns by showing them that a crisis also creates opportunity.

Overthrows: Aries and Libra Suns when it shakes them to the core.

Galvanizes: Taurus and Virgo Suns by getting them to think outside the spreadsheet.

Is anyone's guess with: Gemini and Leo Suns by inuring them to life's ups and downs. Sometimes good because nothing really fazes them, sometimes bad because they become desensitized.

Opposes: Cancer Suns. You see others as Chicken Littles. When Uranus is opposite your sign, you don't connect to its energy naturally, which means you always get thrown for a loop until you do. The best way to harness this energy is to let them cycle through their drama. There's no way you're going to convince them that the sky isn't falling or that their world is coming to an end. Let it all go in one ear and out the other until they regain their emotional equilibrium. They'll thank you later for not being judgmental or condescending.

URANUS IN AQUARIUS

It isn't always easy to tell if you're ahead of your time or if your time has come. If you're too ahead of your time, it doesn't matter how brilliant your ideas are, they still fall on deaf ears. What you say just sounds too bizarre and far-fetched. But if, on the other hand, your time has come, then you see all the lightbulbs go off in rapid succession. People immediately get what you're talking about and are ready to sign on. Uranus is at its most electrifying and avant-garde in Aquarius. You can't help but send a jolt through everyone's lives. However, it can also make you a controversial and polarizing figure—a plus if you're looking for a career in arts and entertainment; problematic if you find yourself in a corporate environment or a culture that insists on uniformity. Nevertheless, many people with Uranus in Aquarius are drawn to these situations precisely because this is where their revolutionary concepts and unorthodox approach are needed most. Aquarius Uranus . . .

Electrifies: Aquarius Suns when it's in sync with the higher self.

Gadflies: Capricorn and Pisces Suns because it always makes them one of those things that's not like the others.

Enlightens: Aries and Sagittarius Suns by debunking myths.

Overthrows: Taurus and Scorpio Suns when it becomes a lightning rod for controversy.

Galvanizes: Gemini and Libra Suns by getting them to champion rights and causes.

Is anyone's guess with: Cancer and Virgo Suns because they turn things around. Sometimes good because they get results, sometimes bad because they often have to upset the status quo to achieve anything.

Opposes: Leo Suns. You see others as erratic and volatile. When Uranus is opposite your Sun sign, you don't connect to its energy naturally, so you always get thrown for a loop until you do. The best way to harness this energy is to roll with it. Be open to whatever unfolds. That unexpected twist may turn out to be a disaster, but given Uranus's propensity to turn on a dime, it could also be the best thing to ever happen to you.

URANUS IN PISCES

It's frustrating to foresee how things will play out, to give ample warning, and for people not to believe you. It would be one thing if you were wrong, but you're often right. Afterward there's regret and promises to listen to you next time, but when next time rolls around, the pattern continues. One would think you'd refrain from saying anything at all, but you can't. You have an almost masochistic commitment to telling the truth. And it's not because you need to be right. It's because relating what you see brings relief. It's like getting your feelings off your chest. People with Uranus in Pisces often hold oracular positions, but this isn't exclusive to crystal ball gazing. Many of you go into medicine, finance, and the sciences. You have an uncanny ability to read trends, diagnose symptoms, and decipher data. Do this with charts and graphs and everybody follows you. Try doing it in plain-speak and you'll come up against the same problem as Cassandra—which only goes to prove what prophets have said all along: people want the message, but not the truth that comes with it. Pisces Uranus . . .

Electrifies: Pisces Suns when it transcends the norm.

Gadflies: Aries and Aquarius Suns because it can't help sounding loopy.

Enlightens: Taurus and Capricorn Suns by revealing the hidden meaning.

Overthrows: Gemini and Sagittarius Suns when it whips up a storm.

Galvanizes: Cancer and Scorpio Suns by making them cutting-edge.

Is anyone's guess with: Leo and Libra Suns because it turns them into whistle-blowers. Sometimes good when they perform a public service by exposing corruption, sometimes bad when they have to pay a high price for it.

Opposes: Virgo Suns. You see others as here today, gone tomorrow. When Uranus is opposite your Sun sign, you don't connect to its energy naturally, so you'll always get thrown for a loop until you do. The best way to harness this energy is to enjoy the ride while it lasts. It's not easy given your need for assurances and guarantees, but this kind of unpredictable energy can also be liberating. It forces you to live in the moment, to be more open and spontaneous. And the best thing about rides like these is that there's always another one right behind it.

NEPTUNE

Neptune is the planet of "what I yearn for" in astrology. It works like a movie dream sequence. Neptune fills you with longing for things that appear hopelessly out of reach, but Neptune also teaches you to be careful what you wish for because you might just get it.

The dreams you have when you're asleep aren't the same as the dreams you have for your future. Nighttime dreams are often a jumble—they require interpretation in order to make any sense of them. The dreams you have for your future are Neptune dreams, which are like mirages shimmering in the distance. They may inspire you to make something of yourself, to trudge on out into the desert and give that vision of yours your best shot at realizing it, or they may taunt you with their spectral half-life of *what if*s and *what-could-be* scenarios that always dissolve on touch but are swift to return whenever you think of giving them up. Neptune is the most treacherous planet in astrology. It's also the most redemptive because it's the hope you never stop holding out for.

Under the influence is how we describe someone who's intoxicated, but it's also a good way to think of Neptune. Neptune rules the euphoria that artists, musicians, and poets experience when the barrier between your conscious and your unconscious mind—or this world and the next—lowers and the words, images, and musical notes just come pouring through. It's not the rush that athletes feel when they push their bodies to the limit or that *aha* moment when the pieces of the puzzle click into place. It's that hazy headspace where you empty yourself of you and become the vessel of something greater; something that's wiser, deeper, and freer. Sometimes it comes when you're anguished and heartbroken, sometimes when you're drunk or high. And sometimes it comes when you're still and quiet and are willing to wait. There is no particular way of summoning Neptune energy. It's not play-on-demand. Nor is there any guarantee that when you emerge from its delirium, those wonderful epiphanies you had when you were swimming with the dolphins won't leave you scratching your head in bewilderment later. What felt so infused with meaning and resonant profundity may now appear as scribbles and gibberish—like debris swept up onto the seashore. Neptune is the planet of heightened experiences and altered states, the favorite go-to source for mystics and seers; one can never be too sure if you're drinking from the Fount of Divine Inspiration or the Kool-Aid of Divine Madness. Or as the comedian Lily Tomlin once quipped: "I worry that drugs have forced some people to be more creative than they really are."

The sea has always been mysterious and otherworldly, vast and unfathomable. Neptune's discovery in 1846 coincided with the advent of spiritualism in the United States. Séances, channeling, Ouija boards, and ghost hunting all originated with spiritualism, which transformed the religious landscape of America in the years leading up to the Civil War. Before spiritualism, the afterlife was strictly defined as either heaven or hell—one of two fates that awaited you on Judgment Day. But spiritualists taught that the dead are with us now—and not only are they "alive and well" living in an astral plane of existence, but they also want to bring comfort to the bereaved and help loved ones live a better life. At its height, spiritualism had eight million followers. It planted the seeds for Theosophy, Christian Science, and New Age practices as well as for the women's rights movement.

Neptune gets you to reimagine your life, your world, and your cosmos. Right now there's a lemming rush for the cliffs. Maybe it's driven by apocalyptic fever, or maybe it's driven by self-deception, but the heads of state don't seem to want to believe that global warming is a thing. However, if we keep going the way that we're going, then the polar caps will melt, the seas will overrun the coasts, and this time the great flood will last a lot longer than forty days and forty nights. It may seem like too tall an order to turn things around, but Neptune speaks to the power of the ripple effect. All it takes is a dream of a better world and the willingness to put your vision out there and to see it through. Change the direction of one fish and you can turn around the entire school.

Neptune isn't always about falling down the rabbit hole. That's because the planet travels outside the Earth's orbit around the Sun, which means that it can appear anywhere in your astrological chart. It might be in the same sign as yours or a sign that's completely opposite.

Neptune in the same sign as your Sun sign **sensitizes**. It heightens all your senses—including the sixth one.

Neptune in the sign before or after your Sun sign **mystifies**. This is the area of life you find hopelessly confusing.

Neptune in the sign two signs before or after your Sun sign **inspires**. It gives you a creative vision that others find compelling.

Neptune in the sign three signs before or after your Sun sign **deceives**. Sometimes it's on purpose and sometimes it's for your own good; there's always more to the story where this Neptune is concerned.

Neptune in the sign four signs before or after your Sun sign is an **influencer**. This Neptune gives you a hypnotic effect on people. Please use responsibly.

Neptune in the sign five signs before or after your Sun sign is **anyone's guess**. It's hard to tell if that impossible dream is worth pursuing or if you're just tilting at windmills.

Neptune in the sign six signs away from your Sun sign is a **total disconnect**. You don't identify with this Neptune in any way, so that what happens is it gets projected onto others—particularly in relationships or with close business associates. You may feel like it's the other person who's too vague, spacey, or incoherent.

What if you have Neptune retrograde? Neptune retrogrades have a hard time quitting things. Whether it's taking back someone you know is no good or stopping by a bar on the way home from rehab to see if you're cured, Neptune retrogrades can appear self-sabotaging. Actually, they're more regressive than destructive, which is why you need to treat them like a swimmer caught in an undertow. Resist the impulse to struggle because you'll only be pulled down deeper. Relax, center yourself, and focus on a positive intention. The panic will pass and you'll soon come bobbing back up to the surface.

Although Neptune is considered the co-ruler of Pisces, the traditional rules of domicile, detriment, exaltation, and fall do not apply to Neptune and the other two modern planets: Uranus and Pluto.

NEPTUNE IN LIBRA (1942/43-1955/57)

Infatuation is a mixed blessing. You know it's not to be trusted, but it's an illusion you never grow tired of experiencing. Hope springs eternal when Neptune is in Libra. People don't make the best choices when they're under the thrall of Neptune, and it probably doesn't much matter because an infatuation is really just the prelude to a kiss in a fairy tale. It's only after the spell has been broken and you arise from your slumber that you are truly free to get to know each other. Libra Neptune . . .

Sensitizes: Libra Suns by making them sympathetic.

Mystifies: Virgo and Scorpio Suns by going against their better judgment.

Inspires: Leo and Sagittarius Suns by getting them to visualize in order to realize.

Deceives: Cancer and Capricorn Suns with nonbinding agreements.

Glamorizes: Gemini and Aquarius Suns by enhancing their appeal.

Is anyone's guess with: Taurus and Pisces Suns because it won't abandon hope. Sometimes good because they keep on believing despite dwindling prospects, sometimes bad because they can't always tell the difference between hope and wishful thinking.

Opposes: Aries Suns. You see others as leaving you hanging. When Neptune is opposite your Sun sign, you don't connect to its energy naturally, and you will always be misled until you do. The best way to engage this energy is to ask yourself if you're coming on too strong. The reason for others' vanishing acts may be that they see you as pushy and aggressive. If true, then dial it down and be more collaborative. But also be aware that no-shows may be the result of flaky personalities. In that case, adopt a three-strikes-and-you're-out policy. That way you'll know you always gave them a fighting chance.

NEPTUNE IN SCORPIO (1956/57–1970)

Your capacity to love is made deeper through heartbreak. It sounds counterintuitive, but getting your needs met and desires fulfilled doesn't make for a loving heart. Satisfaction may generate happiness and feel-good sensations, but it doesn't go much further than that. But that doesn't make people who are brokenhearted any more loving. They can be just as stunted—especially if they become resentful and embittered. Pain can be like a jealous lover who infiltrates your life—blocking all calls and shutting you up in its misery. It thrives on being inconsolable. When you have Neptune in Scorpio, you experience grief and loss on a profound level. You can't help it. Which is why you know it's better to plunge into the abyss than it is to forestall it through drugs, alcohol, or meds. Give yourself over to heartbreak and trust in the capacity of the soul to heal itself. Emotions left to run their course often run their course wisely. Scorpio Neptune . . .

Sensitizes: Scorpio Suns by making them forgiving.

Mystifies: Libra and Sagittarius Suns when it hides the answers in plain sight.

Inspires: Virgo and Capricorn Suns by getting them to go deeper.

Deceives: Leo and Aquarius Suns with lies they tell themselves.

Glamorizes: Cancer and Pisces Suns by adding to their mystique.

Is anyone's guess with: Aries and Gemini Suns because it won't let them shut off their feelings. Sometimes good because it keeps them emotionally present, sometimes bad when it gets to be too much.

Opposes: Taurus Suns. You see others as having something to hide. When Neptune is opposite your Sun sign, you don't connect to its energy naturally, and you will always be misled until you do. The best way to engage this energy is to take everything with a grain of salt. It's not that people are out to mislead you. Often they have things going on in their life that they're reluctant to share, which is why you want to let them come to you when they're ready to divulge all. That said, you still have to protect your interests. They may mean well, but their unconscious motives may not.

NEPTUNE IN SAGITTARIUS (1970–1984)

You have always believed in the power of prayer. It guides you when you've lost your way, consoles you in times of sorrow, binds you to the people who touch your life, and sometimes even answers back. You may not have the clearest idea of who you're praying to, but you do know that the Universe is sentient and not just some exhalation of stars that came into being billions of year ago only to be sucked back up into a gaping black hole. There is meaning in it all. You may never grasp what that meaning is, but you don't have to understand it to know that you are living in it. Affirmations, mantras, rituals, and daily devotionals are important to you. They're your way of aligning yourself. Maybe it's to invoke a higher power so you can tap into its healing and uplifting energy, or maybe it's to join other people on the planet who are engaged in the same form of worship as you right at the same time that you are doing it. Yours is a vision of salvation with no soul left behind. Sagittarius Neptune . . .

Sensitizes: Sagittarius Suns by making them true believers.

Mystifies: Scorpio and Capricorn Suns when they pray because they can't help wondering if they're really just talking to themselves.

Inspires: Libra and Aquarius Suns because they don't stop thinking about tomorrow.

Deceives: Virgo and Pisces Suns with promises that things will only get better.

Glamorizes: Aries and Leo Suns with a contagious exuberance.

Is anyone's guess with: Taurus and Cancer Suns because it makes them willing to suspend disbelief. Sometimes good because they understand things on an exalted and symbolic level, sometimes bad because they may be the only ones who do.

Opposes: Gemini Suns. You see others as gullible and hopelessly naïve. When Neptune is opposite your Sun sign, you don't connect to its energy naturally, and you will always be misled until you do. The best way to engage this energy is to turn it into a teaching opportunity. Take the time to really understand what others aren't getting and help them fill in the gaps. Nobody likes being made to feel stupid. It's a real turnoff. Help them see the light and you'll educate rather than alienate.

NEPTUNE IN CAPRICORN (1984–1998)

People sell their souls without thinking. They used to do it for money and power; however, nowadays they're just as likely to do it for likes, votes, or drugs. It's amazing how something that used to carry a steep asking price can so easily be bought in bulk. And the slope just keeps getting slipperier. You're a deeply soulful person. It's why you rarely discuss your beliefs and experiences. They're that sacred. You let orators thunder from the pulpits and gurus expound on karmic shortcomings. You don't pretend to know any better. But what you do know—at least for yourself—is that people should worry more about the means that they take to their ends. You will always take the high road by questioning, challenging, and doubting. Some say you're a cynic, but you're actually being reverential. You know that the silence of God speaks volumes. Capricorn Neptune . . .

Sensitizes: Capricorn Suns by making them contemplative.

Mystifies: Sagittarius and Aquarius Suns when prizes slip through their fingers.

Inspires: Scorpio and Pisces Suns because they won't settle for second best.

Deceives: Aries and Libra Suns with hopes of winning approval.

Glamorizes: Taurus and Virgo Suns by boosting credibility.

Is anyone's guess with: Gemini and Leo Suns by presenting them with no-win situations. Sometimes good because it forces them to think long and hard about their choices, sometimes bad because they feel like they're damned if they do and damned if they don't.

Opposes: Cancer Suns. You see others as father figures. When Neptune is opposite your Sun sign, you don't connect to its energy naturally, and you will always be misled until you do. The best way to engage this energy is to remember that the permission you seek must come from you. It's wonderful to turn to older people for mentorship and guidance, but don't hand over the reins. In the end you're the one who has to live with the decisions you make in life—not them.

NEPTUNE IN AQUARIUS (1998–2011/12)

It's hard to stand by and watch old rich guys trash civilization as we know it. That's why you show up at rallies, demand social justice, and fight for change. But it's not enough to say you're mad as hell and you're not going to take it anymore. There needs to be a vision of something better. But whose vision is it? And how do you get everyone on board? When you're born with Neptune in Aquarius, you have to do more than create a safe space; you have to create a safe planet. And that means factoring in the concerns of everybody from every corner of the globe to come up with a design for living. It feels like an impossible dream, but then again our future depends on it. Aquarius Neptune . . .

Sensitizes: Aquarius Suns by making them universalist.

Mystifies: Capricorn and Pisces Suns when it gets too theoretical.

Inspires: Aries and Sagittarius Suns with a vision of a better world.

Deceives: Taurus and Scorpio Suns with unrealistic expectations.

Glamorizes: Gemini and Libra Suns by making them persuasive.

Is anyone's guess with: Cancer and Virgo Suns because it makes them self-less. Sometimes good because they always give of themselves with no expectation of getting anything in return, sometimes bad because they often get taken advantage of.

Opposes: Leo Suns. You see others as wacky. When Neptune is opposite your Sun sign, you don't connect to its energy naturally, and you will always be misled until you do. The best way to engage this energy is to hear what people have to say. Yes, the Universe may choose strange mouthpieces, but they're mouthpieces nonetheless and you'd be wise to listen because there's still some truth to their take on things. Hear them out a few times and it will all begin to make a strange kind of sense.

NEPTUNE IN PISCES (2011/12–2025/26)

We all have an imagination—full of hopes, wishes, fantasies, and dreams, but sometimes we forget that there's a collective one as well. What makes a song a hit? A cultural phenomenon "a thing"? The collective imagination. Our personal imaginations feed into it like rivers into the sea. It's where our society houses its memories, myths, customs, and tastes. Everything from a universal archetype to the latest conspiracy theory originates here—which is why Neptune is also the planet of popular delusions and the madness of crowds. We still say "There must be something in the water" whenever people inexplicably embrace a trend or sign on for a cause, and having Neptune in Pisces makes you particularly sensitive to what that "something" is.

Maybe you have a sixth sense for when something feels off, or maybe you're the one who put that something there in the first place. In any case you appreciate the power of influence, and whether you use it to everyone's benefit—or your own—is entirely up to you. Pisces Neptune . . .

Sensitizes: Pisces Suns by making them visionaries.

Mystifies: Aries and Aquarius Suns when it gets esoteric.

Inspires: Taurus and Capricorn Suns to follow their dreams instead of the dollar signs.

Deceives: Gemini and Sagittarius Suns with romantic longing.

Glamorizes: Cancer and Scorpio Suns by increasing their allure.

Is anyone's guess with: Leo and Libra Suns because it fills them with abandon. Sometimes good because nothing rivals their bacchanalian wildness, sometimes bad when they have to face the music the day after.

Opposes: Virgo Suns. You see others as leading you astray. When Neptune is opposite your Sun sign, you don't connect to its energy naturally, and you will always be misled until you do. The best way to engage this energy is to recognize that your resistance is what makes you susceptible. You can't outsmart something that you secretly want to seduce you. We all live in bubbles—even people who believe in facts and stats. Be honest about yearning for more magic in your life and maybe you'll have some fun. After all, if you're going to be led up the garden path, you might as well smell the roses while you're at it.

NEPTUNE IN ARIES (2025/26–2038/39)

There are different kinds of crusades—moral, political, environmental, and even antiwar ones. Sometimes sanctified and sometimes spur-of-the-moment, they can quickly take on a life of their own—overflowing their banks and overwhelming the very leaders who got them started. More than a movement, but not quite an army, crusaders gather together under one banner and are driven by a single vision. When you have Neptune in Aries, you have a propensity to get caught up in the zeal and appeal of a popular cause, and once enlisted you will fight to the finish. Hopefully, this is more a battle of ideas than a battle of fists because the latter can get bloody. Mars, ruler of Aries, was named after the Roman god of war, so there's an us-versus-them animosity streaming through this Neptune; however, it can be redirected into more positive outlets like healthy competition, vigorous contesting of staid norms, and a celebration of individuals who rise above the fray. Your crusade shouldn't be focused on fighting the good fight but on ennobling and improving the lives around you. Aries Neptune . . .

Sensitizes: Aries Suns by making them honorable.

Mystifies: Taurus and Pisces Suns when it offers to fall on its sword.

Inspires: Gemini and Aquarius Suns to get involved.

Deceives: Cancer and Capricorn Suns with assurances that the cream always rises to the top.

Glamorizes: Leo and Sagittarius Suns by magnifying their fabulousness.

Is anyone's guess with: Virgo and Scorpio Suns because it mobilizes them. Sometimes good because it gets them to act before it's too late, sometimes bad when they adopt extreme and radical positions.

Opposes: Libra Suns. You see others as alarmists. When Neptune is opposite your Sun sign, you don't connect to its energy naturally, and you will always be misled until you do. The best way to engage this energy is to get to the bottom of things right away and then present the facts as evenly and as fair-mindedly as possible. But you can't just sound like Mr. Spock. You have to make your case in an equally compelling way. You need to be the sober voice of reason when that's the last thing anyone feels like listening to.

PLUTO

Like plants and animals, we all have a fate encrypted inside us. Call it a genetic code, hereditary traits, or a psychological inheritance that's been passed down through the generations. There is a deep, dark part of us that already knows the end of the story before it plays out. It's the part of us that knows that certain things were meant to be, that other things can't be helped, and that there are make-or-break times in life when it either all comes together or falls apart. If the Sun symbolizes the self in your horoscope—the person you're always growing into—then Pluto symbolizes the seed.

And like a seed, Pluto carries the knowledge of everything that's come before. Pluto knows what shape you will take, the things you need to survive and thrive, and that you have to push through the darkness because if you don't you will surely perish. It's Pluto's job to get you through the rough passages. It does this at the beginning of life when you're squeezing through the birth canal. It does this with every crisis you face, every trauma you suffer, and every accident you walk away from. And it does this at the end of life, when it's time for your body, soul, and spirit to part company and go their separate ways. Pluto symbolizes the will to live that's greater than conscious choice, resolve, or hope: a will that's so indefatigable that it insists there's life after death—which is ironic given that the planet was named after the Roman god of the dead.

"Why not call it Pluto?" asked eleven-year-old Venetia Burney when news of a planet lying beyond Neptune's orbit was announced in the British papers on March 14, 1930. Contrary to popular belief, Burney didn't name the planet after Mickey Mouse's dog. The girl knew her classical mythology and she knew her planets. (Besides, the dog's name came later.) Burney proposed the name over breakfast with her grandfather, a retired librarian of the Bodleian Library at Oxford, who passed it along to a friend at the Royal Astronomical Society, who then sent a telegram to the Lowell Observatory in Arizona, where the planet was first spotted. There was initial hesitation—some scientists thought it sounded too gloomy—but in the end everyone agreed it was a fitting name for a heavenly body so remote and icy.

Although the story of Pluto's naming is quaint and rather charming, there was nothing cheery about when it was discovered. Months after the stock market crash of 1929 and smack-dab between the outbreak of World War I and the end of World War II, Pluto's appearance coincides with one of our civilization's darkest chapters. Mass destruction, the Holocaust, and the threat of nuclear annihilation are just a few of the grim realities to arise from this period. No longer would natural disasters, plagues, or God decide humankind's future. That prerogative would now reside with us.

"What's bred in the bone will out in the flesh" is a good way to think of Pluto. It sounds fatalistic, but Pluto isn't concerned about your fate; it's concerned about your true nature.

Pluto is not an easy planet to know. Like the lord of the underworld, it lies beneath the floorboards of your horoscope. You don't go to it as much as it comes to you when the time is right. And those times aren't pleasant. Pluto is the planet of ordeals and the transformations that arise from them.

Pluto's ordeals are pretty brutal. They often involve cruelty, injustice, grief, and loss. Sometimes they're inflicted on you, and sometimes you inflict them on others. And that's the thing about Pluto. You don't really know what lies beneath those floorboards. It might be buried treasure or it could just be rot. Saturn may be the planet of tests, but Pluto lays bare who you've been all along.

Reincarnation is often associated with Pluto. Reincarnation is a religious belief that originated in agriculturally based civilizations. When you think of the way plants flower, die, and then reappear every spring, it wasn't a big leap to ask: If plants can come back from the dead, why can't we? In many prehistoric societies the dead were buried in fetal position—placed back into the womb of the earth lovingly like a baby. This is where Pluto's connection to rebirth comes from. It doesn't rise from the ashes as much as it returns—richer and more realized than it was before. Pluto always rewards those who suffer its ordeals because it's only by going down into the depths that you activate that mysterious process responsible for your evolution as a being. But even in reincarnation, Pluto maintains the same you. An indomitable you. It's the you who keeps coming back.

Pluto isn't always dragging you down to hell and back. That's because the planet travels outside the Earth's orbit around the Sun, which means that it can appear anywhere in your astrological chart. It might be in the same sign as yours or a sign that's completely opposite.

Pluto in the same sign as your Sun sign **transforms**. It continually works to bring out the person you are underneath.

Pluto in the sign before or after your Sun sign **torments**. This is the one area of life you can't make peace with.

Pluto in the sign two signs before or after your Sun **plays for keeps**. This Pluto means serious business.

Pluto in the sign three signs before or after your Sun sign is a **power struggle**. These are the battles you fight as if your life depended on it.

Pluto in the sign four signs before or after your Sun sign **regenerates**. You keep coming back no matter how many times you're cut down.

Pluto in the sign five signs before or after your Sun sign is **anyone's guess**. It's hard to tell if that thing you're fixated on is worth the trouble or will wind up costing everything you hold dear.

Pluto in the sign six signs away from your Sun sign is a **total disconnect**. You don't identify with this Pluto in any way, so that what happens is it gets projected onto others—particularly in relationships or with close business associates. You may feel like it's the other person who's too obsessive, intense, or self-destructive.

What if you have Pluto retrograde? Pluto retrogrades are known for long gestation periods. They're so long that you can go years—even decades!—completely oblivious to this hidden side of yourself until it emerges full-bodied, seizing your life with a wild ferocity. It's both exciting and unsettling because you're filled with this urge to make up for lost time. And you will. But the thing about Pluto retrogrades is that once spent, this wild part of you goes back to sleep again—leaving you wondering why you did the things you did and if it will ever come back again. Meanwhile the landscape of your life has been irrevocably altered.

Although Pluto is considered the co-ruler of Scorpio, the traditional rules of domicile, detriment, exaltation, and fall do not apply to Pluto and the other two modern planets: Uranus and Neptune.

PLUTO IN LEO (1937/39–1956/58)

You never grow old. Your skin may wrinkle and your hair may turn gray, but you'll always approach life like a child—full of wonder with a carefree heart and a love of play. You have made yourself practically immune to the forces of cynicism and disillusionment. It's because you refuse to buy into a negative worldview that says you are anything less than. You will always be fabulous, special, and gifted for as long as you live. It's why you shut out haters, beat back critics, and take sideswipes at punks who call you "boomer." You were born young at heart and nobody's going to take that away from you. But being an eternal child isn't all it's cracked up to be. You can't evolve if you're forever young. Children don't understand accountability, giving back, or putting somebody else first. They also don't know when it's time to leave the stage. Passing the keys on to the next generation may feel like psychic suicide, but it actually allows you to take on a more fulfilling role: adult. Leo Pluto . . .

Transforms: Leo Suns when they acknowledge others' truths.

Torments: Cancer and Virgo Suns when they're not being authentic.

Plays for keeps with: Gemini and Libra Suns because they're all in.

Grapples with: Taurus and Scorpio Suns for the final say.

Regenerates: Aries and Sagittarius Suns by reconnecting them with what matters most.

Is anyone's guess with: Capricorn and Pisces Suns because it makes them self-deprecating. Sometimes good because they can poke fun at their own faults, sometimes bad when people mistake it for low self-esteem.

Opposes: Aquarius Suns. You see others as sucking all the oxygen out of the room. When Pluto is opposite your Sun sign, you don't connect to its energy naturally, so you will always be overpowered by it until you do. The best way to deal with this self-absorbed energy is to interrupt and then redirect the conversation to someone else. It may seem rude, but it's no ruder than the person who's going on and on about themselves. Besides, everyone will thank you for it later.

PLUTO IN VIRGO (1956/58–1971/72)
Over the years you've been called a control freak, a micromanager, and even OCD, but you don't mind. You understand that it comes from a good

place. It's why you take it as a sign of affection. The people in your life know that everything would have gone to hell in a handbasket long ago if not for you. Yet for someone who's so hands-on, it's remarkable how strong the hands-off signals you transmit can be. The way you juggle responsibilities, multitask, and ask to reschedule get-togethers at the last minute because of work isn't exactly inviting. And even then, you still go to bed worrying that everything could crash and burn tomorrow. It could—so what's the point of all the worry and stress? When you have Pluto in Virgo it's important to live the life you have *now* rather than the one you're saving it all up for. Virgo Pluto . . .

Transforms: Virgo Suns when they find their own voice.

Torments: Leo and Libra Suns by putting off until tomorrow what they can enjoy today.

Plays for keeps with: Cancer and Scorpio Suns because the ends always justify the means.

Grapples with: Gemini and Sagittarius Suns by being a hard sell.

Regenerates: Taurus and Capricorn Suns because it will keep on keeping on.

Is anyone's guess with: Aries and Aquarius Suns because it never rests on its laurels. Sometimes good because they will always work to improve a situation, sometimes bad because they rarely stand back and admire what they've done.

Opposes: Pisces Suns. You see others as commandeering your life. When Pluto is opposite your Sun sign, you don't connect to its energy naturally, so you will always be overpowered by it until you do. The best way to engage this energy is to distinguish what's *yours*, *mine*, and *ours*. The clearer you are about this, the more respectful the other person will be. Good fences make good neighbors because everyone knows where they stand.

PLUTO IN LIBRA (1971/72–1983/84)

Tolerance doesn't necessarily make you tolerant. It's like sitting down to tea with someone you can't stand. You go through the pleasantries of making conversation and passing the sugar, but it doesn't mean you'll grow to like each other. And that's all right because the fact that you're not at each other's throats is a victory in and of itself. The peace and harmony that Pluto in Libra brings is rarely popular or appealing. It doesn't have to be, as long as it succeeds in getting people to get along. Desegregation, assimilation, and affirmative action will always be hot-button topics, but we all know that something must be done to balance the scales for those who feel treated like second-class citizens. But scales are rarely static. The more one side rises, the lower the other side sinks until everything becomes a vicious circle. Equality isn't easy. And then there's the bigger sticking point: What do you do with people and views that really shouldn't be tolerated? And that's where judgment comes in. Hopefully, in your efforts to improve society you don't become the very thing you're trying to rule out. Libra Pluto . . .

Transforms: Libra Suns when they are equal parts just and compassionate.

Torments: Virgo and Scorpio Suns by engaging in discussions for the sake of argument.

Plays for keeps with: Leo and Sagittarius Suns because it's always about the principle of the thing.

Grapples with: Cancer and Capricorn Suns when it makes them bend the knee.

Regenerates: Gemini and Aquarius Suns with every pledge they keep.

Is anyone's guess with: Taurus and Pisces Suns because it never strays from the middle path. Sometimes good because they avoid extremes, sometimes bad because they come across as hedging their bets.

Opposes: Aries Suns. You see others as didactic. When Pluto is opposite your Sun sign, you don't connect to its energy naturally, so you will always be overpowered by it until you do. The best way to engage this energy is to bring the conversation back to what's really going on. Feelings get disconnected once the jargon appears and people start backing up their cases as if they were in a court of law. Words can be a thin veil for what lies underneath. Tell them you'd rather hear what they want to say instead of what they feel they *have* to say.

PLUTO IN SCORPIO (1983/84–1994/95)

Pluto is the planet of black holes, and nowhere is it more gaping than in Scorpio. That means you are constantly fixated on what's missing. Maybe it was denied to you as a child or taken away. Then again, it could have been something you had but was spoiled by cruelty, separation, or shame. Whether it's unrequited love or a grudge that remains unsatisfied, you can't give it up. Yet giving it up is exactly what you must do. Obsession, like other things that aren't good for you, is uniquely designed to keep you hooked. The more you stay focused on something you can't have, the more the anger, ache, and desperation stokes obsession's infernal fire. The general rule for treating obsession is if you think you can't live without it, chances are you can. Closing the door on fixation opens the window to fulfillment, and suddenly that bottomless pit doesn't seem so bottomless anymore. Scorpio Pluto . . .

Transforms: Scorpio Suns by struggling with its inner demons.

Torments: Libra and Sagittarius Suns when it keeps peeking behind the scenes.

Plays for keeps with: Virgo and Capricorn Suns because they have a superior BS meter.

Grapples with: Leo and Aquarius Suns by reopening old wounds.

Regenerates: Cancer and Pisces Suns when they wind up being stronger than they thought.

Is anyone's guess with: Aries and Gemini Suns because it makes them single-minded. Sometimes good because they concentrate only on the most important essentials, sometimes bad because their idea of what's *un*important doesn't always agree with everyone else's.

Opposes: Taurus Suns. You see others as never being satisfied. When Pluto is opposite your Sun sign, you don't connect to its energy naturally, so you will always be overpowered by it until you do. The best way to engage this energy is to stop pandering to people. Just say no. It's Taurus's favorite word. But you may also want to examine why you keep inviting them to make demands on you in the first place. That need to please can get you into a lot of trouble if you're not careful about it.

PLUTO IN SAGITTARIUS (1995/96–2008)

It's hard to believe there's a higher purpose when you're staring disaster in the face—like when fires wipe out your neighborhood, economic down-turns erase your fortune, or illness seizes your body and holds it hostage. These are the times when we get religion, become spiritual, or call on a higher power for help. But what happens when a hater defiles your sacred space? Where do you turn then? Pluto in Sagittarius shakes your moral values to the core—whether you're religious or not. Most people would abandon their faith, but not you. If anything, it becomes stronger, more resilient— and in the most strange and inexplicable ways. It doesn't harden like a resolve, but it deepens. It knows that God cannot protect because God is not a supernatural agency that can be summoned, but rather a living light that exists inside us all. Pluto in Sagittarius teaches that the only higher power we have to turn to resides within ourselves. Sagittarius Pluto . . .

Transforms: Sagittarius Suns by making them rise again.

Torments: Scorpio and Capricorn Suns because nothing is sacred.

Plays for keeps with: Libra and Aquarius Suns because there will always be minds to change and souls to save.

Grapples with: Virgo and Pisces Suns by insisting they get back in the saddle.

Regenerates: Aries and Leo Suns when they keep the faith.

Is anyone's guess with: Taurus and Cancer Suns because they won't call it quits. Sometimes good because they'll keep going long after everyone else has given up, sometimes bad because maybe everyone else had the right idea.

Opposes: Gemini Suns. You see others as proselytizing. When Pluto is opposite your Sun sign, you don't connect to its energy naturally, so you will always be overpowered by it until you do. The best way to engage this energy is to hear them out if you have the time. Being a Gemini, you're naturally curious and are always willing to see things from another perspective as long as it's interesting. Just remember that what's fun for you is serious for them. You don't want to offend someone who sincerely thought you were asking in earnest.

PLUTO IN CAPRICORN (2009–2023)

You were born old. You've always been more serious, reflective, and disciplined than a person your age should be. And it's not like you were a precocious child, because you were never really young. You've always been your parents' confidant, your friends' mentor, or a sounding board to a teacher or coach. You have no problem being accountable. Taking responsibility is empowering, not burdensome. The wonderful thing about the buck stopping with you is that you wind up richer than those who passed it along in the first place. By essentially putting you in charge of the decision making they have no choice but to do what you say—even if they're your boss or client. The downside to Pluto in Capricorn is that it gives you a world-weariness that you haven't really earned. You may feel like you've seen it all, but you haven't. You're still a kid playing at being a grown-up. Making that adjustment—putting aside the child's idea of an adult to make room for the real one who's coming of age—is a tricky passage you'll be navigating well into your forties. It only goes to show that you're never too old for growing pains. Capricorn Pluto . . .

Transforms: Capricorn Suns through austerity.

Torments: Sagittarius and Aquarius Suns by making things harder than they need to be.

Plays for keeps with: Scorpio and Pisces Suns because they can always wait.

Grapples with: Aries and Libra Suns by being a hard-ass.

Regenerates: Taurus and Virgo Suns when they rebuild.

Is anyone's guess with: Gemini and Leo Suns because it turns them into late bloomers. Sometimes good because they come into their own right at that time in life when everyone else feels stuck in a rut, sometimes bad because it isn't always easy taking longer than the rest.

Opposes: Cancer Suns. You see others as harsh and unfeeling. When Pluto is opposite your Sun sign, you don't connect to its energy naturally, so you will always be overpowered by it until you do. The best way to engage this energy is to dig beneath the surface. Chances are you'll unearth very good reasons for why they are the way they are. A more sympathetic understanding of what makes them tick allows you to speak to the person they really are underneath.

PLUTO IN AQUARIUS (2023/24 —2043/44)

You don't believe in fate. Destiny is what you make of it. If people can re-shape their bodies to match who they are underneath, it only makes sense that they can design their own futures. All it requires is making more informed choices about where to go from here. But how informed are those choices? Better life through technology seems like a no-brainer until you realize that our capacity to create things has outpaced our ability to make good decisions. We can modify food, alter the genetic code of species, and even talk about transhumanism without sounding like a sci-fi nerd, but does any of it make us better people? Just because we're capable of something doesn't mean we're meant to do it. Our history is full of Pandora's boxes that we keep opening as if they were Christmas presents tucked beneath the tree. It's the nature of Pluto in Aquarius to see the future as a better place and the past as something in need of correcting—if not casting off altogether. But a future without a past is doomed to repeat it. Aquarius Pluto . . .

Transforms: Aquarius Suns by approaching matters holistically.

Torments: Capricorn and Pisces Suns when it gets too far ahead of itself.

Plays for keeps with: Aries and Sagittarius Suns by pushing the boundaries.

Grapples with: Taurus and Scorpio Suns over ideological differences.

Regenerates: Gemini and Libra Suns when they defy expectations.

Is anyone's guess with: Cancer and Virgo Suns because it enables them to step out of the situation. Sometimes good because it makes them impartial so that they don't take things personally, sometimes bad because they're eliminating the very thing that makes their insight special.

Opposes: Leo Suns. You see others as *them*. When Pluto is opposite your Sun sign, you don't connect to its energy naturally, so you will always be over-powered by it until you do. The best way to engage this energy is to meet people individually. Talking one-on-one will do a lot to break down preju-dices and assumptions and maybe even open your mind up to other points of view.

YOUR ASTROLOGY CHART AS PERSONAL CALENDAR

YOUR ASTROLOGY CHART
AS PERSONAL CALENDAR

The first step in turning your astrology chart into a calendar is to *not* read it like an astrology chart.

The reason for this is that an astrology chart is read with the planets moving in a clockwise direction. This is great for reading a clock, but a clock isn't going to tell you the time of year any more than a calendar is going to tell you the time of day. That's why we don't cover the rising sign, houses, or planetary placements in this book. That will be in the next book. The focus of this book is exclusively on turning your astrology chart into a Cosmic Calendar, and to do this we will be using the modes, seasons, and elements.

Begin with Your Birthday

To unlock your chart and use it as a yearly planner, you need to do three things:

1. Find your season.
2. Determine what mode you are—is your zodiac sign cardinal, fixed, or mutable?
3. Identify the element that your Sun sign is in.

Once you've done this, everything will fall into place.

Let's use Pisces as an example. If you were born under Pisces (Feb. 18–March 19), you know that:

1. You were born in the late winter.
2. You're a mutable sign.
3. Your element is water.

Your next step is to divide the year into quarters according to the **mutable** signs.

MUTABLE SIGNS

Pisces = late winter

Gemini = late spring

Virgo = late summer

Sagittarius = late autumn

In Season/Out of Season

If you are a Pisces, you are in season in the late winter when the Sun is closest to your birthday, and you are out of season in the late summer (Virgo) when the Sun is farthest away from it. You always want to begin things in late autumn (Sagittarius) when the Sun is approaching your birthday and end things in late spring (Gemini) when the Sun is departing it.

Approaching

The season before yours is when the Sun is approaching your birthday. It's increasing in solar strength, which means this is the time to clear away the deadwood, plant seeds for any new projects, and invest energy in those budding prospects that look like they're going to go somewhere. It's also perfect for meeting and greeting new friends and associates as well as updating your dating profile, because your solar energy is building. For Pisces, whatever's begun when the Sun is in Sagittarius will flower when the Sun enters the sign of the Fish.

In Season

The Sun in your own zodiac sign is your peak time of year. This is you at your strongest and most robust. You always want to do the things that matter most when you are in season because the Sun is showing you off in your best light. You're at your most flavorful, appealing, and luscious. The Sun in your birthday sign is hot and bright and makes you ripe for the picking.

Departing

The season after yours is when the Sun is departing your birthday. This is the time for closing deals, settling accounts, and finalizing agreements because what peaks in Pisces fades in the sign of the Twins. It's also a good time to take stock. Did you have a bumper crop or slim pickings? If it's a bumper crop: great. You know you're on the right track and will want to invest more energy in what you're doing and take things to the next level. If it's slim pickings, you'll want to pull the plug on those things that didn't pan out: leave the dead-end job, take your house off the market, or call it quits with that person who could never make a commitment. You can always try again in six months.

Out of Season

When you are out of season, you're likely to feel lethargic, unrecognized, and totally at others' beck and call. And you are because your solar energy is at an all-time low. It's still there, but it feels like it's gone underground. The Sun in your opposite sign is like the midnight Sun. It's cold and dark, and you can't find your way. Needless to say, it's not a great time for big decisions or taking on important responsibilities, because you just aren't up to it. The good news is that this is also the time when the Sun starts moving toward your birthday to begin reigniting your fire again.

Next, Add the Elements

Now that you've figured out when you are in season and not, let's turn to the elements. These are important because they identify the signs that you will do well in (good times of year) versus the ones where your performance will be less than stellar (bad times of year). You might want to take out pen and paper so you can make a list of favorable and unfavorable times according to your Cosmic Calendar.

Elements

FIRE	Aries	Leo	Sagittarius
AIR	Gemini	Libra	Aquarius
EARTH	Taurus	Virgo	Capricorn
WATER	Cancer	Scorpio	Pisces

If you're a Pisces, you are a water sign. That means the other two water signs—Cancer and Scorpio—are favorable for you.

| CANCER | SCORPIO | PISCES |
| (June 21–July 21) | (Oct. 23–Nov. 21) | (Feb. 18–March 19) |

So not only are you in peak season in late winter, but you are also "in your element" when the Sun is in Cancer (early summer) and Scorpio (mid-autumn). This is good because we just added two months to your list of advantageous times of year.

Each element gets a complementary element. A complementary element is an element that likes you, but you're not really BFFs. Water's complementary element is earth.

EARTH

| TAURUS | VIRGO | CAPRICORN |
| (April 19–May 19) | (Aug. 22–Sept. 21) | (Dec. 21–Jan. 18) |

Think of watering the soil to make plants grow and you'll see why these two elements get along. For Pisces, the earth signs Taurus and Capricorn are the most predisposed to helping you out because they are closest to your sign in the calendar. This means Pisces can add mid-spring (Taurus) and early winter (Capricorn) to your list of good times of year. Now you're up to five months that are advantageous to you.

Virgo, although an earth sign, is not favorable to Pisces because Virgo (late summer) is when the Sun is opposite Pisces's birthday (late winter). Virgo goes in the minus column.

VIRGO
(Aug. 22–Sept. 21)

Air and fire are not always friendly to water, but they're complementary to each other—for instance, air fans a flame. This isn't to say they're hostile to water, but imagine a game of rock-paper-scissors. It's a constant one-upmanship among these three elements as they battle it out for the upper hand. Fire evaporates water, but water douses a flame; water drowns air, but a fish out of water will suffocate.

The times of year when Pisces feels out of their element is when the Sun is in air signs—Gemini (late spring), Libra (early autumn), and Aquarius (midwinter) . . .

AIR

GEMINI
(May 20–June 20)

LIBRA
(Sept. 22–Oct. 22)

AQUARIUS
(Jan. 19–Feb. 17)

. . . and then again when the Sun is traveling through the fire signs—Aries (early spring), Leo (midsummer) and Sagittarius (late autumn).

FIRE

ARIES
(March 20–April 18)

LEO
(July 22–Aug. 21)

SAGITTARIUS
(Nov. 22–Dec. 20)

This may seem like there are more bad times than good, but the negative effects are lessened in the uncomplementary signs that flank your birthday because you are in season.

AQUARIUS
(Jan. 19–Feb. 17)

ARIES
(March 20–April 18)

However, you still have to be careful about the timing because these adjacent signs are not always reliable. It's iffy ground but it's not rough going.

And conversely, be sure to note that the negative effects are heightened in the uncomplementary signs that flank your opposite sign, which means that if you're a Pisces, you need to watch your back when the Sun is in Leo and Libra as well.

LEO
(July 22–Aug. 21)

LIBRA
(Sept. 22–Oct. 22)

Now you might say: But I thought Sagittarius was the time for Pisces to begin things, and Gemini was the time for Pisces to wrap things up? Why would these be "bad" times? But ask yourself how many times you have been ready to go at your start date. Doesn't it take a while to get things up and going before you find your groove? And what about deadlines? How often do you find yourself racing the clock to get the job done? The times of year when you are out of your element aren't necessarily bad as much as they're the times when you feel the most anxious, uncertain, or under the gun.

Elemental Compatibility

Water complements earth; incompatible with air and fire

Earth complements water; incompatible with air and fire

Air complements fire; incompatible with water and earth

Fire complements air; incompatible with water and earth

Incorporating the Planets

Now that you've worked out your list of good times versus bad times of year, it's time to incorporate the planets.

Go back to your chart and make a list of all the planets and the zodiac signs they're in. Be sure to include the elements. This will give you an idea of the elemental balance in your chart. Don't expect the elements to be evenly distributed. Often you can have your Sun in one element with the rest of your planets strewn about in the other three.

When Planets Are Team Players

Any planet in like or similar element to your Sun sign is on your team. They work to your benefit—and that even includes the hard-to-manage ones. For instance, combative Mars becomes emboldening when it's in a sign of like or similar element to your Sun sign, while Saturn brings discipline and Uranus is more enlightening. These are good things to know, but what's even better is knowing how to use these planetary placements to plan accordingly. If you know the months when you can expect to feel emboldened, focused, or inventive, then you know when to ask for a raise, take on a heavy-duty project, or do your best brainstorming. They're the months when the Sun is passing through the signs that these planets are well disposed in.

What to Do When the Planets Are Not in a Good Place (for You)

But what if you have these planets in elements that aren't friendly? Mars will become more hostile, Saturn more onerous, and Uranus more unpredictable. But this is still useful information because now you know what to expect. However, planets in unfriendly elements aren't landmines waiting to go off as soon as the Sun passes over them. You can use these times to grow as a person. Let's say you have a lack of water in your chart. Then the Sun passing through the water sign months tells you when you'll be dealing with intense emotional issues that make you feel out of your depth. These are sink-or-swim times for you. Ignore what's going on and you'll surely sink; learn from these experiences and you'll swim. Obstacles can become opportunities for growth when the Sun is passing through out-of-season signs.

There's No Such Thing as a "Bad" Chart

The Sun moving through the zodiac signs of like or similar elements can also help you deal with a difficult planetary placement in your own astrology chart. Let's say you were born with Saturn, the planet of tests, in your Sun sign. This is a burdensome placement, as it just hands you one thankless task after another—and usually around your birthday. Yet when the Sun travels through a zodiac sign of a like or similar element—water signs if you're a Pisces or complementary signs like Taurus and Capricorn—it will actually shift the weight of Saturn's energy so that it's not so crushing. It's not unlike living in a basement apartment that's usually dark and gloomy but suddenly gets light between the hours of twelve and two. The Sun traveling through signs of like and similar elements opens up as times of the year when you might feel the depression lift, get a handle on that problem you've been struggling with, or even make headway with an uphill climb. Things are never fixed in your astrological chart because the Sun is in constant motion. It may take days, weeks, or months, but the Sun will always "come out tomorrow" because at some point it will be in season or it will pass through a zodiac sign of a like or similar element.

Follow the Sun

We all know that there's a time to sow and a time to reap, but there's also a time to do other things as well—like fall in love, build, or cast away. You can use the signs that your planets are in to find out what these times of year might be for you:

The Sun traveling through the sign that your Moon is in is a time for conceiving.

The Sun traveling through the sign that your Mercury is in is a time for buying and selling.

The Sun traveling through the sign that your Venus is in is a time for love.

The Sun traveling through the sign that your Mars is in is a time to fight.

The Sun traveling through the sign that your Jupiter is in is a time for luck.

The Sun traveling through the sign that your Saturn is in is a time for tests.

The Sun traveling through the sign that your Uranus is in is a time for breakdowns or breakthroughs.

The Sun traveling through the sign that your Neptune is in is a time for creative inspiration or delusion.

The Sun traveling through the sign that your Pluto is in is a time for ordeals or transformations.

Putting It All Together

Now that you have a template for the year, you can go ahead and chart your good times and bad times based on when you're in season or out of season. Be sure to note the signs of like elements and the ones that are not. This is especially important for determining which planets in your chart will be helping you (and when) and which planets will be hindering. Remember that even planets that are hindering still present opportunities for growth as long as you're willing to incorporate their unfamiliar elements. You may even come to see them as hidden strengths.

Your Cosmic Calendar

We may all live under one calendar, but each of our personal calendars is different. Some of us are fast out of the gate while others are late bloomers. There are people who go through life on a tear and people who slog through long plateau periods before hitting on something that's truly enlivening and fulfilling. The beauty of having a Cosmic Calendar that's unique to you is that it teaches you to do things in your own time. You don't have to act before you're ready, stay with something you don't like, push to produce, or fret over lost opportunities if you're in sync with your Cosmic Calendar. You'll know when the time is right. Your Cosmic Calendar also teaches you to own your time, and this is perhaps the greatest gift of all. Time is often something we waste by worrying about it. Nothing is lost, stalled, or running out if you're living the life you're meant to live.

Quartering Your Year, à la Mode

This quartering of the year can be applied to any sign, but it must be done by mode. Identifying the modes is like setting up four points on a compass, but instead of directions, you'll be using seasons.

If you're cardinal, you divide by cardinal signs; if you're fixed, you divide by fixed signs; and if you're mutable, you divide by mutable signs.

Here's how it looks:

Aries (cardinal) will rise and shine in Capricorn (Dec. 21–Jan. 18), peak in Aries (March 20–April 18), wrap it up in Cancer (June 21–July 21), and feel out of sorts in Libra (Sept. 22–Oct. 22).

Taurus (fixed) will rise and shine in Aquarius (Jan. 19–Feb. 17), peak in Taurus (April 19–May 19), wrap it up in Leo (July 22–Aug. 21), and feel out of sorts in Scorpio (Oct. 23–Nov. 21).

Gemini (mutable) will rise and shine in Pisces (Feb. 18–March 19), peak in Gemini (May 20–June 20), wrap it up in Virgo (Aug. 22–Sept. 21), and feel out of sorts in Sagittarius (Nov. 22–Dec. 20).

Cancer (cardinal) will rise and shine in Aries (March 20–April 18), peak in Cancer (June 21–July 21), wrap it up in Libra (Sept. 22–Oct. 22), and feel out of sorts in Capricorn (Dec. 21–Jan. 18).

Leo (fixed) will rise and shine in Taurus (April 19–May 19), peak in Leo (July 22–Aug. 21), wrap it up in Scorpio (Oct. 23–Nov. 21), and feel out of sorts in Aquarius (Jan. 19–Feb. 17).

Virgo (mutable) will rise and shine in Gemini (May 20–June 20), peak in Virgo (Aug. 22–Sept. 21), wrap it up in Sagittarius (Nov. 22–Dec. 20), and feel out of sorts in Pisces (Feb. 18–March 19).

Libra (cardinal) will rise and shine in Cancer (June 21–July 21), peak in Libra (Sept. 22–Oct. 22), wrap it up in Capricorn (Dec. 21–Jan. 18), and feel out of sorts in Aries (March 20–April 18).

Scorpio (fixed) will rise and shine in Leo (July 22–Aug. 21), peak in Scorpio (Oct. 23–Nov. 21), wrap it up in Aquarius (Jan. 19–Feb. 17), and feel out of sorts in Taurus (April 19–May 19).

Sagittarius (mutable) will rise and shine in Virgo (Aug. 22–Sept. 21), peak in Sagittarius (Nov. 22–Dec. 20), wrap it up in Pisces (Feb. 18–March 19), and feel out of sorts in Gemini (May 20–June 20).

Capricorn (cardinal) will rise and shine in Libra (Sept. 22–Oct. 22), peak in Capricorn (Dec. 21–Jan. 18), wrap it up in Aries (March 20–April 18), and feel out of sorts in Cancer (June 21–July 21).

Aquarius (fixed) will rise and shine in Scorpio (Oct. 23–Nov. 21), peak in Aquarius (Jan. 19–Feb. 17), wrap it up in Taurus (April 19–May 19), and feel out of sorts in Leo (July 22–Aug. 21).

Pisces (mutable) will rise and shine in Sagittarius (Nov. 22–Dec. 20), peak in Pisces (Feb. 18–March 19), wrap it up in Gemini (May 20–June 20), and feel out of sorts in Virgo (Aug. 22–Sept. 21).

REMINDER: These Sun sign dates are an approximation because they sometimes change every year by a day. The Sun might transition zodiac signs one day earlier or one day later. But it will never be more than by one day. You'll want to keep that in mind when plotting out your yearly calendar. You can find the explanation for this in the Sun chapter on page 43.

ACKNOWLEDGMENTS

I want to thank Megan Newman, my publisher; Lisa DiMona, my agent; and Marian Lizzi, my editor. These are the people every writer dreams of working with.

A special thanks to my students, who taught me more than I could possibly teach them: Michelle Argentine, Sam Barket, Rob Barnes, Annie Bills, Megan Brown, Sandy Burkett, Jan Burnell, Tammy Carlston, Marty Cooke, Nick Critchlow, Stephanie Nelson Cunningham, Martsie Earl, Angie Fernandez, Stef Garcia, Laura Godenick, Kadian Grant, Karah Gray, Melissa Hadley, David Harrington, Wanda Hatton, Colleen Hoyt, Mary Ann Hughes, Emilie Jensen, Larissa Jones, Tomarra LeRoy, Shawn Lerwill, Susan Lundstrom, Marie Manuchehri, John Neider, Shan Neider, Pat Nelson, Tonya Nemanic, Kristen Nicole, Sasha Nydegger, Katy Okelberry, Wendi Record, Shelly Riley, Cresta Schiefer, Sue Shorey, Jillian Spartan, Pamela Thompson, Emmy Thomson, Jean Timpson, Richard Valverde, Sara Vegulla, Suzanne Wagner, Robby Woodliff, Jerre Wroble, and Elle Young.

And finally a reverent bow to my patron goddess, Leslie Soref.

ABOUT THE AUTHOR

Born and raised in Menlo Park, California, Christopher moved to New York City when he was eighteen to attend the Juilliard School of Drama. While studying acting and then playwriting, he also studied astrology under Carolyn Asnien, who taught him valuable consulting skills, how to read a birth chart wherever and whenever, and to always "keep it real." This came in handy as he built up his clientele in the 1980s and 1990s reading tarot cards in the VIP rooms of various discotheques and after-hours clubs while interpreting astrology charts in clients' penthouses, basement apartments, and SoHo art galleries. The result of all this "hoofing it" was a monthly horoscope column for *Allure* magazine (Condé Nast), a daily Sun sign column for the *San Francisco Chronicle*, and his first book, *Ruling Planets*, published by HarperCollins.

Currently, Christopher runs RulingPlanets.com, an online subscription website based on his best-selling book, while teaching astrology classes and workshops around the country. He lectures about the history of astrology in America from pre-Revolutionary to modern times with special emphasis on the history of pop astrology in America (it's older and more colorful than you think), astrology in the American Civil War period, astrology and the queer identity, and the entwined histories of New Age astrology and Christian fundamentalism. He is married to Adam Sklute, artistic director of Ballet West in Salt Lake City, and the proud owner of Juno, an Anatolian shepherd, who has a peculiar taste for the *New York Review of Books*. Nylabones and rawhides won't deter her.